XPath, XLink, XPointer, and XML

XPath, XLink, XPointer, and XML

A Practical Guide to Web Hyperlinking and Transclusion

Erik Wilde

David Lowe

✦✦ Addison-Wesley

Boston • San Francisco • New York • Toronto • Montreal
London • Munich • Paris • Madrid
Capetown • Sydney • Tokyo • Singapore • Mexico City

The publisher offers discounts on this book when ordered in quantity for bulk purchases and special sales. For more information, please contact:
  U.S. Corporate and Government Sales
  (800) 382-3419
  corpsales@pearsontechgroup.com

For sales outside of the U.S., please contact:
  International Sales
  (317) 581-3793
  international@pearsontechgroup.com

Visit Addison-Wesley on the Web: *www.awprofessional.com*

Library of Congress Cataloging-in-Publication Data

Wilde, Erik
    XPath, XLink, XPointer, and XML : a practical guide to web hyperlinking and transclusion / Erik Wilde, David Lowe.
        p.   cm.
    Includes bibliographical references and index.
    ISBN 0-201-70344-0 (alk. paper)
    1. Web site development. 2. Hypertext systems. 3. XML (Document markup language)
  4. World Wide Web.   I. Lowe, David.   II. Title

TK5105.88.W546 2002
005.2'70--dc21   200206566

ISBN 0-201-70344-0

Text printed on recycled paper

1 2 3 4 5 6 7 8 9 10—CRS—0605040302
First printing, July 2002

Contents

List of Figures   *xi*

List of Tables   *xiii*

Foreword   *xv*

Preface   *xvii*

About the Authors   *xxiii*

Introduction   xxv

    Information Linking   xxvi

    The Web   xxvii

    XML   xxviii

    Conclusions   xxx

PART I   FOUNDATIONS: THE WEB WE WANT   1

1 Current Technology   3

    1.1 The Internet Environment   3

        1.1.1 Connecting to the Internet   4

        1.1.2 How the Internet Works   5

    1.2 The World Wide Web   7

    1.3 Information Linking in the WWW   8

        1.3.1 The Web's Linking Model   8

        1.3.2 A Broader View of Linking in the Web   10

        1.3.3 Shortcomings of the Web Linking Model   11

        1.3.4 Current Solutions   18

    1.4 Conclusions   20

2 Hypermedia Concepts and Alternatives to the Web   21

2.1 What Is Hypermedia?   21
    2.1.1 History of Hypermedia   22
    2.1.2 Definition of Hypermedia   23

2.2 Hypermedia Concepts   25
    2.2.1 Representing Information Associations   25
    2.2.2 Formalizing Linking Concepts   37

2.3 Usage Scenarios: Hypermedia Support for
    Information Utilization   42
    2.3.1 Scenario Description   42
    2.3.2 Discussion   44

2.4 Conclusions   48

3 Conceptual Viewpoint   49

3.1 References versus Links   49

3.2 Resource Identification: URL, URI, and URN   54

3.3 Persistence of Identifiers and References   56
    3.3.1 Persistence of Identifiers   57
    3.3.2 Persistence of References   57

3.4 Third-Party Links and Linkbases   59

3.5 Multi-Ended Links   62

3.6 Generic Links   63

3.7 Typed Links   64

3.8 Conclusions   66

PART II   TECHNIQUE: THE WEB'S NEW LOOK   67

4 Related Technologies   69

4.1 XML Core Standards   71

4.2 XML Namespaces   75

4.3 XML Base   79

4.4 XML Inclusions   80
    4.4.1 XML External Entities   80
    4.4.2 XLink   80

4.5 XML Information Set   81

4.6 Extensible Hypertext Markup Language   88

4.7 Extensible Stylesheet Language   89
     4.7.1 XSL Transformations   90
     4.7.2 XSL Formatting Objects   92

4.8 Resource Description Framework   92

4.9 Conclusions   94

5 XML Path Language   95

5.1 General Model   96
     5.1.1 Root Node   99
     5.1.2 Element Node   99
     5.1.3 Attribute Node   100
     5.1.4 Namespace Node   100
     5.1.5 Processing Instruction Node   101
     5.1.6 Comment Node   101
     5.1.7 Text Node   101
     5.1.8 Example   102

5.2 Location Paths   103
     5.2.1 Location Steps   105
     5.2.2 Axes   106
     5.2.3 Node Tests   115
     5.2.4 Predicates   116
     5.2.5 Abbreviations   118
     5.2.6 Examples   120

5.3 Expressions   121

5.4 Functions   123
     5.4.1 Boolean Functions   125
     5.4.2 Number Functions   126
     5.4.3 String Functions   128
     5.4.4 Node Set Functions   131

5.5 Examples   133

5.6 Future Developments   136

5.7 Conclusions   137

6 XML Pointer Language   139

6.1 General Model   143
     6.1.1 XPointer Data Model   144
     6.1.2 XPointer Data Model Examples   148

6.2 XPointer Forms   150
     6.2.1 Bare Names   150

6.2.2 Child Sequences   151
6.2.3 Full XPointers   153

6.3 Functions   156

6.4 Using XPointers   161
6.4.1 XPointer Character Escaping   162
6.4.2 XPointers and Namespaces   163
6.4.3 How to Compose XPointers   165
6.4.4 Persistence   166

6.5 Future Developments   167

6.6 Conclusions   168

7 XML Linking Language   169

7.1 Embedding Links into XML Documents   170

7.2 Link Types and Element Types   171
7.2.1 XLink Link Types   172
7.2.2 XLink Element Types   177

7.3 Attributes   180
7.3.1 Element Type Attribute   180
7.3.2 Locator Attribute   181
7.3.3 Semantic Attributes   182
7.3.4 Behavior Attributes   184
7.3.5 Traversal Attributes   188

7.4 Interpretation of XLinks   188
7.4.1 Processing   188
7.4.2 Conformance   189

7.5 Usage   190
7.5.1 XLink Element and Attribute Declaration   190
7.5.2 Extending XLink   194
7.5.3 Using XLink for Linkbases   195

7.6 The Future of XLink   198

7.7 Conclusions   198

PART III   APPLICATION: WEAVING THE WEB WE WANT   199

8 Authoring Aspects   201

8.1 Practical Issues   201
8.1.1 Lack of Presentation Semantics   201
8.1.2 Unclear Processing Model   203

8.1.3 Tool Support   206

8.1.4 Loss of Context   206

8.1.5 Legal Issues   207

8.1.6 More Complex Authoring   208

8.2 Emerging Support for XLink and XPointer   209

8.2.1 Support in Existing Browsers   210

8.2.2 Parsers and Code Libraries   211

8.2.3 Hand-Coded Support   212

8.3 Development Tools   213

8.4 Authoring Approaches   213

8.4.1 Identifying Things to Link   213

8.4.2 Controlling Linking and Ensuring Link Integrity   215

8.4.3 Link Semantics   216

8.4.4 Accessibility and Usability   219

8.5 Conclusions   220

9 Transitioning to a New Model   221

9.1 Alternative Approaches   222

9.1.1 Issues   222

9.1.2 Alternatives   224

9.2 Example Strategies   226

9.2.1 Internal Hybrid, External No Change   226

9.2.2 Internal Hybrid, External Hybrid   230

9.3 Content Negotiation   231

9.4 Migration of Content   233

9.5 Building New Sites   235

9.6 Conclusions   236

Epilogue   237

References   241

Index   251

List of Figures

1.1 Basic linking components   9

1.2 Implementing a multiple-source link in HTML   16

2.1 Simple Web link   26

2.2 Dynamic Web link   27

2.3 Generic link (using a simplification of the Webcosm server)   28

2.4 Message passing in the Microcosm link service architecture   29

2.5 Structural links (using a simplification of Hyperwave)   31

2.6 Example Hyperwave Web page containing structural links   32

2.7 Spatial hypertext   34

2.8 VIKI screen dump   35

4.1 Example XML Infoset tree   87

5.1 Document order of XPath nodes   98

5.2 Example XPath node tree   103

5.3 XPath axes `ancestor`, `ancestor-or-self`, `child`,
and `descendant`   107

5.4 XPath axes `descendant-or-self`, `following`,
`following-sibling`, and `parent`   108

5.5 XPath axes `preceding`, `preceding-sibling`, and `self`   109

6.1 Snapshot of W3C's technical reports page   140

6.2 Container nodes, node points, and character points   146

7.1 Inline extended link   174

7.2 Inline extended link with arcs   175

7.3 Out-of-line extended link   176

7.4 Out-of-line extended link with arcs   176

7.5 XLink and linkbases   196

advanced changes enabled by these technologies, and the implications of these changes for creating effective, maintainable, and usable applications. A practical perspective allows us to understand how these technologies are actually applied by developers, as well as to examine issues related to current tools, environments, and standardization processes.

The Book's Audience

We believe that XML, XLink, and XPointer and, in particular, the new hypermedia functionality enabled by these technologies will fundamentally change the Web. This book focuses on understanding and leveraging these changes and should therefore be interesting and useful for many people.

Web authors, developers, and project managers. So far, this group has been limited by HTML's primitive linking mechanism; and for many applications, an understanding of this new hypermedia functionality will be beneficial. It will enable them to produce more sophisticated applications, both in terms of the way the content that underpins their site is managed, as well as in terms of the functionality that can be created in the application front-end. This book provides an overview of the technology and presents concrete implementation strategies. To assist Web authors, developers, and project managers in being backwards-compatible, the book also provides transition strategies.

Web users. In many cases, Web users are very interested in what the future of Web technology can bring them. In particular, updated features are often the main motivation for upgrading to a newer version of a browser or other software, so Web users should be well informed about the improvements available with the most recent software.

Students. In courses as diverse as information studies, software engineering, information systems, and library studies, students will benefit from understanding how the Web is likely to evolve in the future—particularly with respect to the way information is represented, managed, accessed, and used.

The Book's Content

In this preface, we discuss the changes in the Web and the role that emerging standards can play in developing a richer and more usable Web. In the introduction, we elaborate on this idea by exploring the emerging standards and, in particular, consider what we mean by information-linking and the role it plays within the Web. The introduction provides a context for the broad focus of the book.

The rest of the book is divided into three main parts. Part I focuses on a conceptual framework. It explores the Web we might wish to develop and the emerging linking technologies that may go some way toward providing it. We start in chapter 1 with a consideration of current technology. We focus on the limitations inherent in this technology, particularly with respect to linking and the implications for information handling, navigation, and retrieval. Chapter 2 provides information about the motivation for the types of changes we are promoting. We start by exploring linking issues in much more detail, looking at hypermedia concepts and some of the historical hypermedia developments, which provides useful insights into how information might be better managed. We also provide relevant definitions that clarify much of the terminology used in the rest of the book. This chapter concludes with a typical scenario that illustrates the types of Web changes that might be desirable currently. Chapter 3 begins the process of considering the new and emerging technologies that enable the vision we have begun to establish in the first two chapters. Rather than describing the technologies from the syntactic level (where their applicability may be difficult to put into the context of the discussions in the previous chapter), we first consider standards such as XPath, XPointer, and XLink from a conceptual viewpoint, looking at the types of support they provide for sophisticated linking and content management. This discussion is supported by XML fragment examples as a way of introducing these concepts through a process of illustration.

Then, Part II of the book gets down to the specific details of the new technologies and considers the emerging core standards in some detail. Chapter 4 begins by considering a range of foundation technologies, which provide a supporting infrastructure, if not the core technologies. For example, we look at XML, XML Namespaces, XML Base, XInclude, XML Infoset, XHTML, XSL, XSLT, XSL-FO, and RDF. Readers with a background in the newer Web technologies may wish to skip this chapter and continue with the discussion in the following chapters; however, readers familiar only with the more "traditional" Web technologies, such as HTML and HTTP, should first read this chapter.

In chapters 5, 6, and 7, we look in detail at three of the key technologies that enable our vision: XPath, XPointer, and XLink. In each case, rather than simply presenting the standard, we explain the concepts and, wherever appropriate, the strengths, limitations, and ambiguities of the standard. As such, it is important that these chapters be read in conjunction with the relevant standards. This, in turn, raises an important point: The XPointer and XLink standards have been evolving continually during the writing of this book and are likely to continue to evolve. This means that you will need to be careful in interpreting some of the comments here. In particular, at the time of this writing, the current status and version of the most relevant standards are as follows:

- XML Path Language (XPath): W3C Recommendation (16 November 1999) [Clark & DeRose 99]
- XML Pointer Language (XPointer): W3C Candidate Recommendation (11 September 2001) [DeRose+ 01b]
- XML Linking Language (XLink): W3C Recommendation (27 June 2001) [DeRose+ 01a]

This means that the standards as they are today are not going to change; but since adoption has been slow so far, actual implementations may differ from these standards, and the standards may have to be reworked.[1] Currently, there is no sign that this going to happen, but readers should regularly check the W3C Web site at `http://www.w3.org`—in particular, the technical reports page at `http://www.w3.org/TR/`—to look at the latest versions of the standards. We will also track standard development on the book's Web site—`http://transcluding.com`.

Finally, in Part III, we look at how these technologies can be applied in order to move toward the vision we established in Part I. These discussions are in the context of current practical limitations imposed by available infrastructure, environments, and tools (or lack of tools). In chapter 8, we investigate the authoring of applications to take advantage of XLink and XPointer. Specifically, we look at some general issues affecting how we author and use XLink, then investigate the tools, applications, and environments that are beginning to emerge. In chapter 9, we consider some of the issues that need to be addressed in migrating from a conventional model of Web content to a model that uses the more sophisticated techniques discussed so far in this book. Finally, in chapter 10, everything is drawn together, and we make some final comments, particularly with regard to our own perspectives on the future of XLink and XPointer.

Acknowledgments

The authors would like to acknowledge the assistance of a number of people in the preparation of this book. Obviously, the W3C in general and the developers of the XPointer and XLink standards in particular deserve special

---

[1]This is not the way standards are supposed to develop, but it may happen. For example, HTML standards for some time more or less simply tracked what the two major browser providers had already implemented.

mention. Specifically, we wish to acknowledge the efforts of Steve DeRose, Eve Maler, David Orchard, and Ron Daniel in developing and promoting these key standards.

We would also like to acknowledge the original ground-breaking work of Theodor Holm Nelson on early hypertext systems. Many of the concepts that are only now being woven into the framework of the Web were originally proposed by Ted 30 or more years ago. His contribution to the field is without parallel, and his vision for hypermedia is one that we are still trying to appreciate and live up to.

The assistance and support of the Addison-Wesley editorial staff has been excellent. In particular, we would like to acknowledge the assistance of Mary O'Brien and Marilyn Rash, who never gave up on us, even when we were missing deadline after deadline. Thanks!

And on a personal note, the support of Catherine Lowe and Jacqueline Schwerzmann has been beyond value.

About the Authors

Dr. Erik Wilde is lecturer and senior researcher at the Swiss Federal Institute of Technology in Zürich (ETH Zürich), Switzerland. To find out more about Erik and his activities, visit his Web site at `http://dret.net`.

Dr. David Lowe is an associate professor and associate dean (teaching and learning) in the faculty of engineering at the University of Technology, Sydney. He has active research interests in the areas of Web development and technologies, hypermedia, and software engineering. In particular, he focuses on Web development processes, Web project specification and scoping, and information contextualization. He has published widely in these areas, including a text focusing on Web development (Lowe and Hall, *Hypermedia and the Web: An Engineering Approach,* Wiley, 1999). In the last seven years, he has published more than 50 referced papers and attracted more than Au$1,300,000 in funding. He is on numerous Web conference committees and is the information management theme editor for the *Journal of Digital Information.* David has undertaken numerous consultancies related to software evaluation, Web development (especially project planning and evaluation), and Web technologies. He can be reached at The University of Technology, Sydney, P.O. Box 123, Broadway, NSW 2007, Australia, or `mailto:david.lowe@uts.edu.au`.

Introduction

The World Wide Web has undergone astounding growth since its emergence in the early 1990s. There is a plethora of statistics that attest to this expansion—the number of users, the number of pages that are available, business expenditure on Web technologies, consumer expenditure through e-commerce sites, and so forth.[1] These statistics usually focus on technical growth and tend not to capture the more fundamental and unprecedented changes in business, the world economy, and, perhaps most significantly, social structures.

And these changes will accelerate, as we continue to head toward an ever richer online environment. Commercial interactions and support for business processes will become more complex and, at the same time, more central to both business and government activity. We will see progressively more pervasive, sophisticated, and diverse user experiences as we move toward the emerging vision of a semantic Web (i.e., a Web that supports automated retrieval, analysis, and management of resources).

Of importance in this rapidly evolving environment is the convergence of a substantial number of emerging technologies and standards. These technologies (or maybe acronyms would be a better name!) include, for example, RDF, SMIL, WAP, WebML, DOM, CSS, PICS, PNG, SVG, WAI, and many more. A quick look through the World Wide Web Consortium's (W3C's) list of technical recommendations, proposed recommendations, and working drafts (see `http://www.w3.org/TR/`) illustrates the breadth of work being considered.

One of the most fundamental, widely discussed, and far-reaching technologies is the Extensible Markup Language (XML). Viewed simplistically, XML provides a mechanism for representing in a powerful way the data that underpins the Web. But a representation of the data is not sufficient to enable systems and users to interact with, utilize, and communicate with that data—a representation of the ways in which different data items are

---

[1] At the time of writing, several good sources of Web statistics are the Open Market Internet Index (`http://new-website.openmarket.com/intindex/index.cfm`), the Webreference.com list (`http://www.webreference.com/internet/statistics.html`), and NetFactual (`http://www.netfactual.com`).

interrelated is also required. Effectively, some form of linking model is necessary. For this model to be useful for the Web, it needs to integrate with XML.

This book is intended to help Web developers understand the evolving standards supporting linking within XML and the implications of these standards for managing information and constructing sophisticated applications. In particular, we consider the ways in which these standards will lead to a fundamentally richer Web environment and user experience.

INFORMATION LINKING

Linking is a fundamental concept that forms an important part of the theoretical foundations of the Web. Without linking, the Web is just an extremely large collection of (albeit very sophisticated) distributed information and applications. With linking, the Web becomes a single complex system.

Linking allows us to associate semantically related items of information so that we can support sophisticated techniques for locating those items. But it goes way beyond that. We can link information to tools for manipulating that information. We can link the various steps in processes (such as the steps in buying a book online). But we can also do more sophisticated linking, such as implementing dynamic links that change depending on the context (time, user, history, etc.) or constructing new documents by merging content or applications from diverse (but linked) locations. Linking effectively allows us to create a complexly structured network of distributed resources—a "Web."

The concept of linking information resources has been around for a considerable period of time, predating the Web by at least 45 years. The concept of associations between items of information (at least as a technically supported aid to information management) was originally introduced by Vannevar Bush [1945] in the 1940s. The concept essentially remained an obscure idea until the 1960s when it was revived by farsighted researchers such as Ted Nelson [1993] and Doug Engelbart [1988]. Indeed, it was Ted Nelson who coined the terms "hypertext" and "transclusion." His Xanadu system encapsulates many of the sophisticated information structuring and management concepts now being investigated for the Web. Engelbart's work envisaged the user and the computer in a dynamic symbiosis, which resulted in augmented human capabilities.

This work then spawned a growing body of research and development of a number of systems within the hypertext community. These systems evolved during the 1970s and 1980s and gradually came to include very diverse and sophisticated concepts: set-based association, multiple source and destination links, dynamically adapted links, generic links that are sourced from all content satisfying certain criteria, spatial representations of the link associations, and so forth. This richness in linking concepts reflected the maturing ideas of how information can be managed and, in particular, how we interact with this information.

THE WEB

Then, in the 1980s, Tim Berners-Lee started experimenting with these concepts. In 1990, he developed (at CERN, the European Organization for Nuclear Research) a relatively simple implementation that was initially intended to allow him and his colleagues within the high-energy physics community to collaborate through rapid information sharing [Berners-Lee 92]. In the next decade, Berners-Lee's ideas became the catalyst, along with various related convergent technologies, for a frenzy of business and consumer activity that has completely transformed the world economy and is fundamentally changing our social structure.

The model originally proposed by Berners-Lee—that of a simple communication protocol (Hypertext Transfer Protocol, or HTTP) that allows documents to be requested from remote servers, coupled with a document format (Hypertext Markup Language, or HTML) that supports references to related documents—ignored almost all of the sophisticated linking concepts that had evolved during the previous 30 years.

The linking model adopted by Berners-Lee was very simple: single-source, single-destination links embedded into the source document. This, however, is not a criticism of the choice to adopt this model. Indeed it was almost certainly partly this choice of a simple model that led to the success of the Web.

We should explain what we mean by this. A distributed system such as the Web relies for its success partly on the fact that there is a sufficient body—or critical mass—of information available to make its use attractive. As the number of users increases, the amount of information increases, and the likelihood of additional users (and providers of information) increases. The simplicity of the original model adopted by Berners-Lee made it very easy for people to provide content and set up servers and clients. This in turn rapidly led to a critical mass and the subsequent rapid adoption and evolution of the Web. A more complex model incorporating some of the sophisticated information linking and management functionalities found in other hypertext systems would have slowed the adoption, possibly to the point where the critical mass was not reached.

It is worth pointing out that, apart from the Web, the only commercially successful hypertext systems have been applied to particular niche markets. Hence, there has been a much stronger justification for the effort required to create sufficient content. Hypercard and Storyspace are two good examples of the systems that have managed to develop small but active niche markets. But even these have been tiny efforts in comparison with the Web.

However—and here is a key point—while the simplicity of the original Web model may have led to its initial success (and what a success it was!), it also meant that much of the richness that had been developed in previous hypertext and information management systems was lost. This was not originally a great problem; but as the Web matured and evolved, these limitations began to place constraints on the ways in which the Web could be used. As just one simple example, the lack of any form of state (i.e., memory about the history of interaction between a server and a client) originally led to concepts such as cookies and server session variables, then complicated the issues of secure transactions and ultimately made systems that adapted to users' specific needs unnecessarily complex. Much of the technical evolution and innovation over the last few years has been a consequence of trying to circumvent or remove limitations such as these. In some cases, this has included the integration of richer hypermedia systems into the Web architecture, for example, the development of systems such as Webcosm [Hall+ 96] and Hyperwave [Maurer 96] (both to be discussed later in the book). This has, however, been an uneasy alliance that has struggled to support the true richness of the underlying system.

More recently, various other Web developments have gained attention as ways to circumvent the Web's original limitations. One of the most significant of these has been XML.

XML

XML was originally developed by the W3C to serve as a simpler variant of the relatively complex Standard Generalized Markup Language (SGML), as a means to make user-defined document types available on the Web. The W3C then realized that it would also be ideally suited to overcoming many of the limitations inherent in HTML. Essentially, XML replaces the fixed element set of HTML with an application-specific set of elements. This allows application designers to define their own vocabulary and grammar for documents—the allowable elements and their valid usage. Essentially, the result is that XML documents support (or at least support much better than HTML documents) aspects such as data exchange, automated processing of content, and customized views of the content.

Accompanying XML and supporting it in various ways is a series of related standards and technologies. For example, the Extensible Stylesheet

Language (XSL) is composed of several components: XSL Transformations (XSLT) supports the conversion of XML documents into other (possibly XML) documents, and XSL Formatting Objects (XSL-FO) support turning the results of a transformation into a form that can be rendered. Extensible HTML (XHTML) is the reformulation of HTML as an application of XML, thereby supporting the transition from HTML to XML. XML Schema is a schema language for XML documents, which in the future will probably replace XML's built-in mechanism for defining schemas.[2] Other examples include XML Information Set, XML Query, and XForms.

In effect, the XML family of standards provides an opportunity to introduce into the Web environment some of the richness that was missing from the original Web architecture. An enormous amount has been written about how XML can support improvements in aspects such as information management, business processes, and the user experience—especially when combined with related technologies such as Resource Description Framework (RDF), Cascading Style Sheets (CSS), and Document Object Model (DOM). However, one aspect that has been overlooked to a certain extent is linking. A key piece of the maturing XML jigsaw is the linking model within XML—as provided by the emerging W3C recommendations on XLink and XPointer. This linking model provides a much more sophisticated approach to linking than the original Web model. Indeed, it comes close to the sophistication of the various hypertext models that predated the Web—but within the context of the distributed diversity offered by the evolving Web.

The linking model that underpins XML is being developed by the W3C XML Linking Working Group. As stated by the W3C, "the objective of the XML Linking Working Group is to design advanced, scalable, and maintainable hyperlinking and addressing functionality for XML." The model that has been developed is composed of several components. The first of these is the XML Pointer Language (XPointer). XPointer builds on the XML Path Language (XPath) to provide a mechanism for addressing XML-based Web resources by defining a powerful way to address fragments of an XML document. These fragments may be single XML elements or a collection of elements, text strings, attributes, and so forth that have been merged into one composite.

The second component is the XML Linking Language (XLink). XLink is used to describe complex associations between information resources identified using URIs, possibly with added XPointers. These associations can be simple directional embedded links between two resources (as with

---

[2]This is the Document Type Definition (DTD) mechanism built directly into the XML standard.

HTML), or much more complex associations. Examples include multidirectional links, multiple-destination links, and inlining of content from one source to another, as well as automatically merged fragments sourced from multiple disparate documents.

CONCLUSIONS

In this book we look at the richer linking enabled by the emerging XLink and XPointer standards (as well as XPath, which is the foundation of XPointer). Overall, our goal is to provide a resource that helps you to utilize the emerging XML linking technologies and (in some respects, even more important) to understand the types of support for information access and management available.

Ultimately, we see this book as a motivation for integrating hypermedia concepts into Web-related projects. These concepts may not necessarily always or only map to XLink constructs (though this mapping is the focus of much of this book). At present many of them can be supported using DHTML (Dynamic HTML), tomorrow they will be supportable by XLink, and in five years time they may be supported by some new technology. The key point is that these concepts should be captured somehow, so that they can be made available in whatever form is supported by the current "publishing system." We don't intend to try to sell XLink as the hypermedia technology to end all other hypermedia technologies, but as one step in the evolution of the Web and a good reason to start thinking about the Web as a hypermedia system.

Part I

Foundations
The Web We Want

1

Current Technology

In this chapter, we consider the current technologies and concepts that underpin the Internet and the World Wide Web (WWW). In particular, we move from a consideration of the Internet environment in the first section to looking at how the Web provides a logical layer on top of the physical Internet in section 1.2, "The World Wide Web." We then finish by discussing the Web's current linking model and its limitations in section 1.3, "Information Linking in the WWW."

1.1 THE INTERNET ENVIRONMENT

One of the main results of the Web's success was to bring the Internet into the conciousness of the general public. Before the advent of the Web, the Internet was mainly used by academic institutions for research purposes. Within ten years, however, the Internet has become the backbone of the information society, propelled mainly by the success of the Web and electronic mail. The public often confuses the Internet and the Web because much too often the terms are used interchangeably. However, there is a clear difference between them, defined as follows:

Internet—The entirety of all computers that are interconnected (using various physical networking technologies) and that employ the Internet protocol suite on top of their networking systems. The Internet protocol suite implements a wide-area, packet-switched network that interconnects networks using different protocols and connection characteristics.

World Wide Web—A distributed hypermedia system built on top of some of the services provided by the Internet, the most important being the naming service provided by the Domain Name System (DNS), and

3

the reliable connection-oriented transport service provided by the Transmission Control Protocol (TCP).

This section provides only a very short introduction to the Internet environment on which the Web is built. For more information, a nontechnical introductory book [Comer 00] describes the Internet's architecture in greater detail. More technically oriented general introductions into computer networks (with an emphasis on the Internet) have been published [Halsall 96, Peterson & Davie 99, Stallings 99, Tanenbaum 96]. Additionally, Internet RFC 2235 [Zakon 97][1] gives a time line of the Internet, including numbers of hosts, domains, and Web servers. It is a very good introduction and will help you to get a feeling for the development of the Internet. For answers to the most frequently asked questions, a good resource is Internet RFC 2664 [Plzak+ 99], which also contains many source references for more detailed documentation.

The two main issues related to the technology of the Internet and of interest in this book are how to connect to the Internet, which is described in the next subsection, and what happens after connecting to the Internet, described in section 1.1.2.

1.1.1 Connecting to the Internet

Most computers today are connected to a computer network in one form or another. On the other hand, most individual home computers are not running constantly, or if they are, they are not permanently connected to a computer network, mainly for economic reasons (because connection costs are often based on connection time). It is therefore possible to differentiate between two different connection modes:

- *Dial-up connections.* This kind of connection is opened on demand, for example, if a user wants to view Web content or send or receive e-mails. In most cases, the initial connection between the user and the user's Internet service provider (ISP) is established over a phone line using a modem. The basic modem connection establishes a data path between the user and the ISP, which is then used to send Internet data packets back and forth, often using the Point to Point Protocol (PPP) as standardized in Internet RFC 1661 [Simpson 94]. After the

---

[1]The most recent version of this document can always be retrieved by using the Web server of the Internet Society (ISOC) and requesting the document `http://www.isoc.org/zakon/Internet/History/HIT.html`.

user has finished working on the Internet, the connection is closed, and consequently the user's computer is disconnected from the Internet.

- *Permanent connection.* For many applications (such as servers, which must be available all the time), a permanent connection to the Internet is required or desirable. One popular technology allowing home users to achieve this is a cable modem, which works over a cable television network. Another technology is asymmetric digital subscriber line (ADSL), standardized in ITU-T G.992.2 [ITU 99], which works over phone lines. For corporate users, ISPs often offer leased lines, which have much greater capacities than modem connections. For internal distribution inside a company, local area networks (LANs) are used to interconnect all computers to form a so-called intranet.

The decision about whether to connect a particular computer permanently to the Internet is dictated by a number of issues, such as the purpose of the computer, the remotely accessed services running on the computer, and available ISPs and their connection costs. While today many home computers still are using dial-up connections, this will change with the expansion of existing services and the introduction of new offerings, such as cheap wireless services, ADSL, cable modems, satellite connections, and new buildings providing Internet connectivity as a basic service in the same way water, electricity, and phone lines are provided today.

1.1.2 How the Internet Works

Once a connection to the Internet is established, the connected computers can start to send data to and receive data from all other computers connected to the Internet. But what does it actually mean to be "connected to the Internet"? The technical requirements are defined in Internet RFCs 1122 [Braden 89b] and 1123 [Braden 89a], which basically define which network services a computer has to provide in order to behave correctly as an Internet host. The most basic requirement is that Internet hosts must be able to send and receive data packets (called *datagrams*) defined by the Internet Protocol (IP), which is standardized in Internet RFC 791 [Postel 81a]. IP provides the functions necessary to deliver a package of bits (an *Internet datagram*) from a source to a destination over an interconnected system of networks. And herein lies the strength of the Internet, it does not depend on a specific underlying physical network; it can be used on top of virtually any networking technology.

In the context of Web technologies, the most important protocol is the Transmission Control Protocol, which is standardized in RFC 793 [Postel 81b]. TCP is layered on top of IP to provide a reliable, connection-oriented, flow-controlled transport service for applications. IP is capable of sending datagrams but does not guarantee that these datagrams will be delivered. IP datagrams can get lost, they can be duplicated, or they can arrive at the receiver side in a different order from the one in which they had been sent. TCP deals with all these possibilities and provides applications with a transport service that, for many application scenarios, is better suited than IP's service. TCP does so by assigning sequence numbers to individual packets and employing a number of elaborate mechanisms to make sure that the underlying network is not overloaded. Many Internet application protocols use TCP as the transport protocol, the most relevant being the Web's Hypertext Transfer Protocol (HTTP) and the Simple Mail Transfer Protocol (SMTP), which is used for the exchange of electronic mail.

Apart from providing applications with transport protocols, the Internet environment also includes services. By far the most important service is the Domain Name System, which is standardized in RFCs 1034 and 1035 [Mockapetris 87a, 87b]. DNS implements a globally distributed database, which is used to map domain names to IP addresses. On the protocol level (IP or TCP), Internet hosts are addressed by IP addresses, which are 32-bit numbers, often written in the so-called dotted decimal notation. In this notation, IP addresses have four decimal numbers, such as `129.132.66.9`, the IP address of the Web server of this book's Web site. However, since such a number is hard to remember,[2] a naming system has been introduced that makes it possible to use hierarchically structured names for Internet hosts. The DNS name for this book's Web site is `transcluding.com`; and whenever a browser is trying to download pages from this server, it first has to resolve the domain name to the IP address using a DNS request. Therefore, most Web browser interactions with the Internet involve two steps: first resolving the domain name by requesting its IP address from a DNS server,[3] and then connecting to this address and requesting a Web page.

---

[2]Furthermore, IP addresses may change, for example, if the Web site is moved to another server. This would change the IP address, but it would be very unfortunate if this would also make the Web server's name invalid. A naming service providing a mapping between names and addresses can prevent this from happening by keeping names the same and changing IP addresses only in the naming service's database.

[3]The DNS server's address must be known by the browser, and this is achieved either by manually configuring it within the browser or the operating system or increasingly through methods that dynamically set this address whenever a computer connects to the Internet.

1.2 THE WORLD WIDE WEB

In the previous section, we briefly describe how the Internet is used to support applications that use computer communications in general and how the Internet supports the Web in particular. Apart from the underlying supporting infrastructure provided by ISPs, what are the most fundamental components of the Web? As described in the very first paper published about the Web [Berners-Lee 92], the basic components of the Web are as follows:

- HTML for the content format of hypertext documents
- The concept of the Uniform Resource Locator (URL) for the globally unique identification of resources
- HTTP for the communication between a server and a client

Today, these basic technologies are still the same—even though the concept of the URL has been extended to the Universal Resource Identifier (URI). However, many technologies have been introduced to supplement this basic architecture. The most important technologies for the topic of this book are described in chapter 4. The basic idea of the Web is very simple: a browser requests a document (or some other resource) from a server using the HTTP protocol, which then provides an appropriate response, also using the HTTP protocol. The response may or may not contain the requested document. The requested document will typically be written using an appropriate language (such as HTML) and sections of the document's information (known as *anchors*) will contain references (known as links) to other documents. The user reads the document and can then, if desired, select one of the anchors. The browser then interprets the reference by extracting the URI of the referenced document (part of which is the name of the server on which the document resides), contacting the server (again using HTTP), and retrieving the new document. In today's Web, this basic pattern has not changed much; and by far most innovations on the Web are new content formats, which in most cases can be used for an improved user experience.

However, this diversity of new content formats has also led to many incompatibilities. The interpretation of a specific content format must be implemented in the user's browser, and if there are dozens of content formats all requiring special plug-ins or external viewers, then the Web becomes less universal than it was designed to be. After a period of uncontrolled competition between Netscape and Microsoft in the mid-1990s, during which both companies continually improved HTML and the Web architecture with new inventions incompatible with the contender's products, the situation has greatly improved. The World Wide Web Consortium (W3C), an industry consortium headed by the Web's inventor, Tim Berners-Lee, now strives to define common standards; and the major players are all part of the standardization efforts.

The idea of the *semantic Web,* as described by Berners-Lee in 1999, is a Web in which all of the information available is not only machine-readable (as it is now) but also machine-understandable. To achieve this goal, the basic standards underlying many Web technologies must be able to carry as much semantic information as possible. Put simply, this means that the meaning of the content needs to be somehow encapsulated in the representation of that information.

Essentially, the two most important issues when trying to develop technologies for a semantically richer Web are how to attach meaning to Web content, as can by the done by using the Resource Description Framework (RDF) described in chapter 4, and how to develop a linking model that supports a more diverse range of linking possibilities than the one currently supported by the Web. This book focuses on the second issue, and chapters 2 and 3 explore why Web linking should be improved and how it can be improved.

1.3 INFORMATION LINKING IN THE WWW

In this section we look at the linking model currently dominant in the Web. This model is quite simplistic when compared with the much richer models developed in a diverse range of hypertext systems over the last 30 years. It has, however, been sufficient for the initial development and adoption of the Web. At the end of this section and in the next chapter, we discuss the limitations that this model imposes and the need for a richer model if the Web is to continue to grow and evolve.

1.3.1 The Web's Linking Model

One of the key factors in the Web's growth in the last decade has been the way in which it enables users to move about and explore an enormous information space. Several key characteristics have contributed to this ability. The first is the distributed nature of the Web—the HTTP protocol supports access to information from remote sources in a seamless fashion. The second is the way in which the information is interlinked—it is supported through several mechanisms, but most notably the linking mechanisms associated with HTML and URIs.

At its simplest, a link between items of information requires three components: a source, a destination, and the connection between these two (shown in Figure 1.1). Although these might be quite obvious, it is worth dissecting them a little. The mechanism for representing link sources

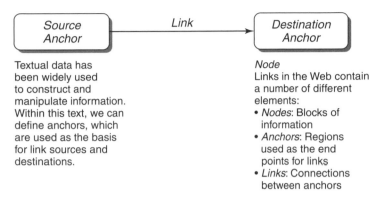

Figure 1.1 Basic linking components

(and possible destinations) is HTML's <a> element. Effectively everything between the start and end tags of this element forms a marked section of text, also called an *anchor*. For example, consider the following HTML fragments:

doc1.html

```
Textual data has been widely used to construct and manipulate
information. We can define <a href="doc2.html#example">anchors</a>
within this text, which are used as the basis for link sources
and destinations.
```

doc2.html

```
<p>Links in the Web contain a number of elements:
<ul>
    <li>Nodes: Blocks of information
    <li><a name="example">Anchors: Regions used as the end points
        for links</a>
    <li>Links: Connections between anchors
</ul>
```

In the second fragment of HTML, the text Anchors has been marked as an anchor—in this case the source anchor for a link in the first HTML fragment. The locator itself is represented as the href attribute of the source anchor. The destination of the link is a URI. The destination can be either an entire document or a location within a document, indicated by a *fragment identifier* (marked by the <a name="example"> tag in the second HTML fragment).

This representation of link sources has several implications. One of the most significant is that the anchors and links are embedded directly into the document being viewed. This means that if we wish to include a link source in a document, then we need to modify that document. Similarly, although we can link to an entire document without modifying the document, if we wish to link to anchors inside a document, then we need to be able to either modify the destination document as well or utilize anchors that have already been placed in the document.

A second implication is that this representation is used for all types of links. If we look at most Web sites, we see that the links are used for various purposes. Typically, there may be structural links, such as links occurring in hierarchical menus to provide information further down (or up) the tree. There will also often be semantic links to related information (such as in the example just given). The representation of links in the Web does not allow differentiation between these different types of links.

1.3.2 A Broader View of Linking in the Web

But is this the only model of linking that the Web supports? It is, if we consider only explicit user-supported navigation. But if we think of links as connections between resources, then the Web also supports some additional forms of linking. For example, consider the following fragment of an HTML document:

```
<html>
 <head>
   <meta name="title" content="Transcluding the Web">
   <meta name="keywords" content="Linking XML XLink">
   <meta name="authors" content="Erik Wilde and David Lowe">
   <title>Transcluding the Web</title>
   <link rel="stylesheet" href="trans.css" type="text/css">
 </head>
 <body bgcolor="#EEEEEE">
   <img src="header.gif" alt="Linking Example">
   ...
 </body>
</html>
```

This example illustrates three other forms of linking. The first is where a document is associated with another one—in this case, a stylesheet. The association is not one based on the content of the document, but rather on the way in which the document is to be presented. This type of relationship is not one that would be explicitly used by (or even be apparent to) a user. Rather, it is used by the software manipulating the document—most likely a browser.[4] Nevertheless, the association between the document

---

[4]Some browsers, such as Opera, allow the user to make explicit decisions about which stylesheet will be used by the browser. This can affect the semantics of how a link to a stylesheet within a document might be interpreted.

and its stylesheet could provide useful information to tools that facilitate access to information (especially where the stylesheet contains named styles). For example, a search engine could use this type of association to allow a user to retrieve all Web pages that contain text paragraphs formatted as `margin-note`.

The second case of linking in the example just given is a little more subtle. We have several `meta` tags containing `name-content` pairs, providing metadata about the document—information that describes the document rather than being part of the document itself. This metadata is typically not displayed by a browser but is used in analyzing or searching the document. In effect, we have information that has been explicitly associated with the document content. This can be viewed as a degenerate case of linking and is usually not even considered to be linking.

The third case is where an image has been embedded into a document. This is similar to the first case just mentioned. Both represent an association between two different files. The difference, however, is in the implied semantics of the association. With the image, the semantics are (usually) interpreted as "when showing this document, show the image embedded into it at this location." The semantics of the association to the stylesheet are that the stylesheet is used to format elements of the document. In other words, the various mechanisms for creating associations in HTML have very different implied semantics.

1.3.3 Shortcomings of the Web Linking Model

The primary linking model for the Web has a number of quite significant shortcomings that will limit its usefulness as the Web matures and becomes more sophisticated. We should again emphasize that this is not a criticism of the model that was adopted—the simplicity of this model is one of the key reasons the Web was originally so successful. A richer, more flexible, but consequently more complex approach to linking would have made Web technologies and concepts more difficult to understand and manage and hence have hindered the early development of the Web. Nevertheless, this simplicity now needs to be addressed as part of the ongoing evolution and maturing of the Web.

So what are these limitations? We shall list some of the more significant constraints and then discuss each of them in turn:

- Embedded anchors limit the ability to link from or into read-only material.
- Embedded unidirectional links make backtracking extremely difficult.
- The lack of overlapping anchors creates problems.

- Links lack any form of inherent contextualization.
- Single-source, single-destination links inhibit the representation of certain types of associations.
- Untyped links inhibit intelligent browsing and navigation.
- Embedded and untyped links restrict effective content management and flexible information structuring schemes.

Inability to Link from or into Read-Only Material

One of the most significant problems is the difficulty associated with linking either from or to content that is either read-only or beyond the control of the link author. This is particularly problematic when content is being reused or is stored in a read-only format (for example, on a CD-ROM). Consider the following scenarios:

- Joe Linker is creating an educational site devoted to XML linking. As part of the educational experience, he would like users to undertake some background reading. This involves reading a specific sequence of material collected from different Web sites. Ideally, he would create a trail though this existing material, either by adding a link to the end of each section, which links to the next, or by creating a new composite page (or node) that contains the relevant extracts (but without "cutting-and-pasting" the material—and hence infringing on the original author's rights).[5] In both cases, the existing HTML model of linking (and document composition) does not allow this.

- Users may often wish to annotate Web pages belonging to someone else with their own comments and observations. For example, Joe Linker is searching for information on XML linking to include in his educational site. He locates a page on a remote server containing relevant information, but finds a small section within the main document with which he disagrees. He would like to add a link (that only he or others using his link set will see) from the section in question to a critique that he has written and is stored on his own server. The Web, however, provides no mechanism to add anchors into content maintained by others.

- Joe Linker finds some additional information on XLink that would be good to provide as a resource, but unfortunately the material is in the middle of a very long Web page containing predominantly unrelated

---

[5]This is a classic example of transclusion, where existing material is *transcluded* into a new document that in reality is only a view onto the underlying original source.

information. The information on XLink is not tagged with a named anchor that can be used as a link destination, so Joe has no way of linking to the information other than to link to the overall page— a rather unsatisfactory solution.

In each case, the scenario described is common but cannot be implemented using the current linking model supported by HTML. There are, of course, ways around these problems (i.e., technical "kludges" such as the use of frames to present related material), but they are invariably cumbersome, often ineffective, and expensive to maintain.

Difficulty in Backtracking through Links

The links supported by HTML are unidirectional and are embedded into the source document. These two factors make it very difficult to locate all documents that link *to* a given target. We can easily determine all the targets to which a given document is linked by searching the document for `<a>` elements and extracting the relevant URIs. Achieving the reverse is extremely difficult. Identifying all of the documents that link to a specific target would require retrieving and checking every single page on the Web to determine whether or not it contained a reference to the target—something that may be theoretically possible but which is rather impractical.

At present a number of search engines maintain linking indexes, so that it is possible to query a search engine for all indexed pages that contain a reference to a certain URI. For example, try submitting `+ml:transcluding.com` to Lycos (`http://lycospro.lycos.com`) or `link:transcluding.com` to Google (`http://www.google.com`). This will return only those pages that reference `http://transcluding.com` and that happen to be indexed by the respective search engines. The list will be anything but comprehensive. Even the most comprehensive search engines are estimated to have only around 25 percent of the Web indexed (see `http://www.searchenginewatch.com/reports/sizes.html` for more details).

One of the major consequences of this problem concerns maintainability of the Web. If an author changes (or deletes) a page, it is very difficult for him to know which other pages may be affected, as it is almost impossible to know which pages may be linked to the one that has been changed. A result of this is that some links are broken and some point to content that is no longer relevant.

Problems with the Lack of Overlapping Anchors

The Hypertext Markup Language has a significant problem with regard to overlapping anchors. Strictly speaking, HTML supports nested anchors, though they are not handled well. For example, consider the following simple Web page:

```
<html>
  <body>
    <h1>A test of overlapping anchors</h1>
    <p><a href="link1">Main anchor<br>
    <a href="link2">Nested anchor</a><br>
    Main anchor again</a>
  </body>
</html>
```

If this is viewed in almost all Web browsers and the nested anchor is selected, then the browser will interpret this as a link to link2 and not both link1 and link2. This case of overlapping anchors may be considered a restriction of the browsers and not HTML itself. However, the inability to represent the following pseudo-HTML fragment (note that it is not valid HTML), where the anchors overlap, is a constraint of HTML itself. This is not a particular flaw in HTML's design but rather something that is a consequence of limitations in the SGML family of languages to which HTML belongs (and which also therefore applies to XML).

```
<pseduo-html>
  <body>
    <h1>A test of overlapping anchors</h1>
    <p><a1 href="link1">Connect to item 1
    <a2 href="link2">Connect to both</a1>
    Connect to item 2</a2>
  </body>
</pseduo-html>
```

This limitation of HTML creates difficulties with both overlapping source anchors (where we might have a section of text that can be linked to several places) and overlapping destination anchors (where we have overlapping material that may be the destination of different links). For example, we may have a document test.htm that contains three sections (A, B, and C), and we want one link that has a destination of sections A and B (test.htm#AandB) and other link that has sections B and C as a destination (test.htm#BandC). This cannot be achieved in HTML.

Link Destination Unpredictability

A significant issue in the use of the Web is the way in which users navigate through the information space. Given a certain page that is being viewed, users must make a decision about which link (or links) are worth following. In order to make a productive decision, they should be able to predict where the link is likely to lead. Links, as represented by HTML, lack any form of inherent contextualization. In other words, the only mechanism that users have for understanding the likely destination of a link is the anchor text (and possibly the context in which the anchor text has appeared). There is an inherent conflict here in that the anchor text is typically part of some broader information and hence is governed by this information and may not be able to be changed to reflect the link destination. This is exactly why it is unclear which form of linking may be more suitable, as illustrated in the following passages:

> An effective way to achieve better linking is through the use of <u>XLink</u>. This would allow the creation of much richer links that do not . . .

or

> An effective way to achieve better linking is through the use of XLink (case studies on the use of XLink are <u>available</u>). This would allow the creation of much richer links that do not . . .

These issues can always be addressed in HTML by modifying both the content and the anchor appropriately, though this can be somewhat cumbersome. A more effective mechanism is to provide a link title, for example:

```
<a href="..." title="XLink Case Studies">XLink</a>
```

The title appears when the link is selected (for example, by moving the mouse pointer over it) but has not yet been activated. This title can therefore be used to provide a brief indication of the link target—a substantial improvement but still confined to a simple (and short) textual description.

Problems Related to Single-Source, Single-Destination Links

HTML links have a single-source anchor and a single-destination anchor. This means that it is not possible to create links with multiple destinations. Consider the following scenario: A user navigates to a Web page that contains a description of a research project. The information includes a link to the project researchers, which when followed opens two separate documents containing, respectively, details about the two main researchers. This is not possible to represent using the linking model in HTML (though it is possible to simulate this behavior using other technologies such as scripting languages).

Similarly the lack of multiple-source links can be problematic. Often content is the target of numerous links. Ideally we would like to be able to create a single link (with a single destination) but with multiple sources. From a user's perspective this would not be any different from multiple single-source links (except that we could no longer query to find out the

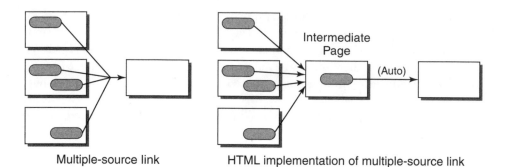

Figure 1.2   Implementing a multiple-source link in HTML

other sources of the link). The major benefit of a multiple-source link is in terms of the link's maintenance. Consider an example where we have numerous links from different places in a site to a single page containing details of the main sales contact person. If this changes to a different person, then we would need to change the destination of all the links; whereas if we have implemented a multiple-source, single-destination link, then we only need to modify a single link.

Again, there are ways to circumvent this problem. For example, we could have all of the single-source, single-destination links point to a single URI and have the content of this URI modified instead of modifying the target anchor. This is somewhat cumbersome. An alternative would be to again have many single-source, single-destination links all pointing to a single URI but have this URI contain a page that immediately redirects the user to the correct destination. In effect, the intermediate page becomes the multiple-source, single-destination link. This is illustrated in Figure 1.2. Again, this solution is somewhat cumbersome.

Inhibiting of Intelligent Browsing and Navigation by Untyped Links

HTML has no mechanism for the typing of links. Indeed it is not possible to add attributes of any sort (other than a name, a title, and an ID) to links. In other words, it is not possible to define different categories of links within an HTML document and then have these categories managed in different ways. This would be particularly useful in supporting more effective browsing and navigation. In many cases it would be useful to be able to show different types of links using different forms of highlighting, as a way of providing additional information to users. For example, a site might contain structural links that relate to the inherent organization of the content, elaborative links that connect to more detailed information on a particular topic, and definition links that provide connections into a glossary. Each type of link could be shown differently (different fonts, colors, and so forth).

As another example, if a link could be supplemented with the name of the link author, then it would be possible for users to selectively view only links created by certain authors. Thus numerous different authors could add links to a given set of Web pages, but a given user could opt to see only those links created by one particular author who creates links that suit that user.

As a final example, different links in a set of educational pages could relate to different levels of learning; and as users learned more, they could switch on certain links and switch off others.

In each case, a fundamental requirement would be that the links could be typed in some form—typically by adding certain additional information to the links and then providing support for interpretation of these link attributes in the browser.

Related to the issue of untyped links is the issue of link semantics. The semantics of links in HTML are very restrictive. Essentially it is assumed that the link defines an association between a source anchor and a destination anchor and that the link primarily exists to be traversed. The only additional semantics that can be specified is the target frame into which the destination of the link should be loaded. This is specified using the `target` attribute of the source anchor. This effectively provides control over whether the target document should replace the existing document or be placed in a different existing frame (or in a new frame altogether).

As an alternative to this restrictive model, consider the following scenario: A user is browsing a Web page that contains multiple components organized into a complex interface and shown on the same page: a map of a local national park, a list of walking trails in the park, a brief history of the park, and a photo showing a waterfall within the park. There is also a sound track of local birdlife playing in the background. If the user selects a link to a trail, then the question is, what aspects of the presentation should be kept, paused, discarded, changed, and so forth? In this situation, the list of walks should be kept, the history should be replaced by a description of the specified walk, the photo should be replaced by a video of the trail, and the sound track should continue unchanged.

Achieving functionality such as this requires sophisticated link semantics, whereby the link includes information on impacts on the media components currently forming the interface. This can be partially simulated in the Web through the use of frames and a scripting language; but as with many of the examples in this section, the techniques are cumbersome and difficult to implement. A good example of a link model that addresses this is the Amsterdam Hypermedia Model (AHM) [Hardman+ 93]. AHM manages this idea by specifying the context for each anchor associated with a link. This context defines the part of the presentation that will be affected when the link is followed. Many of the ideas in AHM have subsequently been included in the Synchronized Multimedia Interchange Language (SMIL) [Hoschka 98] standard.

Restrictive Content Structuring and Management

Links in HTML are used not only to create associations that support users' navigation but also as the primary mechanism for providing structure to the content on a site. The creation of associative links for supporting navigation is largely a local issue; the global issue of overall information structure is just as important.

Content structuring is typically carried out by organizing the content in a site into a hierarchy (though other structures, such as a matrix, are also used). This organization uses the same HTML linking mechanism as other forms of linking (i.e., the <a> element). As such, it is very difficult to effectively maintain the content structures. For example, having the structural links embedded into the documents themselves means that making changes to the structure and browsing the structures that exist are rather difficult. (In chapter 3, we discuss a system called Hyperwave, which stores the structure separately from the content, thereby at least partly resolving this problem.)

1.3.4 Current Solutions

Here are a few ways in which the problems discussed in this chapter are currently being addressed in the Web. As has been discussed, the current linking model supported by HTML creates problems and places restrictions on what can be achieved. Despite this, the need for innovative solutions has led to some creativity. The solutions largely revolve around scripting languages, browser enhancements and plug-ins, and server extensions or enhancements.

Scripting Languages

Scripting languages, such as JavaScript, can be used to support a richer linking functionality than the basic model. The simplest way of achieving this is to associate certain *linking* events with appropriate scripting code. For example, consider the following HTML fragment:

```
<html>
 <head>
  <script type="text/javascript">
  <!--
  function linker(linkname) {
    if (linkname == 'authors') {
      window.open("http://www.eng.uts.edu.au/~dbl/");
      window.open("http://dret.net/netdret");
      return false;
    }
```

```
      if (linkname == 'xmlinfo') {
        window.location = "http://www.w3c.org/xml/";
        return false;
      }
    }
    // -->
    </script>
</head>
<body>
    <h1>Sophisticated linking using JavaScripting</h1>

    <p><a href="" onclick="return linker('authors')">Authors:</a>
    Erik Wilde and David Lowe

    <p>This is a very simple example of using JavaScript to
    create multiple source, multiple destination links. In
    this case there are two links - one to the
    <a href="" onclick="return linker('authors')">authors</a>
    of this page, and the other to information on
    <a href="" onclick="return linker('xmlinfo')">XML</a>.
  </body>
</html>
```

In this example, all source anchors have been associated with the `onclick` event. This event is triggered whenever the anchor is activated. In this case, the event calls a JavaScript function and passes the name of the link to be followed to the function. This means that multiple-source anchors are able to pass the same link name as an argument—hence we have a mechanism for supporting multiple-source anchors. In the example just given, both anchors related to *authors* use the same link.

The JavaScript function that handles the link activation event accepts the link name and then triggers the appropriate action. With the `xmlinfo` link, the event handler simply replaces the current document with a new document—effectively achieving the same behavior as a normal HTML link.[6] The `authors` link, however, results in two new windows being opened, each with a different destination document. As such, we have implemented a simple multiple-destination link.

Additional JavaScript code could be added to make this approach much more sophisticated. For example, attributes could be added that allowed the `linker` function to change the navigation behavior based on user configuration or other characteristics.

Although this approach allows a richer solution to linking than is possible with simple HTML and is quite flexible, it requires a relatively high

---

[6]Note that the JavaScript function returns `false` in order to stop the anchor triggering its own link as specified by the `<a>` element's `href` attribute. Although we have left the `href` attribute without a value (to avoid confusion), in practice a URI would normally be included in case scripting was disabled.

degree of technical knowledge to manage and maintain. Furthermore, it requires additional functionality in the browser, which must be able to execute JavaScript code.

Server Extensions

Web servers can be enhanced in a number of ways. As an example, it is possible to modify a server so that links are stored in a separate linkbase rather than being embedded into documents. They are then merged with documents dynamically as the documents are retrieved. Webcosm (discussed in the next chapter) is a good example of a Web server that follows this pattern. Once links are stored in the linkbase they can then be managed in flexible ways, such as by allowing the addition of numerous link attributes, which are then used in selection or adaptation of the links. It also means that the integrity of the links can be easily ensured by the server.

The server can also be used to manage the content structure. For example, documents can be registered with the server and added to specific structural locations. Additional functionality can also be added. Examples include access control, automatic creation of indexes and site maps, and more sophisticated structures such as guided tours through the content. The Hyperwave server (also discussed in more detail in the next chapter) illustrates well this type of support for very effective content and link management, while still providing a conventional Web-based interface.

1.4 CONCLUSIONS

The Web infrastructure developed and adopted during the 1990s has been highly successful. One of the factors that led to the incredible growth of the Web was the combination of power and simplicity that the HTML/HTTP standards represented. The simplicity allowed developers to focus on creating applications that were usable in a very heterogeneous environment. The simplicity has, however, also led to restrictions that are now beginning to become more apparent as the Web grows and matures. In this chapter, we have looked at many of these restrictions.

In the next chapter, we look at how many of these limitations have been addressed in other systems and develop a deeper understanding of the underlying concepts of hypermedia, information management, and support for information structuring. In particular, we develop some insights into how the Web might evolve and how the various emerging technologies (especially those surrounding XML—XLink, XPath, and XPointer—though also including numerous others) might be utilized to create effective Web-based hypermedia systems and applications.

2

Hypermedia Concepts
and Alternatives
to the Web

The previous chapter showed how the link model that underpins the Web has problems with regard to support for certain types of information management and access. In this chapter, we look at these concepts in much more detail—going back to some first principles regarding concepts from hypermedia, information retrieval, and information management. In particular, we show that there exist much more sophisticated linking models that can be used to provide a richer level of user interaction.

This chapter illustrates why we would benefit from improving the Web's referencing and linking technologies and provides some indications of the directions in which these technologies might usefully be taken—especially with respect to the use of XLink and related technologies such as XPath and XPointer.

In section 2.1, we begin by considering hypermedia itself, looking at some of the historical origins of the field. We then move on to consider basic terminology and concepts (section 2.2) and a range of typical scenarios that illustrate the substantial gains that can be obtained through effective implementation of these ideas (section 2.3).

2.1 WHAT IS HYPERMEDIA?

As we have discussed, two of the key concepts of the Web are the way information can be interlinked and how these links can be used to support user navigation and information access. The linking that is inherently supported by the Web is, however, only a very simplified version of what has been much more deeply investigated within the hypermedia community.

Hypermedia is one of the fundamental concepts underpinning the Web. The terms *hypermedia* and *hypertext* are both in common usage. Historically, hypertext was the original term; but as the concepts extended to include media other than text, the term *hypermedia* became common. The terms are now largely used interchangeably, though purists would still argue that hypermedia is really applicable only when the links can be from and to both text and other forms of media such as graphics, animation, video, audio, and so forth. We use the term hypermedia unless we explicitly are referring to only textual issues.

Hypermedia is the basis for the associative linking that provides much of the Web's flexibility. Hypermedia is, however, potentially much more powerful than the simple links we see in Web pages. The Web implements only a very simplistic version of hypermedia concepts. To explain this, let us go back several decades and look at some of the historical roots of hypermedia concepts and what they tell us about information linking.

2.1.1 History of Hypermedia

In 1945, Vannevar Bush published a paper titled "As We May Think" [Bush 45]. In it, Bush discussed the increasing volume of recorded information and our growing inability to effectively manage this information. In particular, he discussed a hypothetical system called Memex that allows users to establish recorded associations between different elements of information:

> Our ineptitude in getting at the record is largely caused by the artificiality of systems of indexing. . . . The human mind does not work that way. It operates by association. With one item in its grasp, it snaps instantly to the next that is suggested by the association of thoughts, in accordance with some intricate web of trails carried by the cells of the brain.
>
> Man cannot hope to fully duplicate this mental process artificially, but he certainly ought to be able to learn from it. In minor ways he may even improve, for his records have relative permanency. The first idea, however, to be drawn from the analogy concerns selection. Selection by association, rather than by indexing, may yet be mechanized.
>
> Consider a future device for individual use, which is a sort of mechanized private file and library. It needs a name, and to coin one at random, "memex" will do. A memex is a device in which an individual stores all his books, records, and communications, and which is mechanized so that it may be consulted with exceeding speed and flexibility. It is an enlarged intimate supplement to his memory.

Bush went on to describe the Memex as a mechanical device that allowed connections to be established between items of information stored on microfiche. These connections could be used to retrieve information that was associated with the information currently being viewed. Bush wasn't so much concerned with technical implementations (though he described some interesting ideas) but with how information could be managed and accessed effectively. He also went on to discuss concepts such as *information trails,* where information designers could create sequences of connections that could be used by others.

However, it wasn't until approximately 20 years later that these concepts were developed further. Several researchers, including Doug Engelbart and Ted Nelson, began looking at systems that embodied some of Bush's ideas. Doug Engelbart envisaged the user and the computer in a dynamic symbiosis, which resulted in augmented human capabilities. He developed a system called *NLS* (for oN-Line System) for managing documentation that included rudimentary techniques for creating associations between documentation elements [Engelbart 88].

At roughly the same time, Nelson was also looking at similar concepts. He introduced the term *hypertext* in 1965 to refer to the way in which associations between information can be explicitly represented. Indeed, Nelson saw hypertext as a means of extending the way information could be used [Nelson 93]:

> We would not be reading from paper any more. The computer screen, with its instant access, would make paper distribution of text absurd. Best of all, no longer would we be stuck with linear text, but we could create whole new gardens of interconnected text and graphics for the user to explore! (It would be several years before I would choose the word "hypertext" for this vision.) Users would sit holding a light-pen to the screen, making choices, browsing, exploring, making decisions. This would free education from the tyranny of teachers! It would free authors and artists from the tyranny of publishers! A new world of art! knowledge! populism! freedom! The very opposite of what everyone thought computers were about!

Nelson proposed a system called Xanadu (after the place of magic in one's literary memory in Samuel Taylor Coleridge's poem *Kubla Khan*) that included many of his hypertext and related concepts. Xanadu has yet to be completely implemented, though it has been the basis for introducing a number of additional ideas and terms, including micropayment systems, transclusion, and transcopyright. *Transclusion,* put rather simply, refers to the ability to include content by reference (a form of linking) rather than the more common cut-and-paste paradigm seen in computer systems today.

Over the ensuing three decades, the ideas established by Bush, Engelbart, and Nelson were expanded and incorporated into a diverse range of hypertext systems. Illustrative examples include ZOG [Robertson+ 81] (which evolved into KMS in the early 1980s), Hyperties [Shneiderman 87], NoteCards [Halasz+ 87], and Intermedia [Yankelovich+ 85] in the mid-1980s, HyperCard [Apple 89] in 1987, and Hyper-G (which was commercialized as Hyperwave) [Maurer 96] and Microcosm [Hall+ 96] in the 1990s.

2.1.2 Definition of Hypermedia

So what was the outcome of all this work on hypertext systems? It is the creation of explicit associations between information elements and establishing how these associations became the key unifying concepts—though the ways in which these associations are actually used varies significantly. Let us look briefly at some of the definitions developed for hypertext:

- Text that is not constrained to be linear [W3C 95]
- The combination of natural languages text with the computer's capacity for branching, or dynamic display [Nelson 67]
- A database that has active cross-references and allows the reader to jump to other parts of the database as desired [Shneiderman & Kearsley 89]

It is worth noting that the concept of *nonlinearity* often appears in discussions of hypermedia and hypertext. This does not imply that the user navigates along more than one path (though this may indeed be the case). Rather it means that the user has a range of options—hypertext provides explicit support for a network of potential or possible paths through the information.

The underlying theme of all of these definitions is the use of information interrelationships to provide support for flexible access and information management. The support hypermedia provides for information interlinking allows us to navigate the network of information (often referred to as the information space) in complex but flexible patterns, primarily so that we (or software agents acting on our behalf) can identify specific items of information or information patterns. The associative linking of information parallels the mechanisms by which our minds retrieve information. It is also worth commenting that there is a similar argument for using multiple forms of media. This is because of the ability of other forms of media (such as images and audio) to convey certain forms of information much more rapidly.

We shall adopt the following as our working definition of hypermedia for the rest of this book.

Hypermedia—An application that uses associative relationships among information contained within multiple media data for the purpose of facilitating access to and manipulation of the information encapsulated by the data. [Lowe & Hall 99]

This definition states that the reason for supporting hypermedia concepts—and especially the fundamental idea of associations between information elements—is to allow users to gain improved access to information. For much of the rest of the book we will be demonstrating how the evolving technologies of the Web effectively support this idea.

So, this definition tells us what hypermedia *is,* but it doesn't really help us understand the elements that are used in constructing and managing these important information associations or how they can be most effectively utilized. In the next section, we will look at the underlying concepts in much more detail and how these concepts help in improving information utilization.

2.2 HYPERMEDIA CONCEPTS

In this section, we introduce and formalize the basic concepts and terminology that underpin the management of associations between and organization of content. In particular, we focus on the key concepts of hypermedia in the context of a large-scale, open, distributed information management system such as the Web. The logical place to start is to look at how associations are typically represented.

2.2.1 Representing Information Associations

More interesting than the systems themselves (at least when considering what hypermedia is) are the ways in which different systems implement hypermedia concepts. At the core of almost all of the systems was the creation of explicit representations of associations between information. There are, however, very significant differences in both the form the representations take and the types of associations represented.

Associations between information can be unidirectional, bidirectional, or nondirectional. Where associations are directional, there can be a single source or multiple sources, a single destination or multiple destinations. The associations can be typed or untyped; they can be structural or semantic.

Similarly, the associations can be represented in numerous ways. One of the most fundamental is as links between the information sources. Alternatively, they can be reptresented as members of a common set. The associations (be they links or some other form) can be embedded directly into the content or stored separately in a *linkbase* (i.e., a database for links). They can refer to explicit content or be generic to any content that meets certain requirements. They can even be computed dynamically as required (something common in adaptive hypertext systems, where the associations change to adapt to the user or conditions). A few examples might make this bewildering variety of hypertext concepts a little clearer.

Simple Web Link
One of the simplest examples of information associations is the ordinary HTML link. Consider the example HTML code shown in Figure 2.1. This

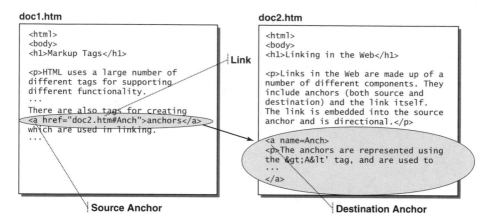

Figure 2.1   Simple Web link

is a simple static, directional, single-source, single-destination link that is embedded into the source document. It is static because the link never changes (unless it is explicitly modified by an author). It is directional because the link has an explicit direction of association (and hence, usually, an explicit primary direction of navigation). It is single-source because the link has only one point from which it can be triggered. It is single-destination because the link has only one information element that is *accessed* when the link is activated. The link is embedded into the source document (indeed, it is embedded within the source anchor) because the description of the connection between the source and destination anchors exists within the source anchor.

Dynamic Web Link

Figure 2.2 shows a slightly more complex example. Like the previous case, this is directional, single-source, single-destination link that is embedded into the source document. The major difference is that the link is dynamic rather than static. The link is to a computer-generated interface (CGI) program (in this example, a Perl script) that analyzes relevant input data and determines a suitable document to be returned (either directly or through an appropriate HTTP redirect response). For example, the CGI program may return a time-dependent page based on the current time or a user-specific page based on users previous navigation (as stored in cookies). In other words, the destination may change each time the link is followed. Note also that the link is not multidestination, despite the existence of multiple possible destinations. Each time the link is activated, only a single destination is retrieved.

Whether the link is viewed as embedded in the source document is somewhat unclear. The first half of the link (i.e., from the source anchor

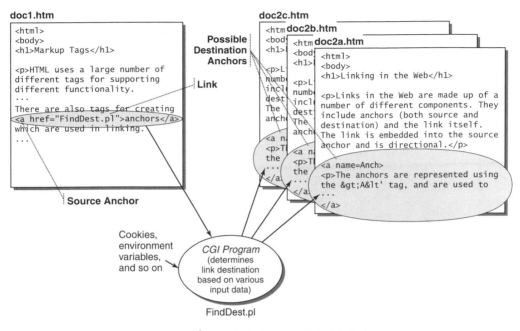

Figure 2.2 Dynamic Web link

to the CGI program) is embedded in the document containing the source anchor, but the identification of the possible link destinations is embedded in the CGI program.

Generic Link (in Webcosm)

Another example of linking is the generic link. In this case, we have a link that is defined independently of the source material but that is instantiated for each occurrence matching the specified anchor.

Consider Figure 2.3, which shows a typical document retrieved through a Webcosm Web server [Hall+ 96]. In this example (which is rather simplistic and does not demonstrate the full capabilities of Webcosm), we have a source document (doc1'.htm) that initially contains no links. When this document is retrieved from the Webcosm server, the server first compares it to a list of links in the currently selected linkbases. Whenever a potential link anchor is located within the source document, a relevant anchor and link are added into the document. Consequently, the document that is returned to the user contains appropriate anchors for each occurrence of the generic link.

The result is effectively a multiple-source, single-destination link. Although the source anchors and the link, as seen by the user, are embedded

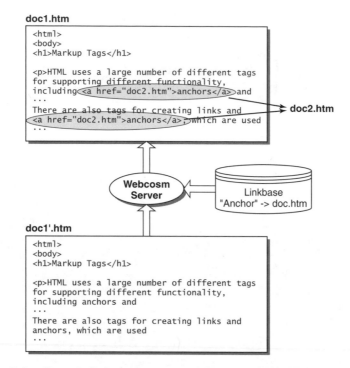

Figure 2.3   Generic link (using a simplification of the Webcosm server)

into the source document, this embedding is a consequence of the HTML presentation. The link (and indeed the anchor) is not stored with the source document. Rather it is stored in a separate linkbase. The link is also still static and still directional.

It is worth noting that the architecture of Webcosm allows a much richer degree of link management than that illustrated by this example. Figure 2.4 shows the architecture of the Microcosm link service (the system from which Webcosm was developed). In Microcosm, documents typically do not contain explicit links that are selected. Rather the user can select a section of a document and request to see or follow the links in this section.

When a user triggers an action (such as selecting a region of text and then requesting the system to follow any links in this region), the action is passed to the Document Control System (DCS). The DCS dispatches information associated with the action (content of the selected part of the source document, the action chosen by the user, and so forth) to the Filter Manager as a message. The Filter Manager then passes the message through a series of filter programs that can manipulate it.

One example of a filter is the Linkbase filter. This recognizes an action to follow a link. It looks up the source anchor (i.e., the selected content) in

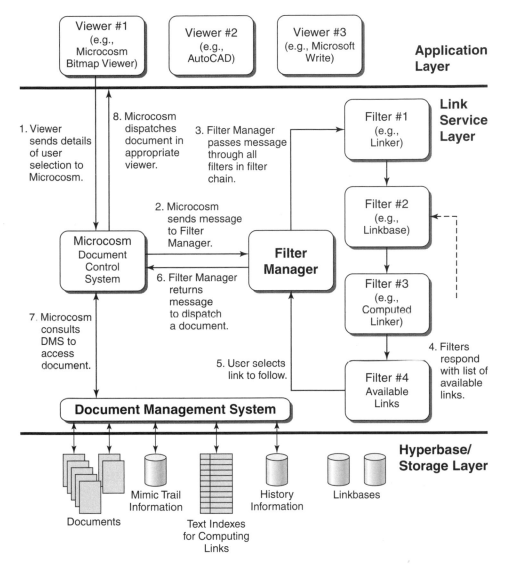

Figure 2.4 Message passing in the Microcosm link service architecture.
Reproduced by kind permission of Wendy Hall [2001].

the database of links. If it can find any relevant links, it generates a new message requesting that the DCS dispatch the document (or documents, if the link has multiple destinations) to the user and show the section of the document that forms the destination anchor.

The architecture also allows more sophisticated functionality. For example, the last filter in the chain can be a program that recognizes all the messages requesting documents to be displayed (i.e., the destinations of any identified links) and replaces them with messages asking the user to select the link he or she wishes to follow. This way if the user selected a section of text that contained multiple links and requested the system to retrieve related documents, the response would be a list of links (and destination documents) from which the user could choose. The structure also allows the creation of computed link filters. Such filters might create dynamically computed links—automatic links that are created based on a comparison of the selected information and the content of other available documents.

The linkbases in Microcosm allow the specification of three primitive link types. The first is the specific link. This is similar to the links in the Web, where the link is associated with an anchor at a specific location in a document. The second link type is the local link. This is associated with the occurrence of a specific piece of information, irrespective of where it occurs in a document. The third type is the generic link, as described earlier. The system can also use multiple linkbases, allowing users to select linkbases that are suitable to their particular needs. In other words, the same set of documents can have different linkbases (and hence links) depending on the way in which the documents are used or the preferences of the user. We could, for example, provide a linkbase developed by the original author, a linkbase containing personal annotations of the user, and a general linkbase containing generic links into a glossary, dictionary, or similar reference source.

Finally, it is worth noting that Webcosm, the Web-based version of Microcosm, is naturally constrained by the architecture of the Web and so cannot provide quite as flexible an approach as that described by the Microcosm link service. Nevertheless, the broad approach to managing links is still significantly richer than that for conventional Web servers.

Structural Links (in Hyperwave)

Not only can links be managed in different ways, but they can also serve very different purposes. This is commonly seen in the Web where many pages have both structural links, such as menus, and associative links, such as cross-site references.

A good example of how these can be managed in an effective way is to store the structure of the site separately from the actual content. Consider Figure 2.5. In this example, the associations between various information nodes (in this case, documents) are stored in a linkbase. The associations include both structural relationships and associative links. When a specific document is requested from the server, the server retrieves the document, looks up the linkbase to identify appropriate associations, and then builds

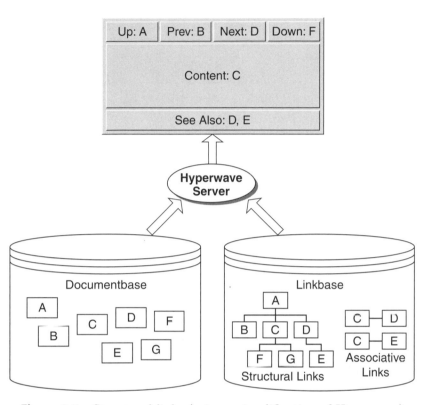

Figure 2.5 Structural links (using a simplification of Hyperwave)

a composite page containing both the document and its relevant links. The generated page is then returned to the user.

The resultant structural links are single-source, single-destination. Like the previous example, they are not embedded into the source document but rather stored separately. A good example of a server that supports this type of functionality is Hyperwave. The Hyperwave server supports the concept of document collections as a way of performing effective document management. Most Web systems address document management very poorly, often leaving it up to the underlying operating system's file management. The developers of Hyperwave (and Hyper-G, the research system on which Hyperwave is based) introduced the idea of document collections. A collection acts as a container for objects (including documents and other collections). Every object must be part of one or more collections, with the result that we have a collection hierarchy. (It is not, however, a tree structure since a document can belong to multiple collections.)

Whenever a new document is added to the server, it must be added to a collection; and since collections can be directly browsed, the document will

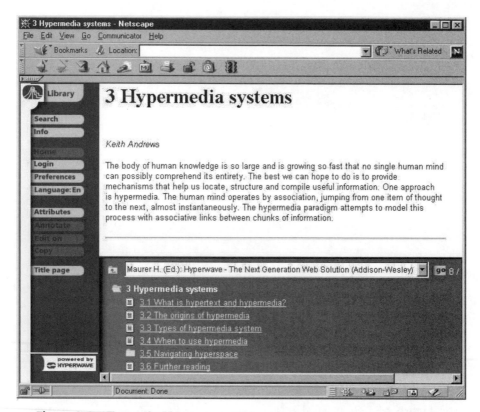

Figure 2.6   Example Hyperwave Web page containing structural links

automatically be available to users, unlike with conventional Web servers where added documents require suitable links to be added from other related documents before they become accessible. Hyperwave uses the document hierarchy as a browsing tool for users. A user can locate a document by browsing the hierarchy like a sequence of menus—following structural links that are automatically created from the collection hierarchy. Figure 2.6 shows a typical example of a Web page constructed by a Hyperwave server. The bottom part of the page contains an automatically generated set of structural links to other elements within a particular collection. The specific format of the generated structural links is highly configurable.

The Hyperwave document management also contains various other features. A collection may contain a special document called the *collection head,* which is shown whenever a collection is viewed (rather than listing the contents of the collection). Hyperwave also supports two special types of collection: the *cluster,* which contains a set of documents that should typically be viewed together in some form (such as for a multimedia presentation); and the *sequence,* which is an ordered collection of documents (or sub-collections) that should be presented in sequence (such as for a guided tour). Also, both documents and collections are supported by a rich attribute model (including attributes such as the owner, name, creation, modification and expiration dates, and access and modification permissions). These attributes allow sophisticated linking, for example, only showing links to documents that the user has permission to access.

Spatial Hypertext Associations

Irrespective of how links are stored and represented, they can be presented in a wide variety of ways. Apart from the conventional link presentation seen in most Web browsers, a number of hypertext systems use spatial representations, where the associations between information components are represented either by actual connections shown in a diagram or through the use of spatial proximity (the closer the items, the more related they are).

Consider Figure 2.7, which shows a screen shot of a relatively simple spatial hypertext system adapted for use on the Web. The left pane contains a representation of the associations between information items—in this case, papers from a conference. Users can zoom into and move around this representation, which is implemented using the Virtual Reality Modeling Language (VRML). They can also select any item and have it displayed in the right pane.

The underlying associations between information items can be represented in any of the ways just presented. They can be extracted from the static links contained in the documents themselves, they can be obtained from a linkbase, or possibly they can even be constructed dynamically by carrying out a suitable semantic analysis of the documents to identify papers with related content. In this last case, the author need not ever explicitly create any form of link. Rather, the association can be determined by an automated analysis. In a case such as this, the association is nondirectional, potentially many-anchored, and certainly not static.

Set-Based Association

All of the examples described so far have represented the associations between information elements as links. This need not be the case. Items can be associated not only by explicitly creating a connection between them, but also by ensuring that they belong to a common set. This was hinted at with Hyperwave, described earlier, where documents belong to a collection (i.e., the association is *represented* by common membership), though the associations are still typically *presented* as a link.

Several research systems have looked at ways of explicitly representing associations between information elements as sets rather than links. There are two levels at which this can be done. We can represent the associations

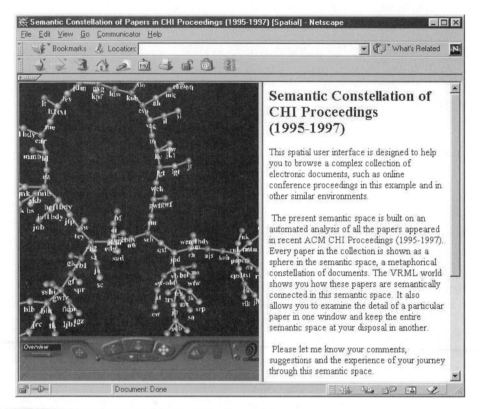

Figure 2.7   Spatial hypertext

as sets but still present them as links, or we can implement user interfaces that allow users to navigate within an information space that is devoid of links but that presents items as belonging to sets. An example of the latter is VIKI [Marshall+ 94]. Figure 2.8 shows how VIKI supports representation of associations between information by spatial proximity and membership in nested collections rather than explicit links. This hierarchy of collections allows users to visualize and utilize the relationships.

Nontextual Link

All of the examples shown so far have revolved around textual information. However, the associations between information need not be between text but may be between other media such as images, video, and audio. Where the association is represented as a link, all we need to do to create nontextual associations effectively is to establish anchors within nontextual data and to be able to refer to these anchors. Doing this in images is not particularly complex—being relatively familiar from HTML image maps,

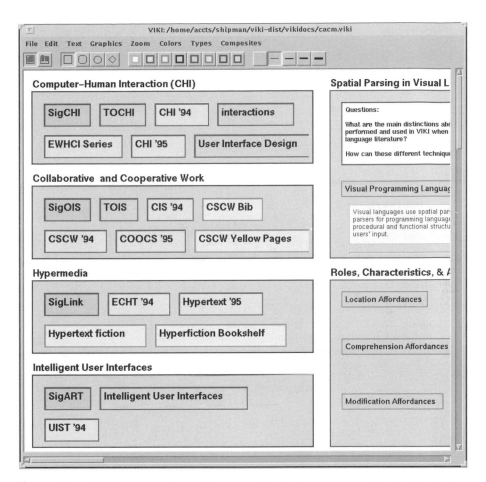

Figure 2.8 VIKI screen dump. Reproduced by kind permission of Cathy Marshall [2001].

where the anchor is defined by specifying the coordinates of the area that forms the anchor (though this mechanism cannot be used to specify destination anchors as targets). The following is an example of an image map being used to define link anchors (areas in the image) and associated links:

```
<html>
  <body>
    <h1>Example of HTML Image Map</h1>
    <img src="transclude_authors.gif" usemap="#auths">
    ...
    <map name="auths">
      <area shape="rect" coords="14,40,48,63" href="dbl.html">
      <area shape="rect" coords="57,71,93,98" href="dret.html">
```

```
      </map>
    </body>
</html>
```

The Synchronized Multimedia Interchange Language (SMIL) provides a more sophisticated way of representing anchors (and links) in nontextual media (allowing both spatial location and time information to be specified). Consider the following example SMIL markup:

```
<smil>
  <head>
    <layout type="text/smil-basic-layout">
      <root-layout width="200" height="200"/>
      <region id="video1" left="20" top="20"
              width="50" height="50" fit="fill"/>
      <region id="image2" left="100" top="20"
              width="80" height="50" fit="fill"/>
    </layout>
  </head>
  <body>
    <par>
      <video src="exampleA.rm" alt="Video clip"
             region="video1" dur="30s">
        <anchor href="blah.rm" coords="25%,25%,75%,75%"
                begin="0s" end="5s"/>
        <anchor href="hmmm.rm" coords="12,27,67,94"
                begin="12s" end="17s"/>
      </video>
      <img src="exampleB.gif" alt="Static image"
           region="image2" dur="30s">
        <anchor href="hmmm.rm" coords="10,10,40,40"
                begin="2s" end="28s"/>
      </img>
    </par>
  </body>
</smil>
```

In this example, the presentation contains both a video clip and an image being presented in parallel (identified by the <par> tag). Each of these media items contains anchors. The anchor specifies the region of the media clip and the time frame over which it is available to be selected. It is up to the presentation program to determine how the anchor should be shown to the user. Like HTML links, the links defined in this way are still single-source and single-destination and are embedded into the source document (though it is possible to define overlapping anchors).

Unlike with HTML links, it is possible to define some additional semantics through the use of specific attributes. The list of attributes includes an id attribute; a show attribute to indicate the presentation semantics (`show="replace"` to insert the media item in place, `show="new"` to insert it into a new window, and `show="pause"` to pause the current media clip); an `href` attribute to specify the target; and `coords`, `begin`, and `end` attributes to define the spatial and temporal location of the anchor within the media.

2.2.2 Formalizing Linking Concepts

The examples just described illustrate the range of link types (and other forms of information associations) that can be used in managing access to and in manipulating information. To aid in the discussions and examples throughout the rest of this book, we now look at formalizing some of these concepts.

However, before we do this there is one point we wish to emphasize. Throughout the previous examples, we discussed information associations at varying levels of abstraction. It is important to clarify these levels. We can view associations at three different levels:

- The first level is how the associations are *conceived*. We can view information associations as being connections (i.e., links) between two or more information items, and these connections can be directional or nondirectional. Alternatively, the associations can be based on common membership of a set or on commonality of some attribute or feature of the information.

- The second level is the way in which these conceptual associations are *represented*. For example, do we represent a connection as a link embedded into the source document or do we store it in a separate linkbase? The particular decisions made regarding the representation of the association will have major implications for what we can achieve in terms of managing the information. For example, with the Web the use of links that are embedded into source documents means that identifying all of the pages that link *to* a given page is possible in theory but impractical.

- The third level is the way in which link information is *presented*. Even when we represent associations in a certain way, we still have many choices about how the system that presents the information will show the associations. Consider the examples discussed previously. If we have simple Web pages, then we can present the links embedded in these pages using the approach adopted by most Web browsers— simply by showing the anchor text in a different font or underlined or by having it stand out in some other way that lets users know they can select the link. Alternatively, we could create a simple program that analyzes the documents and extracts the links and then shows the link structures using a spatial representation, as shown in Figure 2.7. Similarly, with tools such as Webcosm and Hyperwave, the links are stored in linkbases rather than being embedded into documents and provide a much richer model of links. They are still nevertheless used in the creation of HTML documents for presentation in conventional Web browsers.

We need to be able to understand the different models that can be used to represent information associations and the implications of these models. But we also need to be able to separate how the associations are represented from how they are presented. So let us look at formalizing some of the linking concepts. We start with a definition.

Node—A unit of information that should be presented as a whole. Presenting only part of a node will result in a lack of suitable context, and hence the information may lose potential usefulness or may be misinterpreted.

Typically with the Web, nodes will be either single resources (such as text files, audio clips, and images) or a composite of resources (such as an HTML document that includes several images). The situation becomes a little more complex with XML documents, given that we can construct an XSL style sheet that transforms the XML document in such a way that only some sections of the document need to be presented. Indeed, it is possible to create style sheets that generate a document from multiple-source XML documents. In this case, the XML documents would not be viewed as the node. Rather, the node would be the document resulting from the transformation and hence is not represented explicitly as a single document but created as needed from multiple sources.

It is worth noting in passing that determining a valid node size and structure is a significant design issue. Among hypertext and usability researchers, there has been considerable debate and research into node sizes that provide the optimum access to information. Some developers recommend that pages should be kept small (nothing beyond a single screen of information) to emphasize each individual concept and to improve the structuring of the information. Other developers recommend much longer pages that preserve the natural linear structure of the plot or argument (with appropriate interlinking within the page). In our opinion, the size of the presentation nodes will be a function of the application and the way in which the information is being structured, and it is inappropriate to set specific constraints or recommendations.

Within an individual node we will often have many concepts associated with other concepts both within and beyond the node. In representing and utilizing these associations, we need to explicitly identify the concept, as represented by the fragment of the node that captures that concept. These fragments are captured as anchors.

Anchor—A region of a node that can be explicitly addressed and
     identified within the presentation of a node.

An anchor can be the source of an association (and the navigation path that goes with this) or the destination or possibly both. It can be explicitly embedded into the document (as happens with HTML using the `<a>` element). Alternatively, it can be represented externally to the node (as can happen with XPointer fragment identifiers).
     Let's take a closer look at links.

Link—A connection between multiple anchors (and nodes where there is
     an implied anchor that encompasses the entire node) that represents
     an association between the concepts captured by the anchors.

Note that this definition makes no statement about the number of anchors, the direction of the association, or where the link resides. These are all constraints that define particular types of links.
     In HTML the links are directional, with a single-source anchor and a single-destination anchor, and are embedded into the source node. In XLink, the links are much more flexible. It is also worth re-emphasizing that the interpretation of how the links can be used is entirely up to the systems managing the information. The links can be used by a browser to allow a user to select related documents for viewing. Alternatively, the links can be used by a search engine to check whether the related nodes indicate that the information on a given target is relevant to the user's query.
     The way that a link should be interpreted can vary widely. This is referred to as link semantics.

Link Semantics—The attributes of a link that indicate how the link
     should be interpreted (and hence how it might behave under certain
     circumstances).

Consider the following examples. We may have a link that should be followed automatically after a given amount of time has elapsed. An example would be a page that presents an opening screen that is replaced by a main menu after several seconds.
     As another example, we can have links that, when activated, cause a new node to be presented in conjunction with an existing node, rather than replacing the existing node. An example of this is where a link connects a

phrase and a definition of the phrase obtained from a glossary. Selecting the phrase might pop up a window containing a definition.

We could also have a link that causes information to be displayed by inserting the information into the existing document. As an example, we might have a table of contents that contains links from each section. When we select a link, the section name expands into the contents of the section.

As a final example, we may even have links that when followed cause changes in other nodes that are not part of the relationship. As an example, we may have several nodes being presented simultaneously, including an audio track. When we select an anchor and activate a link in a textual document, the browser might load a different textual document, but also cause the audio track to pause.

In each case, we are defining the semantics of the link. This is typically a separate issue from the structure of the link and is often poorly supported. In HTML, link semantics are very poorly supported, being restricted largely to being able to define the window or frame into which the target document should be loaded. Link semantics are somewhat richer in XLink, though still not as rich as in various stand-alone hypermedia systems.

Links can be categorized as static, dynamic, or generic.

Static Link—A link with fixed structure and semantics that does not change based on when, how, or by whom it is used.

Dynamic Link—A link that has structure or behavior that changes over time or with different users or circumstances. Typically, the structure and behavior are not resolved until the link is activated. It is then determined dynamically.

Generic Link—A link whose source anchor(s) is (are) not defined by a specific location, but rather by a particular pattern that can be matched to any relevant content.

Dynamic links effectively change over time. These changes can be with the link structure (such as changes in the link destinations) or with the link semantics (such as changes in the activation time of the link). These types of links can be important for supporting adaptive systems. For example, we may wish to change the destination of a link depending on which pages a user has previously visited. Although HTML has no inherent support for dynamic links, it is possible to create them using server-side technologies such as CGI programs or servlets, possibly in conjunction with other technologies such as HTTP cookies [Kristol & Montulli 00; Moore & Freed 00].

The definition of a generic link has several implications that would be useful to look at briefly. The first is that because the source anchor is defined for a particular pattern, rather than a particular location, it would be more accurate to refer to it as a generic anchor than a generic link. Also, the anchor is typically not resolved until runtime. In effect, the generic link is often viewed as a particular type of dynamic link.

It is worthwhile to note that the pattern can match many locations, and hence we inherently have a multiple-source link (whether the link is also multiple-destination depends on how the link destination is represented and resolved). The mechanism for representing the pattern depends on the particular system and the type of media. For plain text, we can simply define a text string as the pattern—though we could make it more flexible by allowing the definition of various string pattern-matching operations. For image, video, and audio data, the pattern matching becomes much more complex.

For structured text, we can also define other forms of pattern matching. As we will show later in the book, XPointer (and XPath within XPointer) can be used to define patterns for identifying parts of XML documents. These patterns can then be used to create generic links.

Whereas an anchor is typically either specific content or a pattern that matches to content, a pointer is a way of defining an anchor.

Pointer—An identifier that uniquely specifies one or more items.

In other words, a pointer is a mechanism for uniquely identifying a specific anchor or set of anchors. Where we have embedded anchors, the anchor can be labeled with a suitable ID, and the pointer then simply needs to refer to this unique ID. Where the anchor is not embedded, or an ID is not available, then some other mechanism for identifying (or *pointing at*) the anchor needs to be available. With XML documents, this is the purpose of XPointer.

This effectively means that links and pointers are complementary. Links form the connections, but pointers allow the identification of the items that will be connected. Think of items being connected by a rope (i.e., the link). At either end of the rope we have some hooks (i.e., pointers) that connect the rope to the relevant items (i.e., anchors). With XML, we have both XPointer for identifying the participating content (i.e., anchors) and XLink for creating the connections.

Let's look at the concepts of inclusion and transclusion.

Inclusion—The construction of a composite document by replacing a reference with the content of the element that was being referenced.

Transclusion—Reuse of content in such a way that ensures inherent connections between the content used in different contexts.

Going into a little more detail, we see that Ted Nelson (the originator of the term) describes transclusion as follows [Nelson 95]:

> The central idea has always been what I now call transclusion, or reuse with original contexts available, through embedded shared instances (rather than duplicate bytes). Thus the user may intercompare contexts of what is reused, both for personal work (keeping track of reuse) and publication (for deep comprehension and study). Transclusion brings to electronic publishing a copyright method that makes republication fair and clean: Each user buys each quotation from its own publisher, assuring proper payment (and encouraging exploration of the original).

In other words, transclusion is the inclusion of content by reference (i.e., not by cut-and-paste) into a new context (in a way that is often likely to change the interpretation of the content). The connections to the other uses of the content are maintained, and access to the original context is ensured. This is different from inclusion where we include content but don't necessarily do so in a way that ensures that the original context is available.

For example, if this book were written using true transcluding principles, then Nelson's quote would not be included directly in the book. Rather the book would include a link to the original content, and when the book was being read, the quote would be shown in place of the link, but readers would be able to directly see (if they chose) the original context in which the quote was published.

This potentially changes the whole publishing paradigm to one of publishing by reference. Effectively, we can create composite documents that inherently maintain rich cross-linking by the transclusion of document fragments from other sources. As we show later, this model is at least partly supported by XLink and XPointer.

2.3 USAGE SCENARIOS: HYPERMEDIA SUPPORT FOR INFORMATION UTILIZATION

Before finishing this chapter, we provide an example scenario that demonstrate how sophisticated linking can result in significantly improved applications. We describe the scenario and then look at how some of the linking concepts just described might be used in supporting such a scenario.

2.3.1 Scenario Description

Jack is undertaking an online correspondence course on XML and linking. The course includes support for richly linked course content, discussion forums, interactive groupwork, and so forth. Jack is completing some work for the course and, after logging into the main site, goes to the course material for the relevant session on linking concepts. The material provides an initial discussion of some basic concepts and then directs Jack to study a set of readings that have been published elsewhere on the Web (and predate the course material, hence the authors of these readings are oblivious to the existence of the course that Jack is taking).

Jack follows the link to the first article and commences reading. While reading the material, he comes across the term *transclusion*. He clicks on this word, and a window pops up offering him a definition of transclusion provided by his instructor (see section 2.3.2, Note 1). He reads the definition and then closes the pop-up window. He continues reading only to come across the sentence Ted Nelson's definition of transclusion includes the concept of contexts. Again, Jack selects transclusion, but this time a menu pops up providing Jack with the choice of four link destinations. The first choice is the definition he has already seen (see 'section 2.3.2, Note 2), the second destination is Ted Nelson's definition (in its original source), and the third and fourth destinations relate to two different discussions of the relationship between transclusion and context (see section 2.3.2, Note 3). Jack finishes reading the article and returns to the main page for the current week's course material. He continues to read several additional articles, including a very recent essay.

A few days later he returns to the course material and navigates to a discussion that compares the articles. The discussion includes fragments from most of the articles (see section 2.3.2, Note 4). He notices that the discussion compares several definitions of the term *link*, but the definition from the recent essay seems different from what he remembers. He selects the definition and from the main menu chooses to see the original source (see section 2.3.2, Note 5). A second window pops up showing the definition in its original context, and Jack notices that the definition has indeed been changed from the original material.

Jack then returns to the original discussion of links and chooses to see an animation showing how a Web server might support generic links. While watching the animation, he sees a Web server interacting with a linkbase. He is unsure what a linkbase is, but next to the animation is a list of components shown within the animation (server, linkbase, Web pages, network, and so forth). Jack clicks on `linkbase`, and while the list of words remains, the single word linkbase is replaced by a short description (see section 2.3.2, Note 6). The animation is also paused (see section 2.3.2, Note 7). Jack reads this and then clicks on the description. The description is once again replaced by the single word, restoring the list to its original state. The animation begins again, and Jack continues watching but now with a better understanding of the interaction being shown.

2.3.2 Discussion

The following notes explain the issues raised by various aspects of the scenario just described.

Note 1: Adding Links to Read-Only Material

In this case, the course instructor has added links for definitions into material over which he has no control—material that (as far as the instructor is concerned) is read-only. With conventional HTML pages, links must be embedded into the source material, which in this case cannot be modified. As such, the only ways of achieving this using standard Web servers and HTML pages would be either to save the pages locally and modify them to include the new links (which is inefficient and presents copyright problems) or to extend the server functionality to allow it to obtain other pages, modify them dynamically to add new links, and then deliver the modified pages (effectively creating a link-adding proxy—again, rather complex to manage).

This difficulty is a consequence of having to embed links into the source material. A much simpler approach would be to define links independently of the source material. Users could specify (or have specified for them) a set of pages to view and the list of links to use with this content (potentially stored completely independently from the content). The result would be to allow authors to add their own links into content over which they have no control. Indeed, different lists of links could be created for different users or different situations.

As will be shown later, XLink explicitly supports this type of functionality through the use of third-party links and external linkbases.

Note 2: Generic Links

This part of the scenario describes a link with the same link anchor text as the previous example (i.e., `transclusion`). We can create this situation by simply adding a new link anchor (and associated link) for each occurrence of the relevant phrase, but this could become extremely cumbersome and difficult to maintain if the word occurred often.

The use of generic links solves this problem. By defining a link that has as its source anchor *any* occurrence of the relevant text, we effectively create a link that is much easier to maintain. Again, this is relatively easy to implement in XML. For example, the following XPointer refers to any occurrence of the text `transclusion` within element content in a document (though it won't match attribute values and any XML markup such as element or attribute names):

```
xpointer(string-range(//*,"transclusion"))
```

This XPointer can then be used to create a link from all occurrences of this text to the relevant definition of this text in a file containing a list of definitions. For example, the following third-party extended link (a topic explained in much more detail in later chapters) provides a link from all occurrences of the words `'transclude'`, `'transclusion'`, and `'transcluding'` within the `link.xml` file to an appropriate definition in the `defs.xml` file (note that this link can be stored in a third file unrelated to either):

```
<extendedlink xlink:type="extended">
   <loc xlink:type="locator"
        xlink:href="links.xml#xpointer(string-range(//*,'transclude'))"
        xlink:label="phrase"/>
   <loc xlink:type="locator"
        xlink:href="links.xml#xpointer(string-range(//*,'transclusion'))"
        xlink:label="phrase"/>
   <loc xlink:type="locator"
        xlink:href="links.xml#xpointer(string-range(//*,'transcluding'))"
        xlink:label="phrase"/>
   <loc xlink:href="defs.xml#xpointer(//defn[phrase='transclude'])"
        xlink:label="defn"/>
   <go xlink:type="arc"
        xlink:from="phrase"
        xlink:to="defn"
        xlink:show="new"
        xlink:actuate="onRequest"/>
</extendedlink>
```

Note 3: Overlapping Anchors

More is going on in our example than just using generic anchors. Jack is given a choice between four possible destinations. These destinations could be generated from several sources. The first is generated by a generic link from the selected word (`transclusion`) to a definition of the phrase (as described earlier).

The second destination (Ted Nelson's original definition and discussion of transclusion) might have been generated from an outbound link embedded into the content itself. For example, the source content for the page may have looked something like the following:

```
<p id="p23">...so let us consider the issue of context.
<simplelink xlink:href="Nelson.htm" xlink:show="new">
Ted Nelson's definition of transclusion</simplelink>
includes the concept of contexts. What this means is that...
```

In this example, the phrase "Ted Nelson's definition of transclusion" is the anchor for a simple link. But the word `'transclusion'` within this phrase is also the anchor for a generic link, so when it is selected, the user is given the choice as to which destination to follow.

The situation can become more complex still if we add another third-party link with an anchor that overlaps. For example, we could define the following link (abbreviated for clarity):

```
<extendedlink xlink:type="extended">
  <loc xlink:href="doc0.xml#xpointer(string-range(id('p23'),
    'transclusion includes the concept of contexts'))"
    xlink:label="phrase"/>
  <loc xlink:href="doc1.xml"
    xlink:label="discussion"/>
  <loc xlink:href="doc2.xml"
    xlink:label="discussion"/>
  <go xlink:from="phrase"
    xlink:to="discussion"
    xlink:show="new"
  xlink:actuate="onRequest"/>
</extendedlink>
```

This creates a link from the phrase "transclusion includes the concept of contexts" within the specified document to two possible destinations. In other words, we have overlapping anchors. We also have a link that has two possible destinations.

In summary, we have the following:

- A generic (external) link that creates an anchor from "Ted Nelson's definition of <u>transclusion</u> includes the concept of contexts" for a link to the instructor's definition of transclusion.

- An embedded link that creates an anchor from "<u>Ted Nelson's definition of transclusion</u> includes the concept of contexts" for a link to Ted Nelson's original definition of transclusion.

- An external link that creates an anchor from "Ted Nelson's definition of <u>transclusion includes the concept of contexts</u>" for a link to two different discussions of transclusion and context.

When the word `transclusion` is selected, Jack is given the choice of four possible destinations to view.

Note 4: Transclusion—Supporting Composition

This part of the scenario is itself an example of true transclusion. The document being viewed by Jack could be constructed manually, but it makes more sense to build it directly from the original sources. For example, consider the following XML fragment:

```
... Another definition of links has been provided by Joe Bloggs.
Joe has stated that <simplelink xlink:href="bloggs.xml#xpointer
(id('quote32')" xlink:show="embed" xlink:actuate="onLoad"/> ...
```

In this case, the content from the remote resource is embedded directly into the document. The `show="embed"` attribute means that the content is viewed directly in the source document rather than being viewed independently. The `actuate="onLoad"` attribute means that the embedding should occur immediately after loading the source document.

Note 5: Transclusion—Supporting Access to Source

In the embedding example just described, readers need not know that the content has been embedded from a different source. However, in the true spirit of transclusion, it is useful for readers to be aware of this so that they can view the material in its original context if desired. In this case, Jack has seen a quote and wants to see its original source. He selects the quote and then selects the appropriate menu option (which is, of course, dependent on the particular implementation).

The browser could then retrieve the `Bloggs.xml` document and highlight the section indicted by the XPointer `xpointer(id('quote32'))`.[1] In effect, Jack has been able to see the transcluded content in its original context.

Note 6: Link Semantics—Embedding Content

This part of the scenario illustrates an alternative way of embedding content. In this case, we have a list of words that forms the basis for anchors. When a word is selected, the relevant link is traversed; and rather than causing a new document to be viewed (either in a new window or by replacing the existing document), the content is embedded into the existing document. For example, consider the following fragment:

```
<components>
  <comp>
    <simplelink xlink:href="desc.xml#xpointer(//desc[name='server'])"
      xlink:show="embed" xlink:actuate="onRequest">Server
    </simplelink>
  </comp>
  <comp>
    <simplelink xlink:href="desc.xml#xpointer(//desc[name='linkbase'])"
      xlink:show="embed" xlink:actuate="onRequest">LinkBase
    </simplelink>
  </comp>
  ...
</components>
```

---

[1]The single quotes have been chosen here because the `xlink:href` attribute's value in the example just given has been delimited with double quotes. XML would also allow delimiting the attribute value using single quotes, in which case the string value of the XPointer would have been delimited with double quotes.

Each word is an anchor for a link. The link, however, creates embedded content only when it is activated. Thus when Jack selects a component name, the name is replaced by the description of that component. Effectively, the result is that the system can be viewed as a partial folding browser.

Note 7: Link Semantics—Controlling Context

The final part of the scenario illustrates an even more complex situation. In this case, the document contains several media components. When we activate a link in one component of the document (i.e., by selecting a text name), we wish to cause a change in the behavior of another component of the document (i.e., to pause the playing of an animation). The current version of XLink does not allow behavior such as this to be explicitly specified, but it does provide an *extension* mechanism. XLink supports a `show="other"` attribute value and explicitly states that this could be used to instruct an application to look for other information determining the presentation. We could then include suitable markup that explicitly defined the behavior just described—possibly by appropriate use of style sheets (and in particular use of the `multi-switch` and `multi-property-set` XSL-FO formatting objects) or suitable scripting.

2.4 CONCLUSIONS

Note that the previous scenario really only touches the surface in terms of looking at some of the flexibility that a richer linking model can provide. Much more sophisticated functionality should be possible—though naturally it will be limited by the support of the underlying tools and systems for these concepts.

It is also useful to acknowledge that most (if not all) of the described scenario could in fact be implemented using only DHTML (i.e., HTML, CSS, DOM, and a scripting language). The important point, however, is that to do so would require considerably more effort than would be required to implement this using XML's linking technologies, and it would result in a site that was much more difficult to maintain.

In this chapter, we have looked at the hypermedia concepts that underpin the Web and how these concepts can be used to support effective information management and utilization. The key point is that a model that is more sophisticated than the simple model inherent in HTML can lead to a much richer user experience and more effective information management.

3

Conceptual Viewpoint

In the previous chapter, we looked at hypermedia concepts and the types of linking that support effective access to information. This provided a basis for demonstrating the more sophisticated forms of interaction that advanced hypermedia concepts can support and hence prompting the use of technologies such as XPath, XLink, and XPointer.

New technologies such as these can sometimes be confusing (especially in the absence of well-developed, widespread, and diverse applications and tools). Rather than describing the technologies from the syntactic level (where the applicability may be difficult to put into the context of the discussions in the previous chapter), we first consider standards such as XPath, XPointer, and XLink from a conceptual viewpoint. We'll take a look at the types of support they provide for sophisticated linking and content management.

We support this discussion with numerous XML fragments that demonstrate the concepts. These may appear confusing at first—given that we haven't yet discussed the syntax of these standards—but we believe they will help illustrate the ideas being discussed. Much more detailed discussions of the actual syntax will follow in later chapters.

We begin by considering the concept of references versus links (and dip into some of the XLink-specific terminology), then move on to look at how these concepts might be implemented in XML.

3.1 REFERENCES VERSUS LINKS

It is very easy to get confused by the difference between references and links, especially when we also throw in concepts such as resources, arcs, pointers, ranges, and anchors. This issue is exacerbated by the use of different terminology in HTML and XML, along with numerous different hypermedia systems. So let's look at these concepts and see if we can clarify the situation a little.

We begin with the simplest situation, which is HTML linking. In HTML, we normally refer only to anchors and links: an *anchor* is an identified region of a document, and a *link* is the connection between two anchors (or between an anchor and a resource, where the entire resource is assumed to be the destination anchor). This is, however, too simplistic for what we wish to support in XLink.

In XML linking, we can start with the concept of a resource—something that is universal to the World Wide Web [Berners-Lee+ 98]. A *resource* is defined as an addressable unit of information or service—in other words, basically anything that we are able to request, including files, images, audio clips, and program outputs. Indeed, it is possible to refer to (almost) arbitrary subsections of those resources (subresources) and hence those subresources themselves can be viewed as resources.

A key word in this definition is *addressable*. In other words, having resources is not sufficient. We need some way to identify or refer to those resources—what might be referred to in a programming context as *pointers*. The Web standards—and in particular RFC 2396 [Berners-Lee+ 98]— distinguish between addressing a whole resource (referred to as an *identifier*) and addressing a particular subresource (referred to as a *reference*).

A resource (or subresource) can be used in various ways; but in the context of this discussion, the most common use will be related to linking. In order to do this, we need to define the relevant regions of the resources participating in a link. Within the context of a link, these regions are referred to as *anchors*. In other words, a reference defines a resource (or subresource), which, in the context of a link, is treated as an anchor.

Identifiers are typically implemented on the Web using universal resource identifiers (URIs), discussed later in this chapter. References (i.e., referrals to a section or fragment of a resource) are implemented by attaching a suitable fragment specification to a URI. This specification can take many forms, which typically are specific to the document or resource type. For example, with HTML documents, we simply specify the name of a particular anchor within the resource. With XML, on the other hand, we use XPointer to identify a specific fragment. In other words, XPointer can be used only to identify fragments within XML documents, limiting its applicability to just these types of documents.

So let's consider XPointer and its capabilities. XPointer provides a general way to select sections of an XML document, essentially by writing a set of expressions. The result of evaluating an expression will usually be a set of locations (not surprisingly, referred to as a *location set*). It is possible to select elements, attributes, text strings, and so forth. For example, the XPointer expression

```
xpointer(/child::body[position()=1]/child::p)
```

selects all p children elements of the first body element in the document. As another example, the XPointer expression

```
xpointer(/descendant::*[attribute::name='book'])
```

selects all elements (i.e., all descendants of the document root) that have an attribute called name with a value of book. In effect, the selection mechanisms can be concatenated to progressively identify a specific subset of nodes.

XPointer is actually an application of the XPath standard. XPath was developed specifically to be a foundation for other standards such as XPointer. Another application of XPath is as part of XSL Transformations (XSLT). In XSLT, XPath expressions allow the selection of specific nodes that can then be transformed into an alternative textual form (often for presentation).

Since XPath is intended to be relatively generic (to suit multiple applications), certain sections of documents cannot be specified using XPath expressions. For example, although both of the XPointer fragments just shown are constructed from valid XPath expressions, XPath cannot select an arbitrary string that crosses several nodes. It is in areas such as this that XPointer has extended XPath. For example, the following expression defines the set of all occurrences of the string "links and anchors" within all para elements in the http://a.b/c/d.xml resource, which could not be achieved using just XPath expressions:

```
http://a.b/c/d.xml#xpointer(string-range(//para,'links and anchors'))
```

As one further example, the following URI defines a range that extends from the beginning of the element with an identifier of sect-2.3 to the end of the element with an ID of sect-3.4.

```
http://a.b/c/d.xml#xpointer(id('sect-2.3')/range-to(id('sect-3.4')))
```

Note that, in this case, this may include only parts of nodes (for example, part of a Chapter-2 element and part of a Chapter-3 element)—again, something not possible with XPath.

To summarize, URIs are a form of *identifier* that specifies a desired resource. XPointers are one of many forms of *references* that can specify a fragment of that resource (for XPointers, the resource must be an XML document).

In the context of linking, this means that XPointers can be used to specify anchors—or arbitrary sections of resources that will participate in a link. In XML, they are referred to as *locator elements,* rather than anchors. A locator element is, however, more than just an XPointer—we can also specify the role that the resource will play and provide a title for the resource. For example, consider the following XLink fragment (don't worry too much about the syntax yet—just look at the overall structure):

```
<siblings xlink:type="extended">
   <child xlink:type="locator"
          xlink:href="people.xml#xpointer(id('anna'))"
          xlink:title="Anna"/>
   <child xlink:type="locator"
          xlink:href="people.xml#xpointer(id('bill'))"
          xlink:title="Bill"/>
   <child xlink:type="locator"
          xlink:href="people.xml#xpointer(id('carl'))"
          xlink:title="Carl"/>
</siblings>
```

In this example, we define three locator elements, each of which uses an XPointer as part of the locator required to specify the remote resource that is participating in the link. We also give each locator element a `title`.

Before moving on from the concept of a link, two additional concepts need to be clarified—*links* and *arcs.* This requires an understanding of a third concept—*traversal.* In an HTML link, we have a single-source anchor, a single-destination anchor, and an implied connection between them. When we view an HTML document and activate the anchor (in most user interfaces by simply clicking on it), then the link is *traversed* to the link destination.

The situation is somewhat different with linking in XML. XLink allows the definition of links, but a link does not imply traversal! Rather, in XLink a link is simply an association between a number of resources. For example, consider the XLink example just given. In this example, the link associates three resources but does not specify any traversal semantics among them. There is no link source, nor is there a link destination. This is because XLink has separated the concept of associating resources from the concept of traversal among these resources. In many cases, we may not need to provide traversal information—especially where the association is being defined for a reason other than to support navigational hyperlinking (for example, to define a collection of resources to be analyzed by computer, rather than to be viewed by a human user).

Where we do want to specify traversal information, this is done separately from the specification of the association through the use of an arc.

See, for example, the following:

```
<person xlink:type="extended">
   <name
      xlink:type="locator"
      xlink:href="staff.xml#xpointer(string-range(/,'David Lowe'))"
      xlink:label="src"/>
   <details
      xlink:type="locator"
      xlink:href="David.xml"
      xlink:label="dest"/>
   <go
      xlink:type="arc"
      xlink:from="src"
      xlink:to="dest"/>
</person>
```

Here we specify an association between two resources (defined by locators): the first resource is all occurrences of a given string (`'David Lowe'`) within one XML document, and the second is another XML document (about David Lowe). We then specify the traversal semantics using an arc *from* the first resource *to* the second resource. What this effectively means is that we now have separate mechanisms for specifying an association between resources (a *link*) and for specifying how we might traverse between these resources (an *arc* within that link).

Indeed, we can have a single link involving a number of resources, with multiple different traversal rules. Consider the following example, where we have two arc specifications. Also, note that the second arc specification actually creates three arcs since there are multiple destinations specified by the given *to* label. We end up with arcs from a.xml to b.xml, from b.xml to c.xml, from b.xml to d.xml, and from b.xml to e.xml.

```
<extendedlink xlink:type="extended">
   <loc xlink:type="locator" xlink:href="a.xml" xlink:label="x"/>
   <loc xlink:type="locator" xlink:href="b.xml" xlink:label="y"/>
   <loc xlink:type="locator" xlink:href="c.xml" xlink:label="z"/>
   <loc xlink:type="locator" xlink:href="d.xml" xlink:label="z"/>
   <loc xlink:type="locator" xlink:href="e.xml" xlink:label="z"/>
   <go xlink:type="arc" xlink:from="x" xlink:to="y"/>
   <go xlink:type="arc" xlink:from="y" xlink:to="z"/>
</extendedlink>
```

Before leaving this topic, there is one final comment about some of the definitions in the XLink standard. The standard defines traversal as "using or following a link for any purpose," and it defines an arc as "information about how to traverse a pair of resources, including the direction of traversal and possibly application behavior information as well." This can be a little confusing, insofar as we can have links without arcs (and therefore no definition of traversal behavior), but the links can obviously still be used and therefore (according to the definitions) traversed. All this means is that they are being used (i.e., traversed) in a way determined beyond the XLink specification.

This raises an interesting issue—that XLink can be used to specify the existence of a link without specifying rules for how that link will be used. XLink does support some attributes for defining behaviors—such as how and when an arc should be traversed—but these are optional and when present their interpretation is left to the applications using the XML documents. For example, where multiple arcs emanate from one resource, and that resource is activated, the standard does not say how the application should respond. Example alternatives include traversing all arcs, giving a user the choice of which arc to traverse, or using some internal logic to make the choice.

One mechanism that is supported by XLink is the inclusion of arc roles. For example, consider the following:

```
<extendedlink xlink:type="extended">
  <loc xlink:type="locator"
       xlink:href="a.xml"
       xlink:label="x"/>
  <loc xlink:type="locator"
       xlink:href="b.xml"
       xlink:label="y"/>
  <go xlink:type="arc"
      xlink:from="x"
      xlink:to="y"
      xlink:arcrole="http://q.r/s.dat"/>
</extendedlink>
```

In this case the arc has an `arcrole` attribute that provides a unique role identifier.[1] This identifier may allow the application to obtain information that assists in determining the appropriate behavior when traversing the arc. This, however, is beyond the XLink specification and is application-dependent.

3.2 RESOURCE IDENTIFICATION: URL, URI, AND URN

We mentioned in the previous section that XPointers can be used in the definition of XLink locators—those XLink elements used to identify remote

---

[1]This identifier is expressed as a URI, which need not specify an actual resource. The intention, rather, is to specify a globally unique identifier, in much the same way as for a namespace URI.

resources that are participating in a link. We also alluded to the fact that XPointers on their own are not enough. XPointers can define a fragment of a resource but cannot identify the resource itself. This is the purpose of Uniform Resource Locators (URLs), Uniform Resource Identifiers (URIs), and Uniform Resource Names (URNs).

The most general form of identifier is a URI (defined in RFC 2396 [Berners-Lee+ 98]). URIs are intended to provide a broad mechanism for identifying a resource. This identification can happen in many ways. It can take the form of a specification of the mechanism to access the resource, a unique name for the resource, or a combination of both. As stated in RFC 2396,

> [a] URI can be further classified as a locator, a name, or both. The term "Uniform Resource Locator" (URL) refers to the subset of URI that identify resources via a representation of their primary access mechanism (e.g., their network "location"), rather than identifying the resource by name or by some other attribute(s) of that resource. The term "Uniform Resource Name" (URN) refers to the subset of URI that are required to remain globally unique and persistent even when the resource ceases to exist or becomes unavailable.

URLs were originally defined in RFC 1738 [Berners-Lee+ 94] and RFC 1808 [Fielding 95] (dealing with relative URLs), though they are now viewed as a specific subset of URIs and are defined in RFC 2396. URLs specify resources using two parts. The first part of the URL defines the mechanism used to access the resource (e.g., `http`, `mailto`, `ftp`, and so on). The second part defines a mechanism-specific set of information (e.g., `//a.b/c/d.xml#blah`) that defines the protocol-specific information, which provides sufficient information to uniquely identify the resource. This second part has a syntax that is specific to the scheme. For example, many hierarchical schemes (such as `http` and `ftp`) use the following syntax (some examples are included):

```
"//" [user[":" password] "@"]host[":" port]"/"url-path "?" query
```

```
//erik:test@transcluding.com:81/book/examples/code.html
//transcluding.com/book/tw.pdf
//transcluding.com/book/tw.xml
//transcluding.com/book/tw.pl?chap=3
```

The components of most interest in this case are the `url-path` and `query`. All the components before these provide information on finding the host that offers access to the required resource and any specific details required to obtain this access. The `url-path` specifies how the resource can be accessed on the specific host, and the `query` provides information to be interpreted by the resource.

One of the problems with URLs is that in order to identify a particular resource using them, we need to know both the scheme and the scheme-specific information required to access the resource. For schemes such as `http`, this typically means knowing on which host the resource is located and exactly where. This creates significant problems in several situations. If a resource is moved (for example, because of maintenance changes), then any URLs referring to that resource will become invalid. Similarly, we can have multiple identical resources, but a URL must point to a specific one. If the host for that particular resource is temporarily unavailable, then again, the URL becomes invalid, even though other copies of the resource may be available elsewhere.

URNs are intended to circumvent these problems. As stated earlier in this section, the RFC 2396 standard defines a URN as a subset of URI that requires a global uniqueness and persistence even without the resource. In other words, even when resources are moved, a URN should still be valid! The standard does not discuss implementation issues, though a typical implementation might allow a URN to be resolved dynamically to obtain a specific instance of the resource (through a mechanism similar to the Domain Name Service used to resolve Internet host names into IP addresses). At present such an infrastructure does not yet exist, and URNs are neither used nor supported.[2] Work on URNs is currently highly volatile and changing rapidly.

It is worth noting that once a URN-specified resource has been located, we may still often wish to refer to a particular fragment of that resource. As such, the concept of fragment identifiers (including the use of XPointers) is still relevant to URNs.

Finally, it is worth reiterating that URIs are a generalization of both URLs and URNs.[3] All recent Web standards use URIs rather than URLs. In general, it is preferable to avoid the term URL altogether and use URI whenever possible—given that every URL is a URI and only very rarely are only URLs (and not URNs) permitted.

3.3 PERSISTENCE OF IDENTIFIERS AND REFERENCES

In the previous discussion we mentioned the fact that URNs are intended to provide a persistent identifier for a resource. In other words, given a

---

[2]As a temporary solution to the problem of the volatility of URLs (i.e., the problem intended to be addressed in the longer term by URNs), the concept of a Persistent URL (PURL) has been introduced [Shafer+ 96]. PURLs are adaptation URLs that are resolved into URLs by a special PURL service. For more information, visit `http://purl.oclc.org`.

[3]This, however, does not mean that URIs are always either URLs or URNs. For a discussion of the relevant terms and their interpretation, see the W3C note [Coates+ 01].

particular URN, we will still be able to locate the resource being identified irrespective of whether the location has changed. This concept is important to the Web in general and to linking in particular. Since we regularly define links by specifying references to the resources (or resource fragments) that participate in the links and if the references are not persistent, then we will regularly find links that contain invalid references. The consequences of not having persistent references is evident in the ubiquitous broken links and invalid search engine results found in the current Web. The current solution is typically to regularly check for broken links (there are numerous tools that can automate this process) and to manually rectify any that are found. This is, however, a rather unsatisfactory solution. It requires considerable effort and should not be necessary.

In effect there are two separate and distinct aspects to be considered: persistence of the identifier for a resource, and persistence of the reference for the resource fragment. These two aspects are orthogonal and typically addressed using distinct approaches.

3.3.1 Persistence of Identifiers

Identifier persistence is the ability to locate resources, based on a given identifier, irrespective of changes to the location (or other characteristics) of that resource. One obvious way to attain this is by using URNs in preference to URLs. However, given the current lack of an infrastructure to support URNs, this is not a viable solution at present.

This means that we must consider approaches to ensuring the persistence of URLs as identifiers. The specific approach will be dependent on the particular scheme being used in the URL. For example, with `mailto` URLs, the scheme-specific part defines an e-mail address. We can therefore promote persistence by using mail forwarding if a mail address changes.

More interestingly, with the `http` scheme, the scheme-specific part defines a host and a resource within this host. Utilizing approaches such as Web server aliases allows us to change the physical location of a resource but retain the Web address.

In both of these cases, however, ensuring the persistence of the identifier requires manual intervention. This, in turn, requires an awareness of the potential changes to locations of the resources being identified.

3.3.2 Persistence of References

Even if we are able to correctly identify a resource, we may still have problems with persistence of fragment identifiers. This may be best explained by using an example. Consider the following very simple XML document (called `staff.xml`):

```
<?xml version="1.0"?>
<!DOCTYPE People SYSTEM "People.dtd">
<People>
  <Person StaffID="123456">
    <Name>Anna Smith</Name>
    <Position>Sales Manager</Position>
  </Person>
  <Person StaffID="987654">
    <Name>Bill Black</Name>
    <Position>XML Programmer</Position>
  </Person>
  <Person StaffID="555555">
    <Name>Carl Green</Name>
    <Position>Personal Assistant</Position>
  </Person>
</People>
```

If we wish to create a reference to Carl Green's position, then we could write this in various ways:

```
staff.xml#xpointer(/1/3/2)
staff.xml#xpointer(//Person[3]/Position)
staff.xml#xpointer(//Person[last()]/Position)
staff.xml#xpointer(//Person[@StaffID="555555"]/Position)
```

In the first example, we select the first element (`<People>`), then the third child of this (`<Person StaffID="555555">`), and then the second child of this (`<Position>`). This gives the required information but results in a reference which is not particularly robust. We can edit the document to add a new element at the start, as follows:

```
<People>
  <Company OrgID="546431">
    <Name>ACME Linking, Inc.</Name>
    ...
```

Then `<Person StaffID="987654">` would become the third child element of `<People>` rather than `<Person StaffID="555555">`. In some respects this is worse than a broken reference since we have no indication that the reference is incorrect. It still points to a valid XML element—just the wrong one!

The second reference is somewhat better. It says that we want the third `Person` element, rather than just the third element of any type. This is still potentially dangerous, however, as there is nothing stopping us from adding another `Person` element to the beginning of the document, thereby changing the element we want from the third `Person` to the fourth `Person`.

The third reference is another attempt to solve this, but it too has some obvious limitations.

The final reference is where we select the desired element based on a unique identifier (in this case a specific attribute). The result is a fragment reference that holds up to many (but not all!) possible changes in the document.

So, in effect we have a situation where resource identifier persistence relies on the ability to locate a resource irrespective of its actual location and fragment ID persistence relies on the ability to locate relevant sections of a document irrespective of changes in the document. As we've discussed, resource identifier persistence is currently only poorly supported—though eventually URNs will help. Fragment identifier persistence relies on the good design of the references. Referring to an element by an ID, its type, or the value of an attribute is preferable to referring to it by its position in the document.

3.4 THIRD-PARTY LINKS AND LINKBASES

One of the issues discussed in the previous chapter is the concept of adding links to read-only material. This is a rather unusual concept for people who are familiar only with the Web (as distinct from other more sophisticated hypermedia systems), where all links must be embedded into the source content. Being required to embed all links into the source content is, however, very restrictive. For example, we might want to be able to annotate material that doesn't belong to us with our own links, or the material may be stored on read-only media, or we may want to use different sets of links at different times.

In each case, we may not want to or may not be able to add links directly into the underlying content. Instead, we may want to specify links separately and somehow have them used. With XLink, this is relatively straightforward. Consider the following relatively simple example:

```
<?xml version="1.0"?>
<!DOCTYPE Dictionary SYSTEM "Dictionary.dtd">
<Dictionary>
  <Entry word="Anchor">
    <Pronunciation>...</Pronunciation>
    <Definition>An identified region of a node that can be
      explicitly addressed and identified within the presentation
      of a node.
    </Definition>
  </Entry>
  <Entry word="Link">
    <Pronunciation>...</Pronunciation>
```

```
    <Definition>A connection between multiple anchors (and nodes,
        where there is an implied anchor that encompasses the entire
        node) that represents an association between the concepts
        captured by the anchors.
    </Definition>
  </Entry>
  <!-- Further entries go here -->
  <Xref xlink:type="extended">
    <word xlink:type="locator"
          xlink:href="#xpointer(string-range(//Definition,'anchor'))"
          xlink:label="src"/>
    <defn xlink:type="locator"
          xlink:href="#xpointer(//Entry[@word='anchor'])"
          xlink:label="dest"/>
    <go xlink:type="arc" xlink:from="src" xlink:to="dest"/>
  </Xref>
  <!-- Further cross references go here -->
</Dictionary>
```

In this example, the document contains a series of words and definitions. At the end of the document, we have a set of XLinks, which link
any occurrence of specific words in the definitions to the definition of
those words. For example, the word *anchor* appearing in the definition
of the word *link* would be the starting point for a link to the definition of
anchor.

In this case, the links are termed *third-party* links. This is because they
are not embedded into any of the anchors participating in the link.

We can take this one step further and actually separate the links out
into a separate file. We would then have an XML file (`Dict.xml`) containing
definitions and another XML file (`XRefs.xml`) containing the links. The link
file might look something like the following:

```
<?xml version="1.0"?>
<!DOCTYPE XRefs SYSTEM "XRefs.dtd">
<XRefs>
  <Xref xlink:type="extended">
    <word xlink:type="locator"
          xlink:href="Dict.xml#xpointer
              (string-range(//Definition,'anchor'))"
          xlink:label="src"/>
    <defn xlink:type="locator"
          xlink:href="Dict.xml#xpointer(//Entry[@word='anchor'])"
          xlink:label="dest"/>
    <go xlink:type="arc" xlink:from="src" xlink:to="dest"/>
  </Xref>
  <!-- Further cross references go here -->
</XRefs>
```

This file, containing a series of third-party links, is what is known as a link database, or *linkbase*. The problem then arises as to how to ensure that these link definitions are actually utilized. The simplest way is, where possible, to modify the source information so that it includes a reference to the linkbase. This is supported by XLink using a special form of extended link (i.e., it contains an arc from the content to the linkbase with an `arcrole` attribute with a special value; see section 7.5 for further information). When the XML document is viewed or processed, the link to the linkbase will be traversed, and the linkbase will be loaded. This linkbase will contain links rather than content to be presented to the user or for some other form of processing. It is also worth noting (as we shall see in a moment) that linkbases can include links to other linkbases, creating hierarchies of linkbases.

This solution is fine where we have access to the source information so that we can add a link to our linkbase, but one of the benefits of XML linking is that we can define third-party links for content to which we do not have access to edit. So what do we do in this situation? One solution would be to simply allow the user to specify directly within the browser (or whatever other tool we are using to view or process the documents) the linkbases we wish to use. This is analogous to the functionality supported in some Web browsers of being able to specify a particular style sheet to use for presentation of Web pages.

To further illustrate this concept, consider the following scenario (extending the one described in section 2.3): Joe Teacher is preparing the material for the coming semester's course on XML and linking. To support this, he wishes to provide additional links from numerous external resources. He begins by creating a linkbase for each external document. Then, rather than requiring the students to specify all of these individual linkbases, he creates a master linkbase that all students will utilize. This master linkbase contains a collection of links from the various documents to their relevant linkbases. Here is an example of a link from a document to a linkbase:

```
<otherlinks xlink:type="extended">
 <loc xlink:type="locator"
     xlink:href="http://othersite.com/info/aboutXML.xml"
     xlink:label="src"/>
 <loc xlink:type="locator"
     xlink:href="aboutXML-links.xml"
     xlink:label="linkbase"/>
 <go xlink:type="arc"
     xlink:arcrole="http://www.w3.org/1999/xlink/properties/linkbase"
     xlink:actuate="onLoad"
     xlink:from="src"
     xlink:to="linkbase"/>
</otherlinks>
```

This way, whenever a student (who will have initially specified only the master linkbase) accesses a relevant external document, the appropriate link in the master linkbase is activated, and the additional linkbase for that document is loaded.

3.5 MULTI-ENDED LINKS

Another aspect supported by XLink, but not supported by HTML linking, is multi-ended links. This type of link has a number of important applications wherever we have more than two resources that participate in a relationship. There are several ways we can create links of this type. First, consider the following example (adapted from the XLink standard):

```
<family xlink:type="extended">
 <loc xlink:type="locator" xlink:label="parent"
      xlink:href="Ann.xml"/>
 <loc xlink:type="locator" xlink:label="parent"
      xlink:href="Bob.xml"/>
 <loc xlink:type="locator" xlink:label="child"
      xlink:href="Gina.xml"/>
 <loc xlink:type="locator" xlink:label="child"
      xlink:href="Hank.xml"/>
 <loc xlink:type="locator" xlink:label="child"
      xlink:href="Irma.xml"/>
  <go xlink:type="arc" xlink:from="parent" xlink:to="child"/>
</family>
```

In this example, we have five participating resources. We also have a single arc specification that results in six arcs (Ann–Gina, Ann–Hank, Ann–Irma, Bob–Gina, Bob–Hank, Bob–Irma). In effect, we have three arcs from Ann.xml. If we trigger the link traversal from this resource, XLink does not specify what should happen—though a typical behavior might be to provide users with a list of the possible destinations and allow them to select the appropriate arc to traverse. It is also worth noting that not only does XLink not specify traversal behavior, it also does not specify how to trigger a traversal—that is largely left to XLink applications (except for the standard behavior attributes).

XLink also supports a second form of multi-ended link, though it is a little more subtle than the previous example. Consider the following:

```
<family xlink:type="extended">
   <loc xlink:type="locator"
        xlink:label="parents"
        xlink:href="Family.xml#xpointer(//Person[@type='parent'])"/>
   <loc xlink:type="locator"
        xlink:label="children"
```

```
        xlink:href="Family.xml#xpointer(//Person[@type='child'])"/>
    <go xlink:type="arc" xlink:from="parents" xlink:to="children"/>
</family>
```

In this example, we have a single arc specification that results in just a single arc, so how can this be a multi-ended link? The key is in the XPointer. Essentially, the XPointer selects a location set, which in the case of the `parents` locator can be a set of multiple non-contiguous elements. The same applies to the `children` locator. In effect, we have a single arc from one subresource to another subresource, and both subresources can potentially cover multiple elements.

Again, XLink does not specify the behavior semantics governing how this situation, once specified in XLink, should be interpreted. In particular, the standard states the following:

> Some possibilities for application behavior with non-contiguous ending resources might include highlighting of each location, producing a dialog box that allows the reader to choose among the locations as if there were separate arcs leading to each one, concatenating the content of all the locations for presentation, and so on. Application behavior with non-contiguous starting resources might include concatenation and rendering as a single unit, or creating one arc emanating from each contiguous portion.

Before we finish this section, it is worth pointing out that XLink supports annotating arcs with additional semantics—specifically, titles and roles. We can have two arcs between the same two resources, but with different purposes, as indicated by their roles.

3.6 GENERIC LINKS

One of the concepts discussed in section 2.2.1 is generic linking. A generic link is effectively a link that has a participating resource that is specified not by defining the actual resource, but by naming a set of conditions that must be met for a resource to be included. This can be readily achieved using the functionality of XPointer. In particular, XPointer allows the selection of resource fragments based on criteria such as the following:

- elements of a given type
- elements that have a specific attribute with a given value
- text that matches a given string
- complex combinations of the above

In each case, the resulting location set can contain multiple locations. The result, when the XPointers are used in XLink, is a specification of a generic locator. This locator can be the source or the destination of possible arcs. If used as the source, it embodies the conventional generic link as described in section 2.2.1 and, for example, supported by Webcosm. If used as the destination of an arc, then we potentially have a link that traverses to an aggregation of all references to a particular concept or element.

This type of XLink linking would most often be used for producing universal cross-referencing, such as links from words to their definitions in dictionaries or glossaries.

3.7 TYPED LINKS

Finally, one last feature that is not supported by HTML linking, but is supported by XLink, is typed links. Essentially, a typed link belongs to a particular set of links with common characteristics. The fact that it belongs to that set is typically indicated by the link having a particular attribute with a given value.

The ability to type links can make it much easier to navigate through a web of interlinked resources. For example, we can switch certain links on or off or request certain types of links to be highlighted. So, when initially learning a particular concept, we can make all glossary links visible so that we can readily obtain definitions of unfamiliar terms. As we begin to understand the topic, we may wish to switch off the glossary links to reduce clutter. Apart from the visibility of links (or, rather, resources participating in the links), we might wish to change the traversal behavior of certain link types—changing whether or not confirmation is required, where the destination is displayed, and so forth.

It is also worth noting that since XLink separates the concepts of association (i.e., link) from traversal (i.e., arc), we can also type these two elements independently. In other words, we can have various link types, but we can also support various arc types. So a given link might contain multiple arcs (possibly even between the same resources) with different types.

So how do we actually do typing in XLink? Although not explicitly designed for link typing, the standard provides several semantic attributes that effectively provide this support. In particular, both the `title` attribute and the `role` and `arcrole` attributes can be used to support link typing. The `title` attribute is typically used to describe the meaning of a link or resource in a human-readable form. The standard does not, however, specify how this title could be, or should be, used. It is likely to be used for purposes such as making titles available to visually impaired users, generating tables of links, or providing help text before an arc is traversed. Although we could type links by defining specific titles to use for specific link types, this would be a somewhat cumbersome method and would be likely to interfere with other uses of the `title` attribute.

The `role` and `arcrole` attributes are, however, more appropriate for link typing. The value of these attributes (according to the standard) must be a URI reference that identifies some resource that describes the intended property. We could therefore define a URI that is to be used by all links or arcs that belong to a particular type. Indeed, we could support links or arcs belonging to multiple types by having the `role` and `arcrole` URIs point to a resource that contains a list of the types for that link or arc. Consider the following example:

Family.xml:

```
...
<loc xlink:type="locator" xlink:label="p1" xlink:href="Ann.xml"/>
<loc xlink:type="locator" xlink:label="p2" xlink:href="Bob.xml"/>
<loc xlink:type="locator" xlink:label="c1" xlink:href="Gina.xml"/>
<loc xlink:type="locator" xlink:label="c2" xlink:href="Hank.xml"/>
<loc xlink:type="locator" xlink:label="c3" xlink:href="Irma.xml"/>

<go xlink:type="arc" xlink:from="p1" xlink:to="c1"
    arcrole="http://transclude.com/demo/4682.arc"/>
<go xlink:type="arc" xlink:from="p2" xlink:to="c1"
    arcrole="http://transclude.com/demo/8634.arc"/>
...
```

4682.arc:

```
arc-type: mother
arc-type: guardian
```

8634.arc:

```
arc-type: father
arc-type: guardian
```

In this case, we have constructed a (somewhat arbitrary and trivial) format for the *.arc* files simply to illustrate the point. For astute readers, however, this simplistic example points toward a potential problem. The effective use of link typing requires that a common vocabulary be used for describing the link types. The XLink standard does not make any suggestions in this direction (indeed, this particular use of `role` and `arcrole` attributes is not discussed). We could potentially adapt a standard such as the Dublin Core [Weibel+ 98], which provides a standard set of meta-data, to specify attributes of the link or arc. We would constrain the attributes available to us but not their values. More generically, we could utilize the Resource Description Framework (RDF); but again, we would run into similar problems. RDF is more general than the Dublin Core; it does not define a fixed set of attributes but rather a mechanism for defining a meta-data schema. In order to use RDF in defining link types, we would need to begin by defining a suitable RDF schema.

3.8 CONCLUSIONS

In this chapter, we have explored from a conceptual point of view some of the emerging Web standards that support information linking. In particular, we have examined the sophisticated linking enabled by standards such as XPath, XPointer, and XLink. For example, we have considered concepts such as resource identification, identifier persistence, linkbases, multi-ended links, generic links, and typed links. These discussions have been illustrated with example code fragments. This chapter brings to an end the conceptual part of the book, which looks at the types of systems we would like to develop. In the following chapters, we explore in detail the standards and technologies that enable this vision to be created.

Part II

Technique
The Web's New Look

4

Related Technologies

In this and the following three chapters, we present an overview of the core technologies that make it possible to implement a much better hypermedia system than today's Web. The technologies that are a foundation for, but not the center of, these new possibilities are presented in this chapter; while the three core technologies XPath, XPointer, and XLink are presented in chapters 5, 6, and 7 and are discussed in greater detail. Readers with a background in new Web technologies such as XML, XML Namespaces, and XSL may wish to skip this chapter and continue directly with the discussion of XPath in chapter 5, while readers familiar with only the more "traditional" Web technologies such as HTML and HTTP should first read this chapter and then proceed with chapters 5 through 7.

The Web's success is—in comparison with any other hypermedia system—overwhelming. The main reason for this is not its technical superiority but rather its ease of use for both information consumers and providers. However, as the Web matures, it becomes obvious that while the initial design allowed a rapid adoption and hence expansion of the Web, the same design is now constraining growth and will need to be replaced by more powerful technologies. The initial Web design was based on the three core concepts of HTML, HTTP, and URLs, but new technologies are rapidly appearing—even though a large fraction of them disappear just as quickly. The future of the Web's basic technologies can be seen to be as the following sections describe.

HTML as Common Content Format

The Hypertext Markup Language (HTML) as it is today (the most recent version being HTML 4.01 [Raggett+ 99]) is quite different from its first version (as presented by Tim Berners-Lee in 1992). The most significant difference is that HTML today is embedded into a framework of supporting technologies, the most important being style sheet languages such as Cascading Style Sheets (CSS) [Bos+ 98; Lie & Bos 99], scripting languages such as JavaScript[1] [ECMA 99], and the Document Object Model (DOM) [Wood+ 00a; Wood+ 00b], which specifies how scripting languages interface with HTML. Virtually all Web pages today use one or more of these assisting technologies.[2]

Today, almost all text-based Web content uses HTML, but in the future this will be replaced by XML (as described in section 4.1), starting already with XHTML documents (which can be displayed by today's HTML browsers) and then progressing with other document types based on XML (for which XML browsers are necessary). The future will see a mixture of XML content on the Web, some of it using well-known document types (such as XHTML) and some using application-specific document types.

HTTP as Protocol

The HyperText Transfer Protocol (HTTP) [Fielding+ 99; Franks+ 99] is one of the more stable components of the Web. This can be explained by the fact that most Web users and developers are not so much interested in how the protocol works, as in what kind of content can be delivered with it. However, even though in the first years of the Web HTTP was the only protocol used for delivering content, now there are at least two other major protocols: the Real Time Protocol (RTP) [Schulzrinne+ 96], which is used for transmitting real-time data such as audio and video, and the Wireless Application Protocol (WAP) [WAP 99, 01], which is currently almost invisibly hidden behind WAP proxies but may become increasingly popular and visible with the advent of WAP-enabled devices (though WAP has struggled to gain acceptance).

URL as Resource Identification

Uniform Resource Locators (URLs) have become so commonplace today that they can be found everywhere from TV commercials and billboards to milk bottles and chewing gum wrappers. They have become as ubiquitous as postal addresses. In hindsight, the concept of URLs appears so simple

---

[1]Even though the well-known browser scripting language is always referred to as JavaScript, strictly speaking the language is ECMAScript because it has been standardized under this name by the European Computer Manufacturers Association (ECMA). JavaScript and JScript are simply implementations of ECMAScript by Netscape and Microsoft, respectively.

[2]This is based on the assumption that all browsers support these technologies, which is acceptable given that today the Web is almost exclusively accessed from PCs and workstations. In the not-so-distant future, however, content providers will be forced to deal with a far greater diversity of clients, ranging from the full-blown browser of today to rather thin clients running on personal digital assistants (PDAs) and even Wireless Markup Language (WML) browsers on mobile phones. Successfully dealing with this diversity (and not excluding clients not conforming to current standards set by the major browsers) will be one of the biggest challenges of the Web for the future.

that it is surprising it was not developed earlier. However, early approaches to defining universally unique identifiers for resources available on computer networks failed. One important reason for this is that it was not possible to write these identifiers down in a concise and human-readable form. The concept of URLs has been standardized in RFC 1738 [Berners-Lee+ 94] and RFC 1808 [Fielding 95] (dealing with relative URLs) and has not changed substantially since the Web's invention. The concept has, however, been generalized to the idea of the Universal Resource Identifier (URI) as specified in RFC 2396 [Berners-Lee+ 98], which includes URLs. Therefore, throughout this book we use the term URI rather than URL.

One important aspect of URIs are *fragment identifiers,* separated from the URI by a crosshatch (#) character and consisting of additional reference information to be interpreted by the user agent after the retrieval of the resource has been successfully completed. As such, it is not part of a URI but is often used in conjunction with one. XPointers, described in chapter 6, are designed to be used as fragment identifiers for XML resources and will make the use of URIs with fragment identifiers much more sophisticated than it is today (today's usage of fragment identifiers, described in section 1.3.1, is rather simple).

We assume that readers have basic knowledge of the fundamental Web technologies: HTML, HTTP, and URI. If not, there are countless books available about HTML, although it may be difficult to find a book encompassing the greater picture including HTTP and URI (one example of such a book has been published [Wilde 98]). However, since knowledge of XML and related technologies is not as common, the remainder of this chapter includes introductions to XML and its supporting technologies. It is important to note that even though the XML standard has been finalized (in February 1998), many of the supporting standards are still under development. As such, it is always a good idea to check W3C's Web site at `http://www.w3.org` for the status of any XML-related technology. The following sections are not complete overviews of the individual areas. Rather, they are intended to give readers a basic understanding of the many new technologies referenced throughout this book.

4.1 XML CORE STANDARDS

In an effort to enable the exchange of documents based on user-defined document types over the Web, the W3C introduced the Extensible Markup Language (XML) [Bray+ 98; Bray+ 00] in 1998.[3] The idea of XML is to

---

[3]At the time of this writing, a limited revision of XML is under construction [Cowan 01], but it will address only Unicode issues and not make any substantial changes to the general model of the XML 1.0 specification.

replace the fixed set of elements and attributes of an application-specific document type, such as HTML, with a language that is able to specify application-dependent elements and attributes. The Standard Generalized Markup Language (SGML) [ISO 86], which is the foundation of HTML, was one candidate for this; but SGML was too complex for adoption in the context of the Web. Experience had shown that SGML, although undeniably useful and widely used in different application areas, such as the aviation and publishing industries, is very hard to implement and has too many optional features, making it possible for two SGML-compliant applications not to be able to exchange documents because disjoint subsets of optional features have been implemented in both applications. As a consequence of this lesson learned from SGML, the W3C set out to define a functional subset of SGML (in SGML terms, called a *profile*), and the result of this effort is XML.

Consequently, XML is a proper subset of SGML, and every XML document is an SGML document,[4] which will make it relatively easy for SGML-based applications to convert to XML. Furthermore, a lot of the experience with SGML design and implementation can be applied to XML-based Web applications. The following list of design goals for XML has been taken from the earliest available draft for XML:[5]

1. XML shall be straightforwardly usable over the Internet.
2. XML shall support a wide variety of applications.
3. XML shall be compatible with SGML.
4. It shall be easy to write programs which process XML documents.
5. The number of optional features in XML is to be kept to the absolute minimum, ideally zero.
6. XML documents should be human-legible and reasonably clear.
7. The XML design should be prepared quickly.
8. The design of XML shall be formal and concise.
9. XML documents shall be easy to create.
10. Terseness is of minimal importance.

Although the concepts of XML are relatively straightforward, it is still much too complex to be discussed in detail here. Much has been published about XML, so we will explain only a few selected points that are essential for the understanding of the other concepts described in this book. In 1997,

---

[4]Strictly speaking, XML is not a subset of the original International Organization for Standardization (ISO) standard 8879 [ISO 86], but of the so-called WebSGML adaptations, which have been included as an annex in the latest revision of the SGML standard.

[5]See `http://www.w3.org/TR/WD-xml-961114.html`.

an introductory article about XML was published by Connolly, Khare, and Rifkin [Connolly+ 97]; and many books are available, including the annotated specification to XML 1.0 [DuCharme 98], which still is one of the most useful books (though a little difficult if used as an introduction).

The main aim of XML is to allow application designers to define their own vocabulary for documents. This is achieved by specifying a language for defining a document type definition (DTD), which in essence is nothing more than a grammar describing the elements of a particular element set and their valid usage. For example, the following minimalistic DTD describes a very simple document type:

```
<?xml version="1.0"?>
<!DOCTYPE document [
<!ELEMENT  document  (heading?,section+) >
<!ELEMENT  section   (heading,body*) >
<!ATTLIST  section
           author    CDATA   #IMPLIED >
<!ELEMENT  heading   #PCDATA >
<!ELEMENT  body      #PCDATA >
>]>
```

We will not go into the syntactic details of this DTD. In summary, it defines a document type `document`, where a document consists of an optional `heading` element and one or more `section` elements. Each `section` contains a `heading` and any number of `body` elements. Furthermore, the `section` element has an `author` attribute associated with it, which holds character data. The `heading` and `body` elements have character content. The most important structural elements in this short DTD are element type declarations and attribute-list declarations:

- An *element type declaration* declares an element type by specifying its name and its content model. The content model of an element type defines the allowed content of elements of this type.

- An *attribute-list declaration* declares a number of attributes for an element type. These attributes can be used in the element's start tag. Attributes can have different types. Depending on their declaration, attributes may be required or optional. They may also have default values.

Using this DTD, an XML editor could offer the user only choices to create valid instances of this document type by only providing methods to insert certain content (elements, attributes, or characters) where allowed by the DTD. This is one of the advantages of XML—that the logical structure of a document type can be made available to an application by supplying it with the DTD. A small document for the sample DTD just given could look like this:

```
<?xml version="1.0"?>
<!DOCTYPE document SYSTEM "document.dtd">
<document>
<heading>Transcluding the Web</heading>
<section author="Erik Wilde">
  <heading>Web Technologies</heading>
  <body>some text</body>
  <body>more text...</body>
</section>
<section author="David Lowe">
  <heading>Hypermedia Architectures</heading>
  <body>other text</body>
</section>
<section author="generated">
  <heading>List of References</heading>
  <body>generated text</body>
</section>
</document>
```

This is a very simple example, but it demonstrates the ability of XML to define application-specific document types and then to constrain documents according to this type (in this case a very simple version of this book). It is important to note that XML basically defines two different syntaxes: one for defining schemas using DTDs, and another for creating documents according to these DTDs.[6]

However, this new flexibility of XML in comparison with HTML introduces a new problem. Nothing is now known about the meaning of the elements and attributes (except for the meaning that can be derived from the given names). Therefore, additional ways of associating XML elements and attributes with semantics are required. One important set of semantics is formatting semantics, defined in the Extensible Stylesheet Language (XSL), which is briefly discussed in section 4.7. Another set of semantics is link semantics, which answer the question of how to identify hyperlinks in XML documents, since there is no such thing as HTML's <a> element with its predefined hyperlink semantics. This is what the XML Linking Language (XLink) described in chapter 7 is about—a way to embed hyperlinks in XML documents.

---

[6]In the context of the W3C XML Schema [Biron & Malhotra 01; Fallside 01; Thompson+ 01] effort, an alternative mechanism for specifying schemas has been defined that is more powerful, and more complex, than DTDs. However, in this book we will always use DTDs for defining schemas.

4.2 XML NAMESPACES

XML is designed to be used in the context of the Web and to enable the creation of many different document types (each defined by a DTD or some other schema). However, XML should also allow for the combination of vocabularies from different DTDs, such as with a container document type that may hold entries of many other document types. This scenario widely increases the possible applications of XML and encourages the reuse of document types.[7] However, this scenario also introduces the possibility of *name clashes*, where two independently working schema designers accidentally choose the same name for an element or an attribute. The XML Namespaces standard [Bray+ 99] aims at eliminating the possibility of conflicting names in XML schemas.

The basic idea of XML Namespaces is to introduce the concept of *qualified names*. Within the qualified name, a single colon separates the *namespace prefix* from the *local part*. The namespace prefix maps onto a URI reference (which is used to identify a namespace in a globally unique way), and the local part identifies a name within a particular namespace. The `xmlns` prefix is defined for declaring namespaces within XML documents, and the XML Namespaces specification requires that XML names (used for elements and attributes) not contain any colons, unless the colon is used for specifying a namespace. A very simple example of using a namespace is the following XML document:

```
<?xml version="1.0"?>
<html:html xmlns:html="http://www.w3.org/TR/REC-html401">
  <html:head><html:title>simple example</html:title></html:head>
  <html:body><html:h1>simple example</html:h1></html:body>
</html:html>
```

In this example, the `xmlns:html` attribute is used to declare a namespace prefix of `html` belonging to a namespace URI reference. In this case, the reference points to the specification of HTML 4.01 on the W3C's Web server. However, it is not required that the resource pointed to by the URI contain any machine-readable description of the namespace. The URI serves only as a globally unique identification of the associated namespace. All elements used in the example then come from the `html` namespace (as specified by the prefixes), which means that they are normal HTML 4.01

---

[7]In general, the reuse of XML schemas should be promoted because the usefulness of XML will be greatly reduced if for every single application area an entirely new schema is created. It would be preferable to make the use of XML modules possible (such as pioneered in XHTML 1.1). The modules could then be used to assemble schemas rather than creating them from scratch.

elements. An application supporting HTML 4.01 could therefore render these elements as specified by the HTML 4.01 recommendation.

Prefixes can have any form (with the exception of not having to contain the colon character and observing XML's general rules for names[8]). However, prefixes starting with `xml` are reserved for use by XML and XML-related specifications. The prefix `xml` itself is by definition bound to the namespace name `http://www.w3.org/XML/1998/namespace`. The prefix `xmlns` is used only for the declaration of namespaces and is not bound to any namespace.

It is possible to declare multiple namespaces in one element start tag, and namespace declarations are valid in all descendants of an element that declare a namespace unless they are overridden or explicitly undeclared (by assigning them an empty string). Furthermore, a *default namespace* can be declared by using a declaration with no prefix in it. It is considered to apply to the element where it is declared and to all elements with no prefix within the content of that element. Using a default namespace, the example just given can be simplified as follows:

```
<?xml version="1.0"?>
<html xmlns="http://www.w3.org/TR/REC-html401">
  <head><title>simple example</title></head>
  <body><h1>simple example</h1></body>
</html>
```

To illustrate the idea of namespaces in greater detail, the following example shows a more elaborate XML document using different namespaces for different purposes. This document uses a container format, which can hold content from different schemas.

```
<?xml version="1.0"?>
<container xmlns="http://transcluding.com/xmlns/container"
           xmlns:isbn="http://some.org/ISBN">
  <content>
    <html xmlns="http://www.w3.org/TR/REC-html401">
      <head><title>HTML content</title></head>
      <body>
        <p>some HTML text...</p>
        <p>text with <isbn:isbn>3-540-64285-4</isbn:isbn> numbers
      </body>
    </html>
  </content>
  <content>
    <math xmlns="http://www.w3.org/TR/REC-MathML">
```

---

[8]Thus, an XML namespace name begins with a letter or an underscore and continues with letters, digits, hyphens, underscores, or full stops.

```
      <mrow>
        <mi>a</mi><mo>+</mo><mi>b</mi>
      </mrow>
    </math>
  </content>
</container>
```

In this example, a hypothetical container schema is used and declared as the default namespace. Furthermore, a hypothetical namespace for ISBN numbers is used and assigned the prefix isbn. The consequence of these assignments is that all child elements of the container element that do not have prefixes belong to the container namespace (unless it is overridden), while throughout the document it is possible to use elements from the ISBN namespace by explicitly using the isbn prefix. The content of the container format is structured into two elements: one containing a small HTML document and another containing a small Mathematical Markup Language (MathML) document. By overriding the default namespace in their document element, both the HTML and the MathML documents can appear exactly as if they were used as stand-alone documents.

In addition, it is possible to use the elements from the ISBN namespace within any of the documents. If processed by a namespace-aware XML processor, the ISBN elements can be interpreted as required by the application. If the document has to be exported to a non-namespace-aware environment, the tags for the elements from the ISBN namespace can either be removed from the documents or be substituted by any markup that seems to be appropriate, for example, an HTML <span> element for assigning a class.

In essence, XML Namespaces simply defines a collection of names, which can be used in XML documents as element or attribute names. Elements from one namespace must be allowed to appear in the content model of elements where they are being used, either by being explicitly allowed (i.e., being defined as elements in the DTD) or by using an any content model for these elements. Attributes from namespaces can either be *global*, which means that they are not limited to a specific element type, or specific to an element type (in which case they may appear only on elements of that particular type). This partitions a namespace into three disjoint *namespace partitions:*

- *All element types partition.* This partition contains all element types from a namespace. Each element type has a unique local part, and the identification of the namespace name and the local part uniquely identifies the element type.

- *Global attribute partition.* This partition contains all attributes of a namespace that have been defined to be global within the namespace. These attributes also have a unique local name, and the identification of the namespace name and the local part uniquely identifies the attribute.

- *Per-element-type partition.* Attributes that are not global within a namespace are specific to an element type. These attributes are not required to have a unique name within the namespace and can be uniquely identified by their name and the element's type and namespace name.

A good example of a namespace defining only global attributes is XLink, as described in chapter 7. XLink defines global attributes that can be used with any XML element type to make it recognizable as an XLink element. This use of XML Namespaces has the advantage that any XML element type (coming from any namespace, which may not be under the control of the document author) can be used as an XLink element by using XLink's attributes with that element.

Although XML Namespaces defines a mechanism that is essential for many XML-based applications, currently it is not an integral part of XML, and therefore XML processors are not required to support it. However, it is foreseeable that XML Namespaces will become a widely accepted and used construct, so XML documents should be generally designed to conform to XML Namespaces. The effect of XML Namespaces' naming rules are as follows:

- All element types and attribute names contain either zero or one colon. If they do contain a colon, they are qualified names, consisting of a namespace prefix and a local part.

- No entity names, processing instruction targets, or notation names contain any colons.

Even though currently XML Namespaces is a separate specification, it is likely that it will be integrated into the next major version of XML,[9] which would make it necessary for XML processors to support namespaces in order to be conforming XML processors. Therefore, XML Namespaces should be regarded as a central mechanism of XML and should be supported by all applications. Even today it is not advisable to create documents that do not adhere to XML Namespaces (although they could be perfectly legal XML documents) because almost all standards relevant for XML require that the XML documents must be namespace-conforming. As a convincing example, the three core standards described in this book—XPath, XPointer, and XLink—depend on namespace conformance.

---

[9]As noted earlier, a minor revision of XML (called XML 1.1) is currently under development [Cowan 01].

4.3 XML BASE

One feature of HTML that has proven very useful and that currently is not part of basic XML is HTML's `<base>` element (which is part of the HTML document head). This element makes it possible to specify the base URI for any relative URIs that are being used inside the document. The goal of XML Base is to make this kind of functionality available in XML. Currently, XML Base is a separate W3C document [Marsh 01], but it is possible that it will be incorporated directly into the next version of XML.

The basic idea is that an `xml:base` attribute can be inserted in XML documents to specify a base URI other than the base URI of the document or external entity, which according to the rules specified by XML is normally used to resolve relative URIs. The base URI has to be specified according to the definition given in RFC 2396 [Berners-Lee+ 98].

The `xml:base` attribute sets the base URI Infoset property of the element information item (as described in section 4.5) on which the attribute occurs. Furthermore, the value of the base URI property also applies to all descendants of the element, except where further `xml:base` attributes are applied. If the value of the `xml:base` attribute is itself relative, then it is resolved against the base URI of the element it appears on. This scoping behavior makes it possible to specify a hierarchy of `xml:base` attributes.

In general, applications should resolve relative URIs according to the rules specified in RFC 2396 [Berners-Lee+ 98]. XML Base defines how these rules should be applied to XML documents containing one or more `xml:base` attributes. Sorted by priority, the base URI should be calculated according to the following rules (the highest priority appearing first):

1. The base URI is determined by the scope of `xml:base` attributes in the XML document according to the scoping rules defined by XML Base.

2. The base URI is that of the encapsulating entity. According to XML, the encapsulating entity's URI is that of the document entity, the entity containing the external DTD subset, or another external parameter entity.

3. The base URI is the URI that has been used to retrieve the entity containing the relative URI.

4. The base URI is undefined (i.e., equal to the empty string).

XML Base is not yet part of the XML specification or XML processors; and when the `xml:base` attribute in XML documents is used, it should be taken into account that it will take some time until XML Base is generally supported. However, because the functionality provided by XML Base is very basic as well as useful in practical applications, it is likely that it will be supported by many applications in the near future. Furthermore, the functionality now described by the separate XML Base specification will probably be integrated into the next major version of XML.

In the meantime, support for XML Base is already required by some W3C recommendations. Of the W3C specifications important for this book, only XLink requires XML Base, so any application implementing XLink also has to implement XML Base.

4.4 XML INCLUSIONS

Many existing data formats define inclusion mechanisms, which make it possible to include external resources in a resource. This inclusion usually occurs on a fairly low level, meaning that it is often equivalent or almost equivalent to actually replacing the include statement with the included resource. XML has such a mechanism, called XML Inclusions (XInclude) [Marsh & Orchard 01].[10] At first sight, XInclude could be considered unnecessary because of XML's external entity mechanism (similar to a low-level inclusion) and XLink (a high-level mechanism for associating resources). However, on closer inspection, XInclude can be clearly differentiated from these two methods:

4.4.1 XML External Entities

The biggest issue is that external entities require a DTD (because they are declared in the DTD), which makes it impossible to use them for well-formed documents. XInclude, on the other hand, takes the form of a normal XML element and thus can appear and be interpreted in well-formed XML without validation ever occurring.

On a more formal level, external entities are being resolved at parse time (the parser then interprets the assembled document), while XInclude is defined to merge XML Information Sets, as described in section 4.5, hence operating on independently parsed resources.

It is also worth mentioning that XInclude supports URI references, which makes it possible to use XPointers with XInclude. Consequently, XInclude can be used for assembling fragments of resources rather than just complete resources. The variations between XInclude and XML external entities is probably the biggest difference from a user perspective.

4.4.2 XLink

XLink's transclusion features might seem comparable to XInclude. However, while XLink defines an association mechanism for resources of any

---

[10]At the time of writing, XInclude is still in working draft status. This means that it may change before it becomes a stable recommendation.

kind (it is perfectly legal to transclude content of any media type, as long as the presentation program is able to handle them), XInclude specifies a mechanism regulating how XML can be included in XML and, consequently, defines a complete processing model for this. XLink, on the other hand, does not define any specific processing model, and the actual result of transcluding content into an XML document may differ based on the processing platform.

Furthermore, XLink supports association and traversal semantics, which may be used to associate resources in different ways and to traverse these associations in different ways XInclude, on the other hand, simply is a way to assemble an XML resource from different resources or resource fragments, without any support for making assertions about the association between the assembled parts.

In light of these differences, it is important to recognize that XML external entities are part of XML itself, while XInclude is a separate standard that was created to overcome some of the peculiarities of XML's external entities. Consequently, XInclude is not automatically supported by all XML software, so using XInclude requires an XML processor that implements this standard [Lease 00].

4.5 XML INFORMATION SET

Basically, XML defines a syntax for the specification of grammars of documents (XML DTDs) and a syntax for instances of these grammars (XML documents). However, in many cases applications are not interested in the syntactic details of a document, but only in the information contained in the document. The XML Information Set (XML Infoset) [Cowan & Tobin 01] has been designed to achieve this. It is an abstract description of the information contained in an XML document.

The information described by the XML Infoset is used in other specifications, such as the Document Object Model [Apparao+ 98; Le Hors+ 02; Wood+ 00b], which defines an Application Programming Interface (API) for accessing the XML Infoset. The XML Infoset specification itself does not define any specific kind of representation or interface for the information, and DOM is only one possible way by which XML Infoset information can be made available to applications or programmers.[11] Most important, the XML Infoset enables XML users to think of the content of a document (i.e., the information contained in it) rather than its syntactical representation (e.g., start and end tags of elements).

---

[11]Unfortunately, DOM was defined before the XML Infoset, and even though the models of both are very similar, there are some subtle differences.

Table 4.1 XML Infoset Information Items

Information Item	Page
attribute	83
character	84
comment	85
document	82
document type declaration	85
element	83
namespace	86
notation	85
processing instruction	84
unexpanded entity reference	84
unparsed entity	85

XML Infoset uses *information items* to describe the different types of information available from an XML document (see Table 4.1). Every information item has *properties,* which provide the actual information associated with it. In the following description of information items and their properties, the properties will often use data structures: lists are inherently ordered, while sets are unordered.

document

Each information set has exactly one document information item, and all other information items are either directly or indirectly related to it.

Properties referring to other information items: These include a list of child information items appearing in the document order, consisting of zero or more processing instruction information items and comment information items, exactly one element information item (representing the document element), and possibly a document type information item (if the document has a document type declaration); a set of references to notation information items for each notation declaration in the DTD; and a set of references to unparsed entity information items, one for each unparsed entity declared in the DTD.

Other properties: These cover the base URI of the document entity, if known; information about the character-encoding scheme of the document; an indication of the stand-alone status of the document; and the version number of the XML version being used (all this information is taken from the XML declaration).

element

For each element in the XML document, there is exactly one element information item, starting with the element information item of the document element, which, either directly or indirectly, contains all other element information items.

Properties referring to other information items: These include the element's children as an ordered list of element, processing instruction, unexpanded entity reference, comment, and character information items as they appear in document order; a set of references to attribute information items (excluding possible namespace declarations) for all specified or defaulted (from the schema) attributes; a set of references to attribute information items for all attributes declaring namespaces; a set of all namespaces (as namespace information items) in effect for the element; and the parent of the element (a document or element information item).

Other properties: These cover the element's name, split into a local name (not including a possible namespace prefix including colon) and the URI part of the name, if this is given by a namespace to which the element belongs; the namespace prefix of the element; and the base URI of the element, if known.

attribute

There is one attribute information item for each specified or defaulted attribute in the document instance, including namespace declarations (which appear in an element's namespace attributes property rather than in its attributes property).

Properties referring to other information items: These include the owner of the attribute (an element information item); if the attribute type is IDREF or IDREFS, an ordered list of element information items (the elements referred to in the attribute value); if the attribute type is ENTITY or ENTITIES, an ordered list of unparsed entity information items (the unparsed entities referred to in the attribute value); and if the attribute type is NOTATION, a notation information item (the notation referred to in the attribute value).

Other properties: These cover the attribute's name, split into a local name (not including a possible namespace prefix including colon) and the URI part of the name, if this is given by a namespace to which the attribute belongs; the namespace prefix of the attribute; the normalized attribute value; a flag indicating whether the attribute was specified or defaulted; and an indication of the attribute's XML attribute type.

processing instruction

For each processing instruction in the XML document, there is one processing instruction information item. The XML declaration and text declarations for external parsed entities (i.e., processing instructions with a target of xml) do not, however, result in processing instruction information items.

Properties referring to other information items: These include a notation information item for the notation named by the processing instruction's target, if the processing instruction's target names a declared notation, and the parent of the processing instruction (a document, element, or DTD information item).

Other properties: These cover the processing instruction's target (as a string); the processing instruction's content (as a string); and the base URI of the processing instruction.

unexpanded entity reference

Nonvalidating XML processors are allowed to not expand external parsed entities. If they do so, they must generate one reference to each skipped entity information item for each of these external parsed entities.

Property referring to other information items: The parent of the unexpanded entity reference (an element information item).

Other properties: These cover the name of the entity referenced; the public identifier and/or the system identifier of the entity; and the declaration base URI, which is the URI relative to which the system identifier should be resolved.

character

Each data character inside the document (occurring literally, as a character reference, or within a CDATA section) is represented by a character information item.

Property referring to other information items: The parent of the character (an element information item).

Other properties: These cover the character code according to ISO 10646 [ISO 93]; and a flag indicating whether the character is whitespace (validating XML processors are required to provide this information).

comment

Each comment in an XML document is represented by a comment information item (except for comments within the DTD).

Property referring to other information items: The parent of the comment (a document or element information item).

Other property: This covers the content of the comment represented by a string.

document type declaration

If the XML document has a document type declaration (which does not have to be the case for well-formed XML documents), then it is represented by a document type declaration information item.

Properties referring to other information items: These include an ordered list of processing instruction information items representing processing instructions appearing in the DTD; and the parent of the document type declaration (a document information item).

Other property: This covers the public identifier and/or the system identifier of the external subset, if there is an external DTD subset.

unparsed entity

Each unparsed general entity declared in the DTD is represented by an unparsed entity information item.

Property referring to other information items: This covers the notation information item named by the notation name (if there is such an item).

Other properties: These include the name of the entity, the public identifier and/or the system identifier of the entity, the declaration base URI of the entity, and the notation name associated with the entity.

notation

For each notation declared in the DTD, there is one notation information item.

Properties: These include the name of the notation, the public identifier and/or the system identifier of the notation, and the declaration base URI of the notation.

namespace

For each element in the document, namespace information items represent the namespaces in scope for that element.

Properties: These include the namespace prefix being declared (i.e., without the leading `xmlns:` attribute prefix; and if the attribute name is `xmlns`, then this property has no value), and the namespace name to which the prefix is bound.

Using these information items and their properties, XML Infoset defines an abstract description of the information contained in an XML document. As such, it does not contain all information that is present in the document, but only the parts essential for the document's content. For example, XML Infoset does not report the XML version number, the ordering of attributes in the start tag, or any whitespace within start or end tags.

An XML document needs to be well-formed (i.e., adhere to the syntactic rules defined by XML), but it does not have to be valid (i.e., be conforming to a DTD or any other schema) in order to be represented as an XML Infoset. However, a document does need to conform to the XML Namespaces recommendation described in section 4.2 in order to have an Infoset representation. XML documents not conforming to XML Namespaces cannot be described with an XML Infoset. This limitation is important for XPath, XPointer, and XLink (described in chapters 5, 6, and 7), because all these standards can be applied only to documents having an XML Infoset (i.e., documents that are namespace-conforming).

For an example of the Infoset of an XML document, see Figure 4.1, which is a representation of the following XML document with Infoset information items:

```
<?xml version="1.0"?>
<?example do not process ?>
<!DOCTYPE People SYSTEM "People.dtd">
<People xmlns="http://www.people.org/NS/People1234">
  <!-- List of people -->
  <Person StaffID="123456">
    Who: <Name>Anna Smith</Name>
    What: <Position>Sales Manager</Position>
  </Person>
  <Person StaffID="987654">
    Who: <Name>Bill Black</Name>
    What: <Position>XML Programmer</Position>
  </Person>
</People>
```

In this example, the individual character information items have been aggregated for the sake of clarity. Worth noting is the namespace declaration,

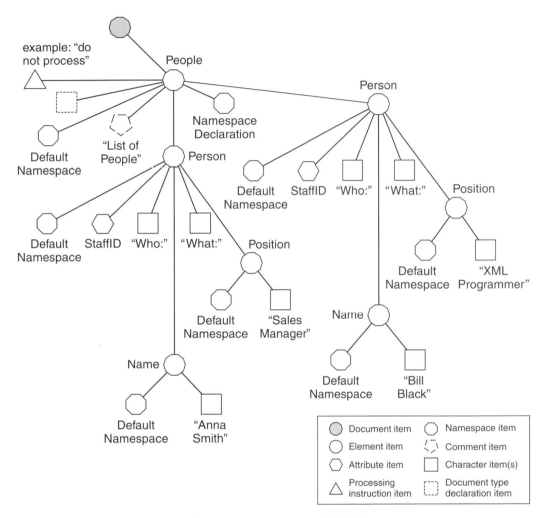

Figure 4.1 Example XML Infoset tree

which results in two nodes on the People element: one for the attribute declaring the namespace and another for the declared namespace.

The XML Path Language (XPath) described in chapter 5 is an application of the XML Information Set and uses the Infoset's information items to define a tree of XPath nodes. See Figure 5.2 in the next chapter for an example of how the Infoset can be used to define a slightly different representation of an XML document's content.

Another (and much simpler) application of the Infoset, Canonical XML [Boyer 01], is an example of how the abstract information specified by XML Infoset information items can be used to define a canonical form of XML documents by simply defining a serialization of an Infoset tree.

Even though the XML Infoset is not directly applicable to many scenarios, it is a very significant standard because it defines what the W3C thinks is important in an XML document. Regarding this issue, there are two important observations:

- There are some things that are not reflected in the XML Infoset, such as whitespace in tags and the order of attributes. The Infoset view of an XML document therefore obviously ignores some aspects of its syntactic representation, and this has been a normative (i.e., definitional) decision that has been made by the W3C. It is therefore safe to assume that the things represented in an Infoset are definitely relevant for a document.

- Some applications may wish to represent additional information that is not part of the XML Infoset.[12] They can do so by defining additional information items. As an example, XML Schema uses this approach to define schema validation as the process of adding information items (describing the result of the validation process) to the XML Infoset of the document being validated.

The XML Infoset is best regarded as an important standard for the modeling of information contained in XML documents, and it is used in many other W3C specifications. More a guideline than a strict standard, it clarifies which aspects of XML documents are considered relevant by the W3C.

4.6 EXTENSIBLE HYPERTEXT MARKUP LANGUAGE

The introduction of XML as a new language for creating application-specific document types raised the problem of a migration path from HTML (which will be the most widely used content type on the Web for a long time to come) to XML. The W3C's answer to that is the Extensible Hypertext Markup Language (XHTML), which in its version 1.0 [Pemberton 00] simply is a reformulation of HTML 4.01 in XML. Only a few things need to be changed when converting a document from HTML 4.01 to XHTML 1.0,[13]

---

[12]A very good example of this type of application is all editor-type applications, which have to retain the original formatting of the XML document through the whole editing process. Editors therefore need to retain many of the syntactic details ignored by the Infoset.

[13]Most of the work to be done is purely mechanical, such as producing full markup as required by XML. There are many publicly available utilities for making this conversion, but many of them should be handled with care because they do have surprising idiosyncrasies. One of the most popular tools is HTML Tidy, which is available at `http://www.w3.org/People/Raggett/tidy/`.

and it is very easy to write XHTML 1.0 documents in a way that makes them compatible with most HTML browsers. Consequently, XHTML 1.0 is the first step toward a migration to XML.

However, W3C's plans for HTML's future development go far beyond making HTML an XML application. XHTML 1.1 [Altheim+ 01; Altheim & McCarron 00, 01] shows the future direction of HTML, which is to use a modular approach. In XHTML 1.1, the document type is no longer a monolithic block, but a number of modules that can be used when needed (for example, for tables or forms). Modularization brings with it several advantages, including the following:

- The provision of a formal mechanism for subsetting XHTML
- The provision of a formal mechanism for extending XHTML
- The simplification of the transformation between document types
- The promotion of the reuse of modules in new document types

This approach makes it particularly easy to include XML document types in XHTML documents that are not a part of XHTML 1.1, such as the Mathematical Markup Language (MathML) [Carlisle+ 01; Ion & Miner 99] or Scalable Vector Graphics (SVG) [Ferraiolo 01]. Although XHTML 1.1 defines most of the same elements and attributes as XHTML 1.0, it does not include the deprecated elements and attributes of HTML 4.01 and therefore is more limited than XHTML 1.0. Consequently, XHTML 1.1 relies on a style sheet mechanism (such as XSL or CSS) for formatting.

The most important observation of this transition from HTML to XHTML is that even text documents using HTML and not XML will increasingly be made available as XML documents in the form of XHTML. As such, even these legacy documents (which can be converted automatically) can be integrated into XML-based scenarios, including those using XPointer[14] and XLink.

4.7 EXTENSIBLE STYLESHEET LANGUAGE

As mentioned in section 4.1, one of the problems of XML is that it associates no semantics with elements and attributes. In HTML, all elements have clearly defined semantics, and therefore clients do not need any additional information to display them properly. For example, if a browser recognizes a `<table>` element, it knows that the material that follows is

---

[14]It is important to remember that, by definition, an XPointer cannot point into an HTML document because it is not XML.

representing content organized in a tabular fashion, and it can present this content appropriately. For a visual browser, this means formatting the content in a rectangular grid; for a voice browser, this may mean reading the table rows, clearly indicating the start of each new column, and maybe repeating the column head. However, in XML an element could have the name table, but this would have no semantic relevance.

Consequently, in order to display (or, more generally speaking, process) XML documents, there must be a way to specify formatting semantics. The simplest way to do this is to use Cascading Style Sheets [Bos+ 98; Lie & Bos 99]; but this method suffers some serious drawbacks, the biggest being the lack of any functionality to reorder content for presentation. It is therefore expected that CSS will be used mainly for HTML and for simple XML documents (such as XHTML documents) but that a more powerful mechanism will be required for more sophisticated applications, where XML content must be reordered, duplicated (for example while creating a table of contents), or otherwise manipulated. The technology to do this is the Extensible Stylesheet Language. Basically, XSL consists of two parts. The first one is XSL Transformations (XSLT), a programming language specifically designed for processing XML documents (described in section 4.7.1). The second part of XSL is XSL Formatting Objects (XSL-FO), a language for specifying formatting semantics (described in section 4.7.2).

Although XSL is not intended to specifically address linking concepts, we feel that it should be mentioned here because some of XSL's features (such as multiple views of a single document) can be used to implement powerful hypermedia systems. In particular, XSLT's ability to transform XML documents programatically makes it ideally suited for all kinds of conversions between XML documents, totally independent of presentation aspects.[15] XSL-FO, on the other hand, is very specifically designed for presentation purposes, and we therefore do not go into significant detail about it.

4.7.1 XSL Transformations

XSL Transformations [Clark 99b] is a programming language designed for transforming XML documents, in most cases (but not necessarily) into other XML documents. XSLT is based on many ideas from the Document Style Semantics and Specification Language (DSSSL) [ISO 96], the

---

[15]In our view, a much better name for XSLT would have been XML Transformation Language, or something along those lines, to avoid implying that XSLT is specific to style sheet (and thus presentation) purposes.

transformation language for SGML, but has diverged significantly during the development process. The most obvious difference is the change of syntax. While DSSSL uses a Lisp-like syntax with many parentheses, XSLT uses XML syntax; and for many people it takes a while to get used to a programming language using a syntax as verbose as XML. A new version of XSLT, XSLT 2.0 [Kay 01a], is currently being developed by W3C.[16]

XSLT is a programming language, and as such it is much too complex to be explained in a book such as this. We recommend the excellent XSLT references published by Kay [Kay 00; Kay 01b] for learning XSLT. There are also other relevant publications slowly hitting the market, such as a book dealing with the specifics of transforming XML into HTML [Fung 00]. However, as with every programming language, it takes a while to get used to XSLT, and there is nothing that can substitute for playing around with little XSLT programs (often referred to as *style sheets*).

Many of the ideas presented in this book are based on the assumption that transforming XML between different document types can be done easily and for doing this in many cases XSLT will be the tool of choice. Currently, XSLT processors read (and parse) both the XML document and the XSLT program before actually performing a transformation, and consequently XSLT is used as an interpreted language. However, making XSLT more efficient is something many people are working on (examples include Sun's Translets and Oracle's XSLT Virtual Machine [Novoselsky & Karun 00]); and in our opinion, performance issues will become less of a concern in the near future.

One of the most important aspects of XSLT is its inclusion of the XML Path Language (XPath), described in detail in chapter 5. Actually, XPath is a result of the work on XSLT because, during work on XSLT and the XML Pointer Language (XPointer) (as described in chapter 6), many overlaps were discovered between addressing into an XML document in XSLT and in XPointer. After a rather long (and uncomfortable) period of hesitation, it was finally decided to base XSLT and XPointer on a common foundation, called XPath. While we do not go into the specifics of the XSLT language itself, we describe XPath in great detail; and mastering XPath is a key point to mastering XSLT.[17]

---

[16]Development of XSLT 1.1 [Clark 01] has been stopped in order to focus all efforts on XSLT 2.0. While XSLT 1.1 fixes the most notorious weaknesses of XSLT 1.0, and some XSLT implementations already support it in their production releases, it no longer is an official version of XSLT.

[17]There are some (minor) points where the differences between XSLT and XPath seem awkward, because the standards are not totally independent; but in general it is pretty easy to get used to XSLT if you know XPath.

4.7.2 XSL Formatting Objects

As stated earlier, XSL-FO, the second part of XSL, define an XML vocabulary for specifying formatting semantics. XSL-FO is specified in the XSL standard itself [Adler+ 01], in contrast to XSLT, which is a separate specification. One of the main goals of XSL-FO is to provide a much more powerful control of formatting than HTML, which is notorious for producing bad-looking hardcopies. XSL-FO provides very fine-grained control over the layout (such as spacing between blocks or footnotes), but does not specify other essential aspects such as line breaking and word spacing. Therefore, XSL Formatting Objects documents must be processed by a formatting program; some XSL-FO processors do the formatting internally. Some produce output in Portable Document Format (PDF) [Adobe 00], or similar formats, while other XSL-FO processors simply transform the input document into the input format for another formatting program—for example, TEX/LATEX [Knuth 86; Lamport 94]—which can then be used to produce a formatted result.

It can be easily observed that there is an overlap between XSL-FO and CSS, which also defines a vocabulary for formatting semantics (even though it is not defined with XML syntax). To avoid any unnecessary friction, the W3C has decided to technically align the formatting model of CSS3 and XSL-FO, so that it will be easy to reuse CSS styles in XSL-FO. The XSL-FO formatting model has been designed mainly with a read-only medium in mind (high-quality printouts), and consequently XSL-FO does not contain many formatting objects for defining interactive documents such as hypermedia. This is a key reason why in the context of this book we will not investigate XSL-FO any further.

4.8 RESOURCE DESCRIPTION FRAMEWORK

Web *meta-data* is the semantic description of Web resources. Although there are some loosely followed conventions about how the meta-data for a Web page should be included (using the `<meta>` element and a number of keywords), this use of meta-data is a very simple approach that relies on the page author's skill in choosing the right keywords (and in the right language). A far more powerful approach is the application of well-defined semantics. The Resource Description Framework (RDF) is the W3C's standard framework for the definition of meta-data.

A small set of standardized meta-data has been defined in RFC 2413 [Weibel+ 98]. It describes the Dublin Core set of meta-data keywords, which defines keywords for use with HTML's `<meta>` element. Because of the lack of support by search engines, the Dublin Core keywords have not been widely adopted,[18] even though they are being used in some newer formats, such as the Open eBook (OEB) format. In general, the Dublin Core and now in a much more flexible way RDF define an *ontology,* which is, according to Webster's dictionary, "a branch of metaphysics concerned with the nature and relations of being." In the context of Web meta-data, an ontology describes the building blocks out of which models for the real world are made. While the Dublin Core is a very simple and fixed ontology, defining a few keywords for the description of a Web document, RDF offers a framework for defining and exchanging ontologies.

RDF as a knowledge representation mechanism has been influenced by many existing approaches to knowledge representation. RDF is not as powerful as modern knowledge representation mechanisms such as the Knowledge Interchange Format (KIF), the de facto standard for exchanging machine-readable knowledge representations. However, RDF has been designed to be easily usable by Web users and to be powerful enough to facilitate meta-data for Web resources in a way not possible before. RDF was influenced by Netscape's Meta Content Framework (MCF) and by Microsoft's Channel Definition Format (CDF) [Ellerman 98] (which in turn was loosely based on Microsoft's earlier Web Collections proposal), which were both used for the description of a Web site's contents, and on other application-specific standards for meta-data.

RDF uses XML for its syntax, but the basic RDF model for structuring meta-data is independent from XML. The RDF model and syntax definition [Beckett 01; Lassila & Swick 99] specify that RDF data consist of nodes and attached name/value pairs. A simple example for this is an RDF model attaching the name "Author" and the value "John Smith" to a document written by that author.

The key idea of RDF is to provide a flexible mechanism for the representation of semantics, rather than defining fixed semantics. RDF therefore does not offer any predefined vocabularies. Vocabularies used in RDF, called RDF schemas [Brickley & Guha 00], are defined by user communities specifically for their needs. RDF defines the root of a hierarchy of schemas (containing basic classes), and users are free to extend this or use other user-defined schemas.

In particular, the information contained in XLink can be regarded as a special case of meta-data about resources (hyperlink-specific meta-data). It is therefore possible to view XLink as an application of RDF, and the W3C has published a note [Daniel 00] discussing the process of generating RDF from XLink. Seen from this perspective, XLink can be represented in

---

[18] A generalized version of the Dublin Core, the Warwick Framework, as described in 1996 [Lagoze 96], defines a container format for different meta-data formats and suffers from the same acceptance problems.

RDF, but the W3C note does not define an RDF schema for XLink. There has been discussion in the W3C about whether XLink should have its own syntax or whether it should simply be seen as some sort of RDF-represented meta-data; but the majority of W3C members voted for defining a specific XLink syntax, which is specified in the current XLink standard.

4.9 CONCLUSIONS

This chapter describes the technologies closely related to the core subject of this book. It gives short introductions to XML, XML Namespaces, XML Base, XInclude, the XML Infoset, XHTML, XSL (with its two components XSLT and XSL-FO), and RDF. The chapter serves as a reference for readers who are familiar with these basic XML technologies but who need a short review.

5

XML Path Language

A common task for many applications based on XML is to identify certain parts of an XML document. Instead of having each application define its own method for doing this, W3C developed the XML Path Language (XPath) [Clark & DeRose 99]. XPath currently is being used by XSLT (as described in section 4.7), XPointer (as described in chapter 6), XML Schema and XML Query (XQuery) [Chamberlin+ 01]. However, it can be used by other applications as well, and W3C's goal is that XPath will be a common foundation for all applications that need to address parts of XML documents. The benefits of such a widespread use of XPath would be the reuse of software developed for it and the opportunity for human users of XPath-based applications to apply their XPath know-how to new application domains. We therefore consider an understanding of XPath as one of the basic skills for working with XML, and it is worthwhile to spend some time learning it. In addition to this chapter, Kay and Fung provide good resources for understanding and learning XPath [Kay 00, 01; Fung 00].

Your personal learning style should determine whether you read this chapter about XPath before or after chapter 6 on XPointer. Even though XPointer builds on XPath, readers with a preference for a top-down approach to learning will find it more suitable for them to read first (or at least skim) the chapter about XPointer and then continue with XPath and the detailed description of what can be done with XPointers. Readers with a preference for bottom-up approaches, on the other hand, may choose to learn about XPath's underlying principle of addressing parts of XML documents before continuing to XPointer's application of this principle for the purpose of defining XML fragment identifiers. Either way, the chapters on XPath and XPointer have a number of interdependencies, making them truly understandable only in combination (at least in terms of supporting linking mechanisms).

The basic point of XPath (and the reason for its name) is to describe the selection of parts of an XML document in a sequence of steps, which are specified in a *path notation*. This is intuitive for people who are used to working with hierarchically organized information[1] and the path can be easily represented in a printable form, which is one of the key requirements for XPath. While XPath in the context of XSLT will often be hidden inside an XSL style sheet, XPointers using XPath will be visible to users (for example, as part of a URI reference, the address bar of a browser) and should be easily readable and exchangeable by nonelectronic means, such as handwriting or even conversation over the phone.[2]

The XPath standard covers a number of areas. The first interesting area to look at is the *general model,* which describes the concepts and data types used in XPath and how the data types can be manipulated. This aspect of XPath is described in section 5.1. The most widely used construct of XPath is a *location path,* which is explained in detail in section 5.2. More general than location paths are *expressions,* which are described in section 5.3. Another important aspect of XPath are *functions,* which can be used in expressions (very similar to a function library in a programming language). They are described in section 5.4. Finally, to illustrate the concepts discussed in this chapter, section 5.5 shows some examples of XPaths and also gives guidelines for constructing XPaths.

5.1 GENERAL MODEL

In order to understand XPath, you must be familiar with some terms and concepts. Most generally, an XPath is an expression that is evaluated to yield an object. This basic model raises two major questions: First, what are the results of the evaluation of an expression? Second, in which context does this evaluation takes place? To answer these questions we need to consider various concepts that form the foundation of XPath:

- *Object types.* XPath knows about four object types: a `node-set`; boolean; number; and string. While the latter three are well known from other application areas, the concept of the `node-set` is less common. Basically, a `node-set` is nothing more than what is implied

---

[1]In an abstract sense, file systems on computers (which are understood by virtually all computer users) and XML documents are similar, in that they represent hierarchically structured information. This common structure often is referred to as a *tree,* which has the file system's root directory or the XML document element as its root and then organizes all information starting from that.

[2]In fact, it is one of the key requirements of URIs (and XPath as the foundation of XPointer will be used in URI fragment identifiers) that they can be printed and even exchanged over the phone.

by its name—an unordered collection of nodes (which themselves can have different types). It is important to recognize that the set of object types defined by XPath is the minimal set to be supported by all XPath applications. XPath applications (e.g., XPointer) are allowed to specify additional object types.

- *Context*. Each expression is evaluated within a given context. In general, XPath assumes that the context is defined by the application sitting on top of XPath (e.g., XPointer or XSLT). A context consists of the following things:

  - A node, which is said to be the *context node*.
  - The *context position* and the *context size*, which determine the location of the context node in the context and the overall size of the context. Both values are non-zero positive integers that are used to put the context node into the context of the containing `node-set`.
  - A set of *variable bindings*, which are mappings from variable names to variable values. The values of variables can be of any object type.
  - A *function library*, which is a mapping from function names to functions. Each function accepts zero or more arguments of any object type and returns a single result of any object type.
  - A set of *namespace* declarations in scope for the expression, which consist of mappings from prefixes to namespace URIs.

  It is important to recognize that the context defined by XPath is the minimal context to be supported by all XPath applications. Because XPath is not intended to be used on its own, actual applications (e.g., XPointer) will be based on it, and they are allowed to specify additional context elements, such as new variables and functions.

XPath's object types as well as the context are minimal requirements that can be extended by XPath applications. Furthermore, the context is defined only on a per-expression base, which means that the context changes while an XPath consisting of multiple expressions is evaluated. A very simple example of this is if an XML document consisted of two levels of hierarchy, and an XPath addressed into one element of the lowest level by first addressing the parent element in the intermediate level and then, in this new context, addressing the target element. It is this design for stepwise (or hierarchical) addressing that makes XPath very powerful.

The concept of the `node-set` has been introduced already, but so far we have not said exactly what a node is. XPath operates on an abstract tree of nodes, which represents the XML document to which the XPath is applied.

(Note that this use of the term *node* is different from the hypertext concept of *node* as a unit of information that should be presented as a whole.) The tree is derived from the XML Information Set (XML Infoset) representation of the document, as described in section 4.5. XPath identifies seven types of nodes, which are explained in detail in the following sections. However, there are some data model concepts not associated with any particular node type, and these are explained in the following list:

- *String value.* For every type of node, there is a way to evaluate the `string-value` of that type. For element nodes and root nodes, this is defined by the `nodeValue` method as specified by the Document Object Model (DOM). The `string-value` of a node is important in XPath because it is used in different contexts to perform certain evaluations and comparisons involving nodes.

- *Expanded name.* Some node types also have an `expanded-name`, which is a representation of a local name (a string) and a namespace URI (empty or a string). More information about XML Namespaces can be found in section 4.2.

- *Document order.* All nodes for a document are arranged in a certain order, called the *document order*. This is determined by the order in which the first character of the XML representation of the node occurs in the XML document. Figure 5.1 shows how the document order would be for elements of an XML document, if they were used

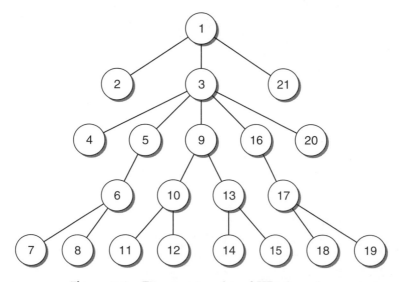

Figure 5.1　Document order of XPath nodes

in the hierarchical structure depicted in the figure.[3] There also is a *reverse document order,* which is the reverse of the document order.

In the document order, all nodes are ordered, not only element nodes. Attribute nodes occur after the element node on which the attribute has been used and before the element nodes of the element's children. Namespace nodes occur before attribute nodes, even if the namespace has been declared after the element's other attributes. The order of attribute and namespace nodes among themselves is implementation-dependent.

- *Node relationships.* The usual terminology for treelike structures applies to XPath, which means that every node (except the root node) has exactly one *parent,* one node can have any number of *child* nodes, and nodes never share child nodes. Finally, the *descendants* of a node are its child nodes and their descendants.

With these common concepts for nodes in mind, we now examine each node type in detail.

5.1.1 Root Node

The *root node* is the root of the tree, and therefore each XML document tree has exactly one root node. The children of the root element are the document element (an element node), and processing instruction and comment nodes for all processing instructions and comments occurring before and after the document element. It is very important to keep in mind that the root node is not the node representing the XML document element, which is represented by a child node of the root node.

The root node's `string-value` is the concatenation of the `string-values` of all text node descendants of the root node in document order.

5.1.2 Element Node

Each element in an XML document is represented by an element node. The children of an element node are the element, comment, processing instruction, and text nodes for the element's content. It is also worth noting that any entity references (both internal and external as well as character references) are resolved, which means that XPath does not provide any means to access the entity structure of a document.

---

[3]It is important to notice that this figure shows only element nodes.

Every element node has an `expanded-name`, which is evaluated in accordance with the XML Namespaces recommendation. Element nodes may also have a *unique identifier* (ID), if the element has an attribute with the type `ID` on it.[4] No two element nodes that are in a document can have the same ID.[5]

The `string-value` of an element node is the concatenation of the `string-values` of all text node descendants of this element node in document order.

5.1.3 Attribute Node

For each attribute of an element, there is an attribute node. Somewhat confusingly, although the element node is the parent of all of its attribute nodes, the attribute nodes are not treated as children of the element node (remember that only element, comment, processing instruction, and text nodes are the children of element nodes). A defaulted attribute is treated as if the attribute has been specified in the document. However, if the default was declared as `#IMPLIED` and the attribute was not defined in the element instance, then there is no attribute node for the attribute.

Some special attributes (such as `xml:lang` and `xml:space`) by definition implicitly apply to all descendants, unless they are overridden. However, this does not mean that all descendants have attribute nodes for these attributes. The attribute nodes for these attributes will appear only at those elements where the attribute was explicitly set in the XML document. Attributes for declaring namespaces (bearing the `xmlns` prefix) will not appear as attribute nodes, but as namespace nodes.

Every attribute node has an `expanded-name`, which is evaluated in accordance with the XML Namespaces recommendation. The `string-value` of an attribute node is its normalized attribute value, with the normalization as defined by the XML recommendation.

5.1.4 Namespace Node

For each namespace in scope for an element, there is a namespace node. As with attribute nodes, the element node is the parent of all of these nodes, but the namespace nodes are not children of the element node. The namespace nodes include the namespace of the `xml` prefix (which is defined by the XML recommendation) and the default namespace if one is in scope

---

[4]Here it becomes obvious that XPath requires DTD processing, because the DTD contains the information about attribute types.

[5]If two elements have the same ID (in which case the document is invalid), then the first element in document order is assigned the ID, while the second element does not have an ID.

for the element. The result of this is that namespace nodes will be present for an element for all of the following cases:

- For every namespace declaration on the element (i.e., for every attribute whose name starts with the prefix `xmlns`).

- For every namespace declaration on an ancestor of the element, unless the element itself or a nearer ancestor redeclares the namespace.

- For an `xmlns` attribute (the declaration of the default namespace), if the attribute on the element or the nearest ancestor where it occurs is nonempty. (Using an empty value for the `xmlns` attribute undeclares the default namespace.)

Every namespace node has an `expanded-name`, where the local part is the namespace URI that belongs to the namespace, and the namespace URI of the `expanded-name` is always null. The `string-value` of a namespace node is the namespace URI that belongs to the namespace (relative URIs are resolved to absolute URIs).

5.1.5 Processing Instruction Node

For every processing instruction in the document, there is a corresponding processing instruction node (the only exception is for a processing instruction in the document type declaration). Every processing instruction node has an `expanded-name`, where the local part is the processing instruction's target, and the namespace URI of the `expanded-name` is always null. The `string-value` of a processing instruction node is the part of the processing instruction following the target until the closing ?>, including any whitespace.

5.1.6 Comment Node

For every comment in the document, there is a corresponding comment node (the only exception is a comment in the document type declaration). Comment nodes do not have an `expanded-name`. The `string-value` of a comment node is the content of the comment, not including the opening `<!--` and the closing `-->`.

5.1.7 Text Node

Character data occurring inside elements is grouped together in text nodes. Each text node holds as much character data as possible, in other words, all the character data between two tags. Text nodes do not have an `expanded-name`. The `string-value` of a text node is its character data. Text nodes always have at least one character of data.

CDATA sections are treated as character data, with every character inside the CDATA section resulting in one character in the text node. The CDATA markers are not included in the text node. Characters in attribute values, processing instructions, or comments do not produce text nodes.

5.1.8 Example

To illustrate the different node types presented in the previous sections, consider the following simple example XML document:

```
<?xml version="1.0"?>
<?example do not process ?>
<!DOCTYPE People SYSTEM "People.dtd">
<People xmlns="http://www.people.org/NS/People1234">
  <!-- List of people -->
  <Person StaffID="123456">
    Who: <Name>Anna Smith</Name>
    What: <Position>Sales Manager</Position>
  </Person>
  <Person StaffID="987654">
    Who: <Name>Bill Black</Name>
    What: <Position>XML Programmer</Position>
  </Person>
</People>
```

We can represent this XML document as an XPath node tree (based on the concepts introduced by the XML Infoset as described in section 4.5), shown in Figure 5.2. This figure shows the various XPath nodes. Note, however, that for the sake of clarity, the text nodes for the whitespace in the XML document have been omitted. It is also important to notice that although this tree is derived from the concepts introduced in the Infoset, there are some differences (such as the absence of the document type declaration and the aggregation of characters into text nodes; see Figure 4.1 for a direct comparison).

One interesting observation about the node tree is that some nodes do not directly correspond to any XML markup, for example, the namespace nodes in the descendant elements of the People element, which inherit the default namespace declaration from the People ancestor element. Another example of nodes not directly corresponding to any XML markup in the document are defaulted attributes taken from the DTD (this case is not shown in the example).

Note that the XML declaration is not part of the tree (only the example processing instruction is represented as a processing instruction node). Another important thing to note is the kind of relationship between nodes. Solid lines in the tree denote "real" treelike relationships, where the upper node is the parent of the lower node, and the lower node is a child of the

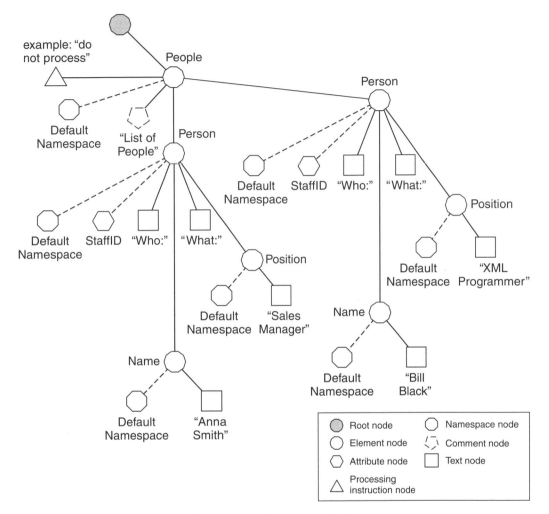

Figure 5.2   Example XPath node tree

upper node. Dashed lines, on the other hand, denote the special kind of relationship, where the upper node is a parent of the lower node, but the lower node is not a child of the upper node. This kind of relationship within the node tree is used for attribute and namespace nodes.

5.2 LOCATION PATHS

Now that we have an understanding of how an XML document is represented by nodes of different types, the next step is to look at how these nodes can be used for addressing content within an XML document. The most important construct of XPath is the *location path*. A location path is used to address a certain `node-set` of a document. This is achieved by concatenating multiple steps, which describe with increasing specificity which parts of the document should be addressed, into one location path. The following definitions are taken from the XPath specification[6] and describe a location path syntactically:

```
[1] LocationPath           ::= RelativeLocationPath
                             | AbsoluteLocationPath
[2] AbsoluteLocationPath ::= '/' RelativeLocationPath?
                             | AbbreviatedAbsoluteLocationPath
[3] RelativeLocationPath ::= Step
                             | RelativeLocationPath '/' Step
                             | AbbreviatedRelativeLocationPath
[4] Step                   ::= AxisSpecifier NodeTest Predicate*
                             | AbbreviatedStep
[5] AxisSpecifier          ::= AxisName '::'
                             | AbbreviatedAxisSpecifier
[6] AxisName               ::= 'ancestor' | 'ancestor-or-self'
                             | 'attribute' | 'child' | 'descendant'
                             | 'descendant-or-self' | 'following'
                             | 'following-sibling' | 'namespace'
                             | 'parent' | 'preceding'
                             | 'preceding-sibling' | 'self'
[7] NodeTest               ::= NameTest
                             | NodeType '(' ')'
                             | 'processing-instruction' '(' Literal ')'
[8] Predicate              ::= '[' PredicateExpr ']'
[9] PredicateExpr          ::= Expr
[10] AbbreviatedAbsoluteLocationPath ::= '//' RelativeLocationPath
[11] AbbreviatedRelativeLocationPath ::= RelativeLocationPath '//' Step
[12] AbbreviatedStep       ::= '.' | '..'
[13] AbbreviatedAxisSpecifier ::= '@'?
```

The syntax of location paths has been designed to be similar to other hierarchical notations used in computer applications, such as URIs or file names. A location path is either absolute or relative. Absolute paths are denoted by a leading slash and a trailing relative location path. Relative location paths are divided into several steps, separated by slashes. These location steps are described in section 5.2.1. XPath also defines a number of abbreviations for the most commonly used location paths and steps, and these abbreviations will be mentioned where appropriate.

---

[6]We list XPath grammar productions only where they help to understand the concepts behind them. The numbering of the productions has been taken from the XPath specification [Clark & DeRose 99], which should be consulted for a complete and authoritative definition of the XPath grammar. It can be found at `http://www.w3.org/TR/xpath`.

Before we go into the details of location steps and what can be done by using and combining them, here are some examples of location paths. XPath supports an abbreviated syntax for location paths (as specified in rules 10 to 13 of the preceding code), which is often used in real-world applications. We explain these abbreviation mechanisms in detail in section 5.2.5. However, in the following examples, we use the full syntax, which is easier to explain and understand:

1. `attribute::name`
   Selects the `name` attribute of the context node.

2. `/descendant::numlist/child::item`
   Selects all the `item` elements that have a `numlist` parent and that are in the same document as the context node.

3. `child::para[position()=1]`
   Selects the first `para` child of the context node.

4. `/descendant::figure[position()=42]`
   Selects the forty-second `figure` element in the document.

5. `/child::doc/child::chap[position()=5]/`
   `child:: sect[position()=2]`
   Selects the second `sect` child of the fifth `chap` child of the `doc` document element.

6. `child::para[attribute::type='warning'][position()=5]`
   Selects the fifth `para` child of the context node that has a `type` attribute with the value `warning`.

7. `child::para[position()=5][attribute::type="warning"]`
   Selects the fifth `para` child of the context node if that child has a `type` attribute with the value `warning`. If there is no such attribute, nothing is selected.

In all these examples, it is apparent that two things are very important in locations paths: the context (the position within the document against which the location path is evaluated) and the difference between relative and absolute location paths (easily identified by beginning with either an axis specifier or a slash character, as defined by rules 1 to 3).

5.2.1 Location Steps

A location step is the most important construct of a location path in XPath, making it possible to select a number of nodes from a given set of nodes according to certain criteria (e.g., selecting only the elements of a `node-set` that have a given name or a given relation to the context node). As defined by rule 3, location steps are separated by slash characters. Each location step is defined as consisting of three distinct parts: an axis, a node test, and a predicate. These parts are the core building blocks of every location step (and therefore every location path as well), as described in sections 5.2.2, 5.2.3, and 5.2.4. To make location steps more compact, XPath also defines a number of abbreviations, discussed in section 5.2.5. Finally, section 5.2.6 gives examples for XPath location paths and also mentions some of the fine points of using them.

5.2.2 Axes

An axis in XPath defines which nodes are selected starting from the context node. For example, the most often used axis is the `child` axis; and based on a given context node, all child nodes of the context node are placed on this axis. Generally speaking, axes can be most easily remembered as a special kind of view from the context node, each defining another particular way to look at the nodes of an XML document.

Table 5.1 lists all XPath axes. In addition to the number of the figure in this book that illustrates the axis, the table also contains two properties of axes:

- *Direction.* The *direction* of an axis determines in which order the nodes on an axis are arranged. If the axis is a forward axis, then the nodes are arranged in document order. If it is a reverse axis, then they are arranged in reverse document order (more about document

Table 5.1 Overview of XPath Axes

Axis Name	Direction	Principal Node Type	Page	Figure
ancestor	reverse	element	109	5.3
ancestor-or-self	reverse	element	110	5.3
attribute	n/a	attribute	110	n/a
child	forward	element	111	5.3
descendant	forward	element	111	5.3
descendant-or-self	forward	element	112	5.4
following	forward	element	112	5.4
following-sibling	forward	element	112	5.4
namespace	n/a	namespace	113	n/a
parent	forward	element	113	5.4
preceding	reverse	element	114	5.5
preceding-sibling	reverse	element	114	5.5
self	forward	element	114	5.5

order can be found in section 5.1). The direction of an axis is very important when nodes on an axis are selected using their position, discussed in detail in section 5.2.4, which deals with location step predicates.

- *Principal node type.* The *principal node type* of an axis determines the type of nodes being selected by the node test ∗ (more about node tests in section 5.2.3), so depending on the node test, it may be important to know the principal node type. However, XPath's rule is that "if an axis can contain elements, then the principal node type is `element`; otherwise, it is the type of the nodes that the axis can contain," so the principal node type can be easily remembered.

Because axes are most easily remembered as views from the context node, Figures 5.3 to 5.5 visualize the axes from the point of view of the emphasized node in the middle of the tree (the context node) and shading

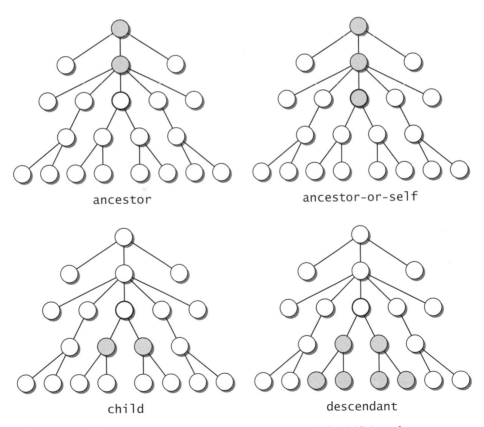

Figure 5.3   XPath axes `ancestor`, `ancestor-or-self`, `child`, and `descendant`

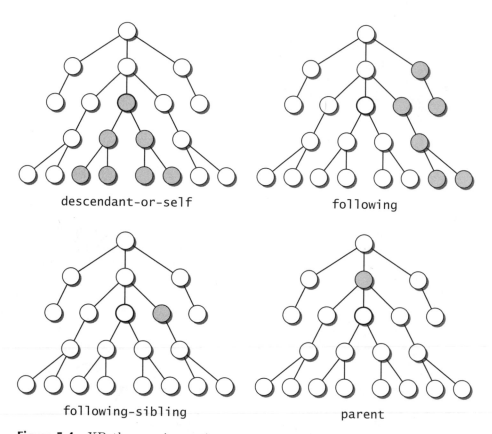

Figure 5.4   XPath axes `descendant-or-self`, `following`, `following-sibling`, and `parent`

the nodes that are part of the individual axes. It should be noted, however, that even though in these examples all axes are non-empty, it is perfectly legal for axes to be empty, one simple example being the `child` axis of an element that does not have any children. Furthermore, the figures show only element nodes, which is why the `attribute` and the `namespace` axes are not shown.[7]

Another important thing to remember is that in XPath's node tree, the XML document element is not the root node but a child (the only element

---

[7]The astute reader will notice that, strictly speaking, the node tree shown in the examples is not possible using element nodes only. One reason is that by definition the root node of an XPath node tree is not an element node. The other reason is that even if the root node would be accepted, it would not be legal for it to have more than one element child. Therefore, in order to keep the examples valid as XPath node trees, the node tree examples can be regarded as the node tree directly under the root node, starting with the document element's node.

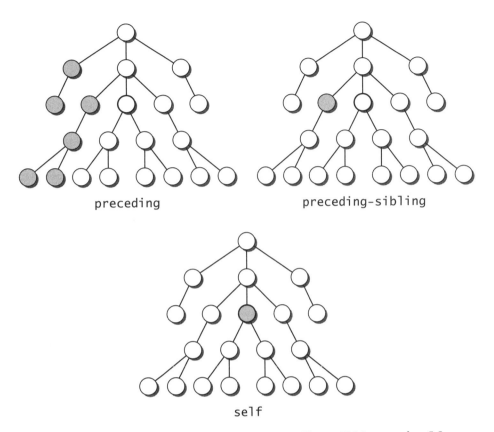

preceding   preceding-sibling

self

Figure 5.5 XPath axes `preceding`, `preceding-sibling`, and `self`

child) of the root node. Consequently, when using axes that select nodes before, above, or after the context node, the root node as well as children of the root node other than the document element node (i.e., comment nodes or processing instruction nodes, but not attribute nodes or namespace nodes) may also be part of these axes.

Before we go into the details of all axes available in XPath, we reiterate that according to rule 4, the axis is the first component in every location step (the only exception being an abbreviation or the lack of an axis specifier, thereby implicitly specifying the default axis `child`, as defined in rule 13).

The ancestor Axis

This axis selects all ancestor nodes of the context node, which are its parent node, the parent node of the parent node, and so on until the root node. Consequently, the `ancestor` axis will always include the root node, unless the context node is the root node (in which case the `ancestor` axis will be empty). An easy way to visualize the `ancestor` axis is to look up the tree starting from the context node. All nodes up to the root are on this axis. Because this view of the nodes starts further down in the tree and goes up, the `ancestor` axis is a reverse axis.

The `ancestor-or-self` Axis

This axis selects all ancestor nodes of the context node and the context node itself. The ancestors of the context node are its parent node, the parent node of the parent node, and so on until the root node. Consequently, the `ancestor-or-self` axis will always include the root node.

The `ancestor-or-self` axis can be seen as the union of the `ancestor` axis and the `self` axis. An easy way to visualize the `ancestor-or-self` axis is to look up the tree starting from the context node. All nodes up to the root are on this axis, including the context node. Because this view of the nodes starts further down in the tree and goes up, the `ancestor-or-self` axis is a reverse axis.

The `attribute` Axis

The `attribute` axis selects all attributes of the context node. If the context node is not an element node, or if it is an element node but the element does not have any attributes, then the `attribute` axis is empty. There are three special things to remember about this axis:

- Nodes on the `attribute` axis are placed in arbitrary order, so it does not make sense to make any assumptions about the position of nodes on the attribute axis. Therefore, the `attribute` axis does not have a direction.

- The `attribute` axis has a principal node type of attribute nodes, so selecting all nodes on this axis using the * node test selects attribute nodes.

- Even though namespace declarations syntactically are XML attributes, they do not appear on the `attribute` axis. Instead, all namespace declarations in effect for an element are selected by the `namespace` axis.

The `attribute` axis is one of XPath's most frequently used axes, and it can be conveniently abbreviated using the @ character, as described in detail in section 5.2.5. Because attribute nodes do not have children, a location step specifying the `attribute` axis usually is the last step that is in a location path.[8]

---

[8]However, an attribute node's parent is the element bearing the attribute, so it is possible to further navigate the tree of element nodes starting from an attribute node.

The child Axis

The `child` axis is the most frequently used axis of all XPath axes, and for this reason it is the default axis. This means that if no axis specifier is given, it is assumed that the `child` axis should be used (this is formally specified in rule 13, which allows an empty abbreviated axis specifier). The `child` axis selects all children of the context node, which are all nodes located immediately beneath the context node.[9] If the context node does not have any children, then the `child` axis is empty. An easy way to remember the `child` axis is that it selects all nodes directly beneath the context node, which in the tree view corresponds to all nodes directly connected to the context node.

Even though in most cases the children of the context node are element nodes (representing the elements directly contained in the element represented by the context node), note that the `child` axis may contain other node types as well, specifically text nodes, comment nodes, and processing instruction nodes. In section 5.2.3, we will discuss how these different types of nodes can be differentiated using node tests. If, however, the node test `*` is specified, then only nodes of the principal node type will be selected, which in case of the `child` axis are element nodes.

The `child` axis is a forward axis (which can be easily remembered by "looking down" the node tree), so all nodes selected by this axis are arranged in document order.

The descendant Axis

The `descendant` axis can be most easily thought of as a recursive version of the `child` axis, selecting not only the nodes immediately beneath the context node but also all nodes indirectly beneath the context node (i.e., the children's children and so on, until there are no more children).[10] If the context node does not have any children, then the `descendant` axis is empty. An easy way to remember the `descendant` axis is that it selects all nodes directly or indirectly beneath the context node, which in the tree view corresponds to all nodes located under the context node.

As with the `child` axis, the descendants of the context node will usually be element nodes, but may also be text nodes, comment nodes, and processing instruction nodes. In section 5.2.3, we will discuss how these different types of nodes can be differentiated using node tests. If, however, the node test `*` is specified, then only nodes of the principal node type will be selected, which in case of the `descendant` axis are element nodes.

---

[9]It is important to notice that, formally, attribute and namespace nodes are not children of element nodes, so these node types are not selected by the `child` axis.

[10]It is important to notice that, formally, attribute and namespace nodes are not children of element nodes, so these node types are not selected by the `descendant` axis.

The `descendant` axis is a forward axis (which can be easily remembered by "looking down" the node tree), so all nodes selected by this axis are arranged in document order.

The `descendant-or-self` Axis

The `descendant-or-self` axis is an extended version of the `descendant` axis and selects all nodes chosen by the `descendant` axis, and the context node itself. If the context node does not have any children, then the `descendant-or-self` axis selects only the context node. An easy way to remember the `descendant-or-self` axis is that it selects the context node and all nodes directly or indirectly beneath the context node, which in the tree view corresponds to all nodes located under the context node.

The `descendant-or-self` axis is a forward axis (which can be easily remembered by looking down the node tree), so all nodes selected by this axis are arranged in document order.

The `following` Axis

This axis selects the nodes that follow the context node. It is rarely used because it is very specific to the order of elements in the document, and usually XPaths are more likely to be based on structural criteria rather than sequence. The axis can be most easily remembered by thinking of the document in its XML serialization (in contrast to its tree representation), with all nodes being selected whose start occurs after the end tag of the context element. (However, attribute and namespace nodes are never selected by the `following` axis.) Therefore, the `following` axis is empty for the last node of the document.

The `following` axis is a forward axis (which can be easily remembered by selecting the nodes following the context node in the XML serialization), so all nodes selected by this axis are arranged in document order.

The `following-sibling` Axis

The `following-sibling` axis selects all nodes having the same parent as the context node and occurring after it in document order. This makes it easy to select the "next" element when thinking of hierarchy levels in the document tree and when it does not matter how many subelements an element may have. The easiest way to visualize the `following-sibling` axis is to look from the context node in a horizontal direction in document order and then to select only the nodes that share a common parent with the context node.

It should be noted that siblings are by definition nodes having the same parent as the context node (otherwise the axis would have been called "cousins of various degrees"), so the `following-sibling` axis does not select all nodes on the same hierarchy level of the XML, but only those nodes with the same parent as the context node. Consequently, if the node is the last child of its parent, then the `following-sibling` axis is empty.

The `following-sibling` axis is a forward axis (which can be easily remembered by looking in the direction of the document order of the node tree), so all nodes selected by this axis are arranged in document order.

The namespace Axis

The `namespace` axis selects all namespaces in effect for the context node. If the context node is not an element node, or if it is an element node but there is no namespace in effect for that element, then the `namespace` axis is empty. For a namespace node to appear on the `namespace` axis of a given element, it is not necessary for that namespaces to be explicitly declared for that element. This is because namespaces are inherited by child elements (see section 4.2 for more information on XML Namespaces).

There are three special things to remember about the `namespace` axis:

- Nodes on the `namespace` axis are placed in arbitrary order, so it does not make sense to make any assumptions about the position of namespace nodes on the axis. Therefore, the `namespace` axis does not have a direction.

- The `namespace` axis has a principal node type of namespace nodes, so selecting all nodes on this axis using the * node test selects namespace nodes.

- Even though namespace declarations syntactically are XML attributes, they do not appear on the `attribute` axis. Instead, all namespace declarations in effect for an element are selected by the `namespace` axis.

Because namespace nodes do not have children, a location step specifying the `namespace` axis usually is the last step in a location path.[11]

The parent Axis

This axis selects the parent node of the context node. If there is no parent node (because the context node is the root node), then this axis is empty. Because by definition each node in a tree has at most one parent node, the `parent` axis never selects more than one node. As a convenient abbreviation (and very intuitive for people used to working with file systems), the location step "`..`" can be used to select the parent node of the context node (it is defined in rule 12; see more about abbreviations in section 5.2.5). Because

---

[11]However, a namespace node's parent is the element bearing the namespace declaration, so it is possible to further navigate the tree of element nodes starting from a namespace node.

the `parent` axis never selects more than one node, its direction (technically being forward) is irrelevant.

The `preceding` Axis

This axis selects the nodes that precede the context node. It is rarely used because it is very specific to the order of elements in the document, and usually XPaths are more likely to be based on structural criteria rather than sequence. The axis can be most easily remembered by thinking of the document in its XML serialization (in contrast to its tree representation), with all nodes being selected whose end occurs before the start tag of the context element (however, attribute and namespace nodes are never selected by the `following` axis). Therefore, the `preceding` axis is empty for the nodes on the leftmost branch of the document tree.

The `preceding` axis is a reverse axis (which can be easily remembered by selecting the nodes preceding the context node in the XML serialization), so all nodes selected by this axis are arranged in reverse document order.

The `preceding-sibling` Axis

The `preceding-sibling` axis selects all nodes having the same parent as the context node and occurring before it in document order. This makes it easy to select the previous element when thinking of hierarchy levels in the document tree and when it does not matter how many subelements an element may have. The easiest way to visualize the `preceding-sibling` axis is to look from the context node in a horizontal direction in reverse document order and then to select only the nodes that share a common parent with the context node.

It should be noted that siblings are by definition nodes having the same parent as the context node (otherwise the axis would have been called "cousins of various degrees"), so the `preceding-sibling` axis does not select all nodes on the same hierarchy level of the XML, but only the nodes with the same parent as the context node. Consequently, if the node is the first child of its parent, then the `preceding-sibling` axis is empty.

The `preceding-sibling` axis is a reverse axis (which can be easily re-membered by looking in the direction of the reverse document order of the node tree), so all nodes selected by this axis are arranged in reverse document order.

The `self` Axis

The `self` axis selects the context node itself. As a convenient abbreviation (one that is very intuitive for people used to working with file systems), the location step "." can be used to select the context node itself (it is defined in rule 12; see more about abbreviations in section 5.2.5). Because the `self` axis always selects at most one node, its direction (technically being forward) is irrelevant.

Although the axes described in the preceding sections may look complex at first, they are the key to creating effective and concise location paths. Of these thirteen axes, `child`, `parent`, `attribute`, `descendant-or-self`, and `self` are used most frequently, often by employing their abbreviations as described in detail in section 5.2.5.

Note that the `ancestor`, `preceding`, `self`, `descendant`, and `following` axes partition the document into five disjoint node sets. They do not overlap, and together they select all nodes of the document (excluding attribute and namespace nodes).

5.2.3 Node Tests

Rule 4 specifies that a node test is the second element of each location step. Once a node set has been selected using a particular axis, a node test is applied to all these nodes, which potentially reduces the number of nodes in the node set. The following rules from XPath's syntax rules for location paths are the most important for the node test:

```
[7]  NodeTest      ::= NameTest
                     | NodeType '(' ')'
                     | 'processing-instruction' '(' Literal ')'
[37] NameTest      ::= '*'
                     | NCName ':' '*'
                     | QName
[38] NodeType      ::= 'comment'
                     | 'text'
                     | 'processing-instruction'
                     | 'node'
```

Rule 7 states that a node test tests either for a particular node name or for a node type (there is a third, special case where only processing instruction nodes of a certain name are selected). If a name test is specified, then only nodes of the principal node type are considered, and the name test may select the following:

- All nodes of the principal node type using the * notation
- All nodes of the principal node and belonging to a certain namespace[12]

---

[12]If a namespace is specified, it is by using its prefix, and the prefix must be specified somewhere. More on XPaths and XML Namespaces can be found in section 6.4.2.

- All nodes of a certain name (which, according to the `QName` definition from the XML Namespaces recommendation, may or may not specify a namespace prefix)

The most frequent use of a node test is as a name test, testing for nodes of a certain name. However, nodes can also be tested for types, and rule 7 states that this case is indicated by using parentheses following the type.[13] Because a name test selects only nodes of the principal node type (the principal node type is shown in Table 5.1), the `node()` node test is the only node test that selects nodes of more than one type. All other node tests select exactly one type.

Since most of the structural information of an XML document often is identified by element or attribute types, in most XPaths, name tests that specify a location step for a certain name are used. This is also apparent through the available abbreviations (described in detail in section 5.2.5), which make it possible to simply use an element's name to specify a location step among the child axis and to use the @ abbreviation for specifying name tests for certain attribute types.

5.2.4 Predicates

According to rule 4, the last component of a location step is an arbitrary number of predicates, though in most cases a location step does not specify any predicate. However, predicates can be used to specify very elaborate filtering criteria and, as such, are important for composing complex XPaths. Essentially, a predicate is nothing more than an expression, which is the most general XPath construct. In particular, predicates themselves can be complete XPaths, which are then evaluated using the current context as the context. Predicates are used for further filtering the nodes selected by the axis and the node test (and possibly other predicates), and they are applied to each node in the node set. If a predicate evaluates to `true`, then the node remains in the resulting node set. Otherwise, it is removed from the node set. This process is repeated for all predicates of a location step, and the resulting node set of the last predicate is the resulting node set of the whole location step.

In order to completely understand predicates, it is necessary to learn more about XPath's expressions and functions, discussed in sections 5.3 and 5.4. However, for a first impression of the use and power of predicates, we give some simple examples in the following XPaths:

---

[13]Otherwise it would be impossible to syntactically distinguish the name test for elements of the `text` element type from the `text()` keyword testing for text nodes.

- /descendant::chapter[attribute::author][attribute::date]
  – This XPath selects all chapter elements within the document and then applies two predicates that contain location paths themselves. In this case, the first predicate filters all chap elements by testing them for an author attribute. The second predicate filters all chap elements that have an author attribute by testing them for a date attribute. As a result, this XPath selects all chapter elements within the document that have an author attribute and a date attribute.

- /descendant::chapter[descendant::figure][descendant::table]
  – Further complicating the previous example, this XPath selects all chapter elements within the document that have figure as well as table descendants. Consequently, it selects all chapters that contain figures and tables.

Using location paths inside location step predicates is a very powerful way of selecting nodes because each predicate is individually evaluated for each node in the node set that goes into the predicate. Constructing this kind of XPath can take a bit of time, but it can also save a lot of programming (in particular if XPath is used in the context of XSLT), and it certainly is more robust and declarative than a program containing several XPaths and combining their results programmatically.

More formally speaking, a predicate filters a node set with respect to the location step's axis in order to produce a new node set. Taking XPath's general model as described in section 5.1, for each node in the node set to be filtered, the predicate is evaluated with that node as the context node, with the number of nodes in the node set as the context size, and with the *proximity position* of the node in the node set determined with respect to the axis as the context position.

The proximity position of a member of a node set with respect to an axis is defined to be the position of the node in the node set ordered in document order if the axis is a forward axis and ordered in reverse document order if the axis is a reverse axis. It is therefore important to know direction of an axis, as shown in Table 5.1.

If the predicate evaluates to true for that node,[14] the node is included in the new node set; otherwise, it is not included. This formal definition

---

[14]If the result of the predicate is not a boolean value, then the result will be converted as if by a call to the boolean function (more about expressions and functions in sections 5.3 and 5.4). However, if it is a number, the result will be converted to true if the number is equal to the context position and it will be converted to false otherwise. This definition can be exploited in several ways, the most popular being the "abbreviation" that is presented in Table 5.2.

Table 5.2 XPath Abbreviations

Abbreviation	Full XPath Syntax
(no axis specifier)	`child::`
@	`attribute::`
.	`self::node()`
..	`parent::node()`
//	`/descendant-or-self::node()/`
[x]*	`[position()=`x`]`

*The x in this case represents any expression evaluating to a number. Technically, this is not an abbreviation because of the rule that if the result of a predicate is a number, it will be converted to **true** if the number is equal to the context position; otherwise, it will be converted to **false**.

again refers to XPath expressions, and we therefore discuss predicates in more detail in section 5.3.

5.2.5 Abbreviations

Because one of the design goals of XPath is to provide a concise notation for selecting nodes from an XML document and because locations paths are the most frequently used form of XPaths (in XSLT style sheets as well as in XPointers), XPath defines some abbreviations for the most frequently used location path components, shown in Table 5.2.

These abbreviations cover only a small portion of XPath's features, but they cover many of the most frequently used constructs. The abbreviations provide a very useful mechanism to not only make XPaths shorter but also to help make them more easily readable. With the help of the abbreviations, the seven examples shown earlier in this chapter can be abbreviated as follows:

1. `attribute::name` → `@name` – Selects the `name` attribute of the context node. In this case (and this is a very frequently used construct), the attribute axis abbreviation helps to make the XPath more readable.

2. `/descendant::numlist/child::item` → `//numlist/item` – Selects all the `item` elements that have a `numlist` parent and that are in the same document as the context node. Interestingly, this abbreviation effectively replaces the two-step unabbreviated location path with a three-step abbreviation. However, because the `descendant` step with a name test can be replaced by two steps (the `//` abbreviation

meaning `/descendant-or-self::node()/`, and an implicit `child` axis specifying the name[15]) without changing the meaning of the location path, the abbreviated form is preferable because of its conciseness.

3. `child::para[position()=1]` → `para[1]` – Selects the first `para` child of the context node. As mentioned before, the predicate does not really use an abbreviation but exploits the mechanism of how predicates are evaluated if the result of the predicate expression is a number.

4. `/descendant::figure[position()=42]` → `/descendant::figure[42]` – Selects the forty-second `figure` element in the document. In this case, the axis cannot be abbreviated because there is no abbreviation for the `descendant` axis. However, the predicate can be specified using the well-known rule for predicates resulting in numbers.[16]

5. `/child::doc/child::chap[position()=5]/child::sect[position()=2]` → `/doc/chap[5]/sect[2]` – Selects the second `sect` child of the fifth `chap` child of the `doc` document element. This XPath exclusively uses the `child` axis and predicates specifying the position of the children. It can be seen that, in this case, the abbreviation mechanism helps to make the XPath much more concise.

6. `child::para[attribute::type='warning'][position()=5]` → `para[@type='warning'][5]` – Selects the fifth `para` child of the context node that has a `type` attribute with value `warning`. Using the `child` and `attribute` axes, all of the XPath's components can be abbreviated.

7. `child::para[position()=5][attribute::type="warning"]` → `para[5][@type="warning"]` – Selects the fifth `para` child of the context node if that child has a `type` attribute with value `warning`. If there is no such attribute, nothing is selected. In the same way as in the previous example, XPath's abbreviation mechanisms help to make the XPath much shorter.

While these examples show only a few cases of how XPaths can be abbreviated, they should be sufficient to demonstrate that the abbreviation mechanisms not only make XPaths shorter but also (and more important)

---

[15]This may sound surprising. However, when the tree representation of XPath's axes is used, as shown in Figures 5.3 and 5.4, it can be easily seen that these two constructs indeed are identical with respect to their result.

[16]A precautionary note: The location path `//figure[42]` does not mean the same as the location path `/descendant::figure[42]`. The latter selects the forty-second `figure` element counting from the root node, while the former selects all `figure` elements that are the forty-second `figure` children of their parents.

more readable. It is therefore advisable to use these mechanisms; and because there are so few of them, getting used to writing abbreviated XPaths is quite easy.

5.2.6 Examples

In the following examples, we show some general techniques to select nodes from an XML document, which provide useful tips for constructing location paths (more general examples that are not restricted to locations paths can be found in section 5.5).

- `//@id/..` – This XPath selects all elements that bear an `id` attribute. It is somewhat computationally expensive because it starts with a `//` location step, but this cannot be avoided when the whole document has to be searched for attributes of a certain name. Note the last location step, which is used to actually select the elements after selecting the `id` attributes.

  As an alternative, the XPath `//*[@id]` could be used, which yields exactly the same results as the first variant. In this second case, the existence of `id` attributes is tested for in a predicate and not using the attribute axis as a location step, as in the first case.

- `//comment()` – Using this XPath, all comments in a document can be selected, making it easy to check a document for any comments.

- `//processing-instruction('xml-stylesheet')/..` – This XPath returns all nodes that contain a processing instruction with the name `xml-stylesheet`. (This name is specified in the standard about associating style sheets with XML documents [Clark 99a].)

- `//a[starts-with(@href,'http://www.w3.org/')]` – This XPath is an interesting example of how predicates can greatly increase the usefulness of XPaths. (It uses two string functions that are not introduced until section 5.4.3.) In this case, assuming that hyperlinks as defined in XHTML are used, all hyperlinks that point to resources on W3C's server are selected by using string functions to further filter `href` attribute values by inspecting whether they start with a certain string.

- `//table//a/ancestor::p[1]` – Assuming an HTML-like document type (e.g., XHTML), this location path can be used to locate all paragraphs that contain hyperlinks (i.e., **a** elements) and occur within a table. It will even correctly work for nested tables, because the predicate of the last location step specifies that in case of multiple **p** ancestors,[17] only the element closest to the a element should be selected. (In this case it is important to know that the `ancestor` axis is a reverse axis.)

These examples show some general techniques for constructing location paths. In particular, in the last example, it becomes obvious that a key point for constructing robust location paths that work in all cases is the knowledge of the document type. Only if the document type is known, is it possible to foresee all possible cases in which a location path has to produce the expected result and to install safeguards against special cases (such as the `[1]` predicate in the last example, which protects against the rare case of a `//table//p//table//p//a` document, which—even though being rather exotic and slightly contrived—would be legal XHTML).

What these examples also show is that location paths are, in themselves, very powerful and the key to mastering XPath. However, location paths also require additional constructs for further specifying criteria for filtering node sets. Predicates as discussed in section 5.2.4 are one such case, and we have already used them in our examples. However, the expressions used within predicates are the most general construct of XPath and therefore can be used as whole XPaths, not only within predicates. Expressions are therefore the basis of every XPath (a location path, on which we have focused so far, is only a special case of an expression), and we discuss them in detail in the following section.

5.3 EXPRESSIONS

An expression is the most basic construct of an XPath, and every XPath is an expression (location paths, as discussed in section 5.2, are only special cases of expressions). The formal syntax rules for an expression defined in the XPath standard are too complicated to be of any use for understanding expressions, but basically it can be stated that XPath expressions are recursively defined as being made up of operators and operands. To make this abstract definition a little more real, the expression 2+3 is made up of two operands (the numbers) and an operator (the plus sign for the additive operator). This XPath expression would evaluate to a number.

Besides being the most fundamental XPath construct, expressions are particularly important because they appear with predicates as described in section 5.2.4. Furthermore, even though expressions can be constructed

---

[17]One such case would be a paragraph inside a table, with the paragraph indirectly containing another table, which in turn contains hyperlinks within paragraphs. This, even though rarely used in practice, would be valid XHTML.

Table 5.3 Overview of XPath Operators and Their Priorities

Operator	Operator Name	Priority
-	negation	1
*	multiplication	2
div	floating-point division	2
mod	remainder*	2
+	addition	3
-	subtraction	3
<	less than	4
<=	less or equal than	4
>	greater than	4
>=	greater or equal than	4
=	equal	5
!=	not equal	5
and	logical and	6
or	logical or	7
		union	8

*This operator calculates the remainder from a truncating division according to IEEE 754 [IEEE 85] (more about XPath numbers and IEEE 754 in section 5.4.2), and in particular, note that it is not the same as the % operator in Java or JavaScript.

from location paths and operands alone, they often use functions, described in detail in section 5.4. Let's look at the details of XPath expressions.

In general, expressions are made up of operands and operators. As is usual in languages for specifying expressions, this pattern can be applied recursively, so that each operand can be an expression. This results in expressions such as 2+3*5, which directly leads to the question of operator precedence (i.e., if this expression is evaluated from left to right, it would evaluate to 25; if the usual arithmetic priorities were applied, it would evaluate to 17). XPath has a number of operators, and these are assigned priorities, so that the example expression indeed evaluates to 17. Table 5.3 lists all XPath operators with their priorities. The rule is that operators with higher priorities (i.e., a lower number) are evaluated first, while operators with equal priorities are evaluated left to right.

If the implicit priorities have to be superseded, it is possible to use parentheses to group expressions to force a certain evaluation precedence, so that (2+3)*5 results in 25. Operators are specific to certain operand types, and depending on the type of operator, operands may be converted implicitly to satisfy these requirements (e.g., when comparing a string and a number, the string is converted to a number). These conversions are always performed as if the explicit conversion functions, described in section 5.4, were used. Even though XPath's operator priorities are much the same as for most programming languages, for the sake of clarity it is advisable to use parentheses in certain cases, such as when mixing calculations and comparisons, for example, (2+3)>(2*3) (which evaluates to the boolean value false).

All operators in Table 5.3, except for the last one, operate on one or several of the common object types described in section 5.1, which are numbers, string, and booleans. The more unusual object type of XPath is the node set, and while most operators accept node sets (in particular, the comparison operators), the most interesting operator is the union operator. The union operator is frequently used to join node sets resulting from location paths. For example, the XPath //ol | //ul | //dl evaluates to a node set containing all ol, ul, and dl elements of a document (these are the three types of list elements defined in HTML). Since location paths themselves are nothing but expressions, they can appear as operands within expressions. An even better demonstration of that is the XPath //a[ancestor::ul | ancestor::ol], which selects all hyperlinks that occur within an ol or a ul element (an alternative solution to this problem would be the XPath //ul//a | //ol//a, which is probably more computationally expensive to evaluate because it contains several // location steps).

As with every expression syntax, XPath expressions are very flexible, and thus it makes little sense to give a large number of example expressions. However, the examples presented so far should be enough to convince the reader to start playing around with XPath expressions and to try to compose powerful XPaths. Combining expressions, functions (to be discussed in the following section), and location paths, section 5.5 presents some complex examples that demonstrate XPath's versatility and expressiveness.

5.4 FUNCTIONS

One of the most important components in XPath expressions, as discussed in the previous section, are XPath's functions. These can be compared to programming languages, which also gain much of their power and versatility by providing a rich set of functions (through function or class libraries), which may be taken for granted. XPath defines the set of core functions listed in Table 5.4. In this table, each function is listed with its name, the result type, and the arguments. Arguments with a trailing question mark may be omitted, while arguments with a trailing asterisk may used as often as required (including not at all).

XPath's core functions must be provided by all XPath implementations, so all XPaths using only the core functions are guaranteed to work with any XPath implementation. XPath is intended primarily as a

Table 5.4 Overview of XPath Functions

Function Name	Result Type	Arguments	Page
boolean	boolean	object	125
ceiling	number	number	127
concat	string	string, string, string*	128
contains	boolean	string, string	128
count	number	node-set	131
false	boolean	n/a	125
floor	number	number	127
id	node-set	object	131
lang	boolean	string	125
last	number	n/a	132
local-name	string	node-set?	132
name	string	node-set?	132
namespace-uri	string	node-set?	132
normalize-space	string	string?	129
not	boolean	boolean	126
number	number	object?	127
position	number	n/a	133
round	number	number	128
starts-with	boolean	string, string	129
string	string	object?	129
string-length	number	string?	130
substring	string	string, number, number?	130
substring-after	string	string, string	130
substring-before	string	string, string	130
sum	number	node-set	128
translate	string	string, string, string	130
true	boolean	n/a	126

*: May be used as often as required.
?: May be omitted.

component to be used by other specifications. Therefore, XPath explicitly
mentions that the core function library may be extended by other standards
building on top of XPath. In particular, the XPointer standard described in
chapter 6 extends the set of functions, and these extensions are described
in detail in section 6.3 (see Table 6.1 for a list of these functions).

In the same way, the document function, which is very convenient in
XSLT style sheets for accessing multiple documents from within one style
sheet, is not an XPath core function but an XSLT extension of XPath.
Additionally, XSLT defines a number of other functions that may be used
within XPaths in XSLT style sheets. However, instead of listing these functions here, we simply want to make the point that this extensibility of the

XPath function library is very useful for extending XPath whenever necessary (in particular, XPath applications) but can be confusing for users moving from one XPath application to another (e.g., applying their XSLT knowledge to XPointer and then seeing that some of the functions are not supported in this new environment). Consequently, whenever a function that has been seen elsewhere in an XPath-based environment is missing, it is probably an extension of XPath and not one of XPath's core functions.

In the following sections, we give detailed explanations of all XPath core functions, grouped by their type (i.e., the type of object they primarily are designed for). Since XPath knows four object types (booleans, numbers, strings, and node sets), there are four sections.

5.4.1 Boolean Functions

Boolean functions return a boolean value, which means their result is either `true` or `false`. Because XPath does not have a way of denoting the boolean values themselves, there are two dedicated functions that always return the same value. Consequently, if it is necessary to denote a boolean value in an XPath, the `true()` or `false()` functions must be used. Other important boolean "functions" not listed here, because they are operators rather than functions, are the logical **and** and **or** operators as well as all of the comparison operators explained in section 5.3. All these operators are frequently used to calculate boolean values, for example, when testing for multiple values as in (@author='dret') or (@author='dbl'). Apart from these operators producing boolean results, XPath defines the following core functions:

- `boolean` – *Converts to a boolean value.*
  Signature: `boolean boolean(object)`
  Conversion to a boolean value can be done with arguments of all possible object types. A `number` is `true` if and only if it is not zero. A `node-set` is `true` if and only if it is non-empty. A `string` is `true` if and only if its length is greater than zero. Any other object type is converted to boolean according to that object type (i.e., as defined in the specification introducing that object type).
- `false` – *Always returns false.*
  Signature: `boolean false()`
- `lang` – *Tests for languages of nodes.*
  Signature: `boolean lang(string)`
  This function is used to test for a specific language of a node. In XML, the language of a node is specified by the `xml:lang` attribute (as defined by the XML recommendation), which specifies the

language according to Internet RFC 3066 [Alvestrand 01]. If the language of the context node (or the nearest ancestor specifying a language, if the context node does not specify one) is the same or a sublanguage of the language specified in the argument, then the `lang` function returns `true`; otherwise, it returns false.

- not – *Inverts a boolean value.*
  Signature: `boolean not(boolean)`
  This function inverts a boolean value, returning `false` when the argument is `true`, and returning `true` when the argument is `false`.

- true – *Always returns true.*
  Signature: `boolean true()`

One important thing to remember is that the `boolean` function often is used implicitly, because location path predicates are always converted to a boolean value (the one exception being a predicate that evaluates to a number, in which case the result is converted to a boolean based on a comparison with the context node for which the predicate is evaluated). For example, the location step `chap[.//figure]` selects all `chap` elements having `figure` descendants.

This location step is equivalent to the variant `chap[boolean(.//figure)]`, which makes explicit the fact that the predicate's value (in this case, a node set) is converted to a boolean value in order to determine whether a node is part of the location step's resulting node set. Only if the node set resulting from evaluating `.//figure` for each `chap` is not empty will the corresponding node become a member of the resulting node set.

5.4.2 Number Functions

XPath relies heavily on IEEE 754 [IEEE 85], a standard for floating-point arithmetics. It is a good idea to rely on a standardized model, but IEEE 754 includes some concepts that, from a mathematical point of view, make sense but can take some time getting used to.

The IEEE 754 standard includes not only positive and negative sign-magnitude numbers but also positive and negative zeros, positive and negative infinities, and a special Not a Number (NaN) value. The `NaN` value is used to represent the result of certain operations such as dividing zero by zero. Except for `NaN`,[18] floating-point values are ordered; arranged from

---

[18]`NaN` is unordered, so the comparison operators `<`, `<=`, `>`, and `>=` return `false` if either or both operands are `NaN`. The equality operator `=` returns `false` if either operand is `NaN`, and the inequality operator `!=` returns `true` if either operand is `NaN`. In particular, `x!=x` is `true` if and only if `x` is `NaN`.

smallest to largest, they are negative infinity, negative zero, positive zero, negative finite non-zero values, positive finite non-zero values, and positive infinity. Positive zero and negative zero compare equal.

For handling numbers according to the rules of IEEE 754, XPath defines the following core functions:

- `ceiling` – *Rounds up a number.*
  Signature: `number ceiling(number)`
  Rounding up a number according to the rules specified in IEEE 754 means to return the smallest number that is not less than the argument and that is an integer. In particular, this means that negative numbers are rounded toward zero (`ceiling(-4.5)` = `-4`).

- `floor` – *Rounds down a number.*
  Signature: `number floor(number)`
  Rounding down a number according to the rules specified in IEEE 754 means to return the largest number that is not greater than the argument and that is an integer. In particular, this means that negative numbers are rounded toward negative infinity (`ceiling(-4.5)` = `-5`).

- `number` – *Converts to a number.*
  Signature: `number number(object?)`
  This function is used to convert its argument to a number. Depending on the type of argument, the function performs this conversion as follows:
  - A `boolean` value of `true` is converted to 1; a value of `false` is converted to 0.
  - A `string` is converted to a valid numeric value if it contains whitespace, followed by an optional minus sign, a number (digits optionally including a decimal point), and whitespace.[19] If the string does not adhere to this formatting, it is converted to `NaN`.
  - A `node-set` is converted as if the original argument has been given as argument to the `string` function, and the resulting string has been converted by using it as a string argument to the `number` function.

  Any other object (i.e., an object other than the basic types defined by XPath) is converted to a number in a way that is dependent on

---

[19]It should be noted that this specification excludes many strings using common number formats (such as exponential notations or notations including thousands separators) from being converted to a number. Improved functionality for dealing with various number formats will be incorporated into future version of XPath (as discussed in section 5.6).

that type and should be specified in the definition of that type. If the argument is omitted, it defaults to a `node-set` with the context node as its only member.

- round – *Rounds to the next closest integer number.*
  Signature: `number round(number)`
  This function returns a number that is the closest to the argument and that is an integer. For the special cases of IEEE 754 values (`NaN`, positive and negative infinity, positive and negative zero), the function returns the value of its argument. For numbers that are less than zero but greater than or equal to -0.5, negative zero is returned.

- sum – *Sums the string-values of all nodes.*
  Signature: `number sum(node-set)`

Even though IEEE 754's definitions of floating-point arithmetic may seem hard to remember at first, remember that most of the arithmetic used with XPath is integer arithmetic and as such is not as complicated. Some of the most frequent uses of numbers in XPath are for context positions, and these are always positive integers, so arithmetic with context positions is rather simple.

5.4.3 String Functions

String functions are frequently used for inspecting attribute or element contents, and because many applications allow some sort of free form data as content, it is very useful to have more sophisticated functions than the simple comparisons that may test strings for equality. In particular, the following core functions operating on strings are defined by the XML Path Language:

- concat – *Concatenates two or more strings.*
  Signature: `string concat(string, string, string*)`
  This function returns the concatenation of its arguments. It must have at least two and can have as many arguments as necessary, all of which must be strings.

- contains – *Tests for containment of one string in another.*
  Signature: `boolean contains(string, string)`
  If the first argument string contains the second argument string, then this function returns `true`; otherwise, it returns `false`. Unfortunately, this function does not provide case-insensitive matching; so if this is

required by an application, it must be specified at the application level.

- normalize-space – *Normalizes whitespace in a string.*
  Signature: string normalize-space(string?)
  The normalize-space function returns the argument string with whitespace normalized by stripping leading and trailing whitespace and replacing sequences of whitespace characters with a single space. Whitespace characters are the same as those defined in XML—space characters, carriage returns, line feeds, and tabs. If the argument is omitted, it defaults to the context node converted to a string.

- starts-with – *Tests if one string starts with another.*
  Signature: boolean starts-with(string, string)
  This function tests whether the first argument starts with the second argument. If this is the case, the function returns true; otherwise, it returns false.

- string – *Converts to a string.*
  Signature: string string(object?)
  The string function is used to convert its argument to a string. The argument may be of any type, and depending on its type, the function performs this conversion as follows:

  - If the argument is a node set, it is converted by returning the string value of the node in the node set that is first in document order. For an empty node set, an empty string is returned.
  - Numbers are converted to strings in the following way:
    - NaN is converted to the string "NaN."
    - Positive and negative zero are converted to the string "0".
    - Positive and negative infinity are converted to the strings "Infinity" and "-Infinity", respectively.
    - Integers are converted to a string of the decimal representation of the number with no leading zeros or separators; negative numbers are preceded by a minus sign.
    - Otherwise, the number is represented as a floating-point number in normal notation with no exponential notation.
  - The boolean values true and false are converted to the strings "true" and "false", respectively.

  Any other object (i.e., an object other than the basic types defined by XPath) is converted to a string in a way that is dependent on that type and should be specified in the definition of that type. If the argument is omitted, it defaults to a **node-set** with the context node as its only member.

- `string-length` – *Represents the number of characters in a string.*
  Signature: `number string-length(string?)`
  The `string-length` function returns the number of characters in a given string. If the argument is omitted, it defaults to the string value of the context node.

- `substring` – *Extracts a substring from a string.*
  Signature: `string substring(string, number, number?)`
  This function extracts a substring from a string. The first argument is the string itself, and the second argument specifies the position from which the substring should be extracted.[20] The optional third argument specifies the length of the string to be extracted. If the third argument is not present, the function returns the substring starting at the position specified in the second argument and continuing to the end of the string.

- `substring-after` – *Selects after a matching string.*
  Signature: `string substring-after(string, string)`
  The `substring-after` function returns the substring of the first argument that follows the first occurrence of the second argument. If the second argument does not occur in the first argument, it returns the empty string. As an example, `substring-after("dret@transcluding.com","@")` returns `"transcluding.com"`.

- `substring-before` – *Selects before a matching string.*
  Signature: `string substring-before(string, string)`
  This function returns the substring of the first argument that precedes the first occurrence of the second argument. If the second argument does not occur in the first argument, it returns the empty string. As an example, `substring-before("dbl@transcluding.com", "@")` returns `"dbl"`.

- `translate` – *Replaces characters in a string.*
  Signature: `string translate(string, string, string)`
  The `translate` function is used to translate the string given as the first argument by substituting all occurrences of the characters in the second argument with the corresponding characters in the third argument.[21] If the third argument string is shorter than the second argument string, then the characters of the second argument string that do not have a corresponding character in the third argument string are removed from the first argument string. A standard application of this function is case conversion; other possible

---

[20]It is important to notice that counting starts with 1 (which is different from Java, JavaScript, or C conventions), so `substring("123",2)` returns `"23"`.

[21]Unix users will notice that this is very similar to the standard `tr` utility.

applications include substituting or removing special characters within strings, such as when using `translate("++41-1-6325132",` `"+-","0")` for converting a printable phone number to the dial string `"004116325132"`.

Even though this repertoire of string functions is useful and sufficient for many applications, it is pretty limited when compared with really powerful string-matching mechanisms, such as regular expressions [Friedl 97]. It would have been nice to have state-of-the-art regular expressions in the XPath language, but the designers chose to concentrate on defining XPath as a language mainly for working on XML structures. If versatile string matching is required by an application, XPath should be used only for extracting the relevant attributes and elements from the XML document, and then a language more appropriate for the task (such as Perl [Wall+ 00]) should be employed.

5.4.4 Node Set Functions

The node set is the most interesting XPath object type, because, on the one hand, it is the object type returned by a location path and, on the other hand, a node set directly corresponds to parts of the XML document. By far the most useful "function" for processing a node set is a location path, which—while not a function in the formal sense—can be regarded as a number of "functions" (the location steps) chained one after the other, each passing its results to the next. However, some functions cannot be achieved using location steps alone (or should be available in predicates), and in particular, this is true for functions returning a result other than a node set (location steps and thus location paths always result in node sets). The following core functions are available for node sets:

- `count` – *Returns the number of nodes.*
  Signature: `number count(node-set)`
  This function returns the number of nodes in a node set. As a simple but useful example, you can count the number of hyperlinks on an XHTML page by using `count(//a)`.

- `id` – *Node set with elements selected by ID.*
  Signature: `node-set id(object)`
  XML elements may be uniquely identified (within the scope of an XML document) with an attribute of the `ID` type.[22] The `id` function

---

[22]It is important to notice that the attribute providing the unique `ID` may have any name, but it has to be declared as being of the type `ID` (remember that the type of an attribute is specified in the document's DTD). Consequently, if a document does not have a DTD, then no element in the document will have a unique `ID`.

can be used to select elements according to this identification as specified by the following rules:

— If the argument is a node set, then the result of the `id` function is the union of applying the `id` function to the string value of each of the individual nodes.

— For other argument types, the argument is converted to a string as if by a call to the `string` function, and the resulting string is then split into a list of tokens separated by whitespace. For each of the tokens, the element having an ID attribute with that value (if present in the document) becomes part of the resulting node set.

As an example, consider a document giving chapters individual IDs via ID type attributes. The function `id("references index")` results in a node set containing two elements, if the document contains two elements with these IDs.

- `last` – *Returns a numeric pointer to the last set member.*
  Signature: `number last()`
  This function returns a number equal to the context size of the context within which the expression is evaluated. A frequently used application, the XPath `//chap[last()]`, returns the last `chap` element of a document.

- `local-name` – *Returns the local part of the first node.*
  Signature: `string local-name(node-set?)`
  The `local-name` function returns the local part of the first node (in document order) of the argument's node set. If there is no such name or if the node set is empty, then it returns the empty string. If no argument is specified, then it defaults to a node set with the context node as the only member.

- `name` – *Returns the expanded name of the first node.*
  Signature: `string name(node-set?)`
  This function returns the qualified name (i.e., the namespace URI as well as the local name) of the first node (in document order) of the argument's node set. If there is no such name or if the node set is empty, then it returns the empty string. If no argument is specified, then it defaults to a node set with the context node as the only member. The namespace URI must reflect the namespace declarations in effect for the node for which the function is evaluated.

- `namespace-uri` – *Returns the namespace URI of the first node.*
  Signature: `string namespace-uri(node-set?)`
  The `namespace-uri` function returns the namespace URI of the first node (in document order) of the argument's node set. If there is no

such URI or if the node set is empty, then it returns the empty string. If no argument is specified, then it defaults to a node set with the context node as the only member.

- position – *Returns a numeric pointer to the context position.* Signature: `number position()`
  The `position` function returns a number equal to the context position of the context node for which the expression is evaluated. A frequently used application, the XPath `chap[position()=3]`,[23] returns the third `chap` child of the context node (or an empty node set if there are fewer than three `chap` children).

The node set functions of XPath are often used in order to get access to information about the XML document itself, such as in the XPath `name(id('intro'))`, which returns the name of the element bearing the ID `intro`. However, the most frequently used node set functions are probably `count` (`count(//a)`: how many hyperlinks are in the document?), `last` (`chap[last()]`: select the context node's last chapter child), and `position` (`chap[position()=3]`: select the context node's third chapter child).

5.5 EXAMPLES

At this point it is worthwhile making a few general remarks about XPath. XPath is essentially a query language for XML documents,[24] and considering that XML documents may be quite big, some performance suggestions should be taken into account when using XPath:

- *Be as specific as possible.* Consider a document type that always contains `chap` elements as children of `part` elements, which in turn are always children of the `doc` document element. An XPath selecting all chapters within this type of document could be specified either as `//chap` or as `/doc/part/chap`. While the results of both XPaths would always be the same, the second XPath could be evaluated much faster because the XPath implementation would not have to search the entire document tree for `chap` elements, as specified by the first XPath. It is important to notice that this kind of XPath optimization requires some knowledge of the document type, and because XPath

---

[23]This can be abbreviated to `chap[3]`, as described in section 5.2.5.

[24]Strictly speaking, it is not a complete query language because it does not allow the recombination of different result sets, but its addressing capabilities cover a substantial area of a query language.

implementations do not interpret or even know about the document type,[25] they cannot make these optimizations.

- *Filter as early as possible.* Even though location steps do not necessarily decrease the cardinality of the node set, they very often do so. In many cases, the node set gets smaller with (almost) every location step. Consider a document containing thousands of `address` elements, which in turn contain `city` elements with a `zip` attribute. Selecting all addresses with a certain zip code could be done either by specifying `//address/city[@zip='94704']/..` or by using `//city[@zip='94704']/parent::address`.

  While the optimization presented in the previous list item required knowledge about the document type, the optimization in this example requires knowledge about the actual document that is being used. If there is a large number of `address` elements and the `city` element only rarely occurs in locations other than as an `address` child, then the second XPath is preferable because it filters more specifically with its second step (after the first abbreviated `//` step) than the first XPath. If, however, the `city` element also frequently occurs more often in other contexts than as an `address` child, then the first XPath may be better, because it restricts the search among `city` elements to `address` children.

While XPath in the context of XPointer may be less of a performance problem, because the XPointer is evaluated only once to select the fragment of the XML document, XPaths in an XSLT style sheet may be evaluated very often, because of loops or recursions in the style sheet. In this case, XSLT's `xsl:key` element and the `key` function can be used to declare keys that can then be handled more efficiently by the XSLT processor.

The questions discussed so far relate to a specific aspect of an XPath—namely, how efficiently it can be evaluated.[26] However, there is another aspect of XPaths, and this is their persistence or robustness, meaning how well they work for different documents of the same document type or how robust they are against changes in the document. This is a very typical problem for XPointer, which is used to point into XML documents, and these pointers should remain valid even if the document is modified, at least to a certain extent. This issue was introduced in section 3.3.2 and is discussed in more detail in section 6.4.3.

---

[25]It would be possible to think of an XPath implementation that actually interprets the document type and uses this information for automatic optimizations, but to our knowledge no such implementations exist at the time of writing.

[26]It could be argued that optimization should be handled by XPath implementations anyway, at least as much as possible.

Here are a few examples showing how the general principles of XPath (location paths, expressions, and functions) can be used to select parts of XML documents in a very concise way. In the following examples, we assume that an XHTML document type is being used, which makes the XPaths more understandable. Instead of explaining the syntactical details of the XPaths, we give the intention behind them and leave it as an exercise to the reader to figure out the exact way it is done (and maybe to compose different XPaths that produce the same result).

- `//a[starts-with(@href,'http:') or starts-with(@href,'ftp:')]` – This XPath selects all hyperlinks referencing resources on HTTP or FTP servers.

- `substring-after(substring-before(//ul[@id='biblio']/li[$x$],']'),'[')` – Assuming a bibliography using an uniquely identified unnumbered list of list items, in which each bibliographic entry is labeled with an identifier occurring between brackets, this XPath selects the label of the xth bibliography entry.

- `//table[not(thead)]` – If a document should be searched for tables that do not specify a table head (which is not required by XHTML, but should be used to clearly mark the head rows of a table), then this XPath can be used to select all these tables.

- `//h2[normalize-space(string())='Erik Wilde']/preceding::h1[1]` – Assuming that each first-level heading is followed[27] by a second-level heading containing the section author's name, this XPath could be used to select all first-level headings of sections written by the specified author. The `normalize-space` function is used here as a safeguard against whitespace charactersin the `h2` element's content.

These examples show only a couple of possible applications of XPath. Possibly the best way to learn XPath is to take some documents from your own application domain and try to write down XPaths that select the required parts of these documents for a number of usage scenarios.

Remember that XPaths are sensitive to object types, and failing to correctly specify an object's type (by using conversion functions or correctly delimiting strings) may result in an XPath that is still valid but behaves unexpectedly. In particular, strings must always be delimited; otherwise, they are interpreted as location paths (if a location path is permitted at

---

[27]It is important to notice that in XHTML, headings do not contain the section's content but precede it. This is unlike most other hierarchical document models, where sections of different hierarchy levels are reflected as hierarchy levels in the document tree.

that place), which will produce a completely different result (but not an error message from the application interpreting the XPath).

5.6 FUTURE DEVELOPMENTS

XPath is stable in its current version (1.0), and a number of implementations are available, most of them integrated into XSLT processors. Since XSLT, with its ability to transform XML documents, is one of the key components of an XML-based infrastructure, it is evolving pretty rapidly. At the time of writing, XSLT 2.0 [Kay 01a] is being developed.[28]

During work on XSLT 1.1, it has become apparent that XSLT lacks some features that cannot be added by simply changing XSLT. Consequently, XSLT 2.0 will be based on XPath 2.0 [Berglund+ 01]. The exact outcome of these activities is still unclear, but generally speaking (and citing from the requirements analysis), the following goals should be accomplished with XPath 2.0:

- Simplified manipulation of XML Schema–type content
- Simplified manipulation of string content
- Support for related XML standards
- Improved ease of use
- Improved interoperability
- Improved internationalization support
- Maintenance of backward compatibility
- Improved processor efficiency

One of the most important observations is that XPath 2.0 should be fully compatible with XPath 1.0, in such a way that each version 1.0 XPath interpreted by a version 2.0 XPath implementation should yield the same result. It is not yet clear whether that goal will be fully reached, but the required changes to the version 1.0 XPaths (if any) will be kept to a minimum.

Being the basis for a number of XML technologies (in particular XSLT, XPointer, XML Schema, and XML Query), XPath receives a lot of attention and also a lot of input from other standardization efforts. The latest development is XML Query (XQuery) [Boag+ 01], which is an effort to define a powerful query language for XML. At the time of writing, XQuery

---

[28]Standardization of XSLT 1.1 [Clark 01] has been stopped to concentrate efforts on XSLT 2.0. However, the draft version of XSLT 1.1 is already implemented by some of the available XSLT processors. XSLT 1.1 still uses XPath 1.0.

still is in its early development stages, but it is very possible that XQuery's development will result in more changes to XPath 2.0 than currently under consideration (at the time of writing, the changes are mostly derived from requirements for XSLT 2.0).

The best thing we can do therefore is to advise readers to frequently check `http://www.w3.org/TR/` for the latest developments in XPath and related standards. However, XPath 1.0 will remain as it is today, and it will also remain the foundation of XPointer for some time to come (at the time of writing, there is no new version of XPointer under development).

5.7 CONCLUSIONS

XPath provides a mechanism for defining fragment identifiers for XML documents, which point into XML documents. XPath works by applying a well-known metaphor—the path through a hierarchy of directories/folders in a file system—to the hierarchical structure of an XML document. This chapter describes in detail how XPath works and how XPath can be used to easily select surprisingly complex structures within an XML document. The chapter also describes strategies for composing robust XPaths, which is important if the XML document that the XPath has been defined for is modified.

6

XML Pointer Language

XPath, described in detail in the previous chapter, provides a common foundation for other standards that need to address into XML documents. One such standard, and the most interesting with regard to implementing hypermedia based on XML technologies, is the XML Pointer Language (XPointer) [DeRose+ 01a], which is used for fragment identifiers for XML resources. According to RFC 3023 [Murata+ 01], XML documents are associated with a number of MIME types.[1] For all these different types of XML resources, it is possible to specify a fragment identifier, which is separated from the URI of the resource itself by a crosshatch (#) character. As defined in RFC 2396 [Berners-Lee+ 98] (the standard for URI syntax), a fragment identifier is not an actual part of a URI but is often used in conjunction with one in the so-called URI reference.

Thus, XPointer can be used for specifying references that point to parts of an XML document, and not to the whole document. As a simple example, while the URI `http://www.w3.org/TR/` references the technical reports page of the W3C (as shown in Figure 6.1), the URI reference `http://www.w3.org/TR/#xpointer(id('xptr'))` specifically points to the entry for the XPointer standard on that page.[2] This mechanism makes it possible to create links that are much more specific than through the use of URIs only. There are, however, several things to keep in mind, as follows:

- *The resource must be XML.* XPointer is a mechanism for addressing into XML documents, so the resource identified by the URI must be

---

[1]The Multipurpose Internet Mail Extensions (MIME) [Borenstein & Freed 92] define (in addition to a multitude of other things not relevant in this context) a mechanism for identifying types of resources by means of a media type (e.g., `text`) and a subtype (e.g., `html`).

[2]The XPointer standard may have changed status since the time of this writing and consequently will not appear on the technical reports page as shown in the figure (and as used in the examples in sections 6.4.3 and 6.4.4). However, the general principle does not depend on the particular status of the standard or the W3C's technical reports page.

2 November 2000, Jon Ferraiolo
Resource Description Framework (RDF) Schemas
3 March 2000, Dan Brickley, R.V. Guha
Candidate Recommendation Phase Ends 15 June 2000.

Working Drafts

The following Working Drafts have been submitted for review by W3C Members and other interested parties. These are *draft documents* and may be updated, replaced or obsoleted by other documents at any time. It is inappropriate to use W3C working drafts as reference material or to cite them as other than "work in progress".

Working Drafts in Last Call

A document in last call is to be reviewed by Working Groups that rely on or have a vested interest in the technology. The duration of the last call review period is listed in the status section of the document in review.

XML Inclusions (XInclude) Version 1.0
17 May 2001, Jonathan Marsh, David Orchard
Last Call Ends 05 June 2001.
User Agent Accessibility Guidelines 1.0
09 April 2001, Jon Gunderson, Ian Jacobs, Eric Hansen
Last Call Ends 04 May 2001.
Composite Capability/Preference Profiles (CC/PP): Structure and Vocabularies
15 March 2001, Graham Klyne, Franklin Reynolds, Chris Woodrow, Hidetaka Ohto
Last Call Ends 05 April 2001.
CSS Mobile Profile 1.0
29 January 2001, Ted Wugofski, Doug Dominiak, Peter Stark
Last Call Ends 01 March 2001.
CSS3 module: W3C selectors
26 January 2001, Tantek Çelik, Daniel Glazman, Ian Hickson, Peter Linss, John Williams
Last Call Ends 01 March 2001.
Character Model for the World Wide Web
26 January 2001, Martin J. Dürst (W3C), François Yergeau (Alis Technologies, Inc.), Misha Wolf (Reuters Ltd.), Asmus Freytag (ASMUS, Inc.), Tex Texin (Progress Software Corp.)
Last Call Ends 23 February 2001.
XML Pointer Language (XPointer) Version 1.0
8 January 2001, Ron Daniel Jr., Steve DeRose, Eve Maler
Last Call Ends 29 January 2001.
Speech Synthesis Markup Language Specification for the Speech Interface Framework
03 January 2001, Mark R. Walker, Andrew Hunt
Last Call Ends 31 January 2001.
Speech Recognition Grammar Specification for the W3C Speech Interface Framework
03 January 2001, Andrew Hunt, Scot McGlashan
Last Call Ends 31 January 2001.
Common Markup for micropayment per-fee-links
25 August 1999, Thierry Michel
Last Call ended 30 September 1999, but implementation experience solicited until 31 March 2000.

Working Drafts in Development

XML Blueberry Requirements
20 June 2001, John Cowan
Document Object Model (DOM) Level 3 XPath Specification
. . .

Figure 6.1   Snapshot of W3C's technical reports page

XML.[3] In the example just given, this is true since W3C makes its pages available in XHTML, the XML variant of HTML. However, the vast majority of documents on the Web are not XML, and consequently XPointer cannot be used to address into them. While it is assumed that XML resources will become more popular in the near future (in particular since XHTML is the successor of HTML), as long as non-XML browsers are still widely used,[4] HTML is likely to remain the most popular language.

As a side note, HTML also supports fragment identifiers, but they are limited to pointing to IDs only (as opposed to the XPath-based addressing capabilities of XPointer). HTML uses its own extremely simple syntax for fragment identifiers, which works by giving the ID as the fragment identifier, so the XML example just given would be equivalent to the HTML version `http://www.w3.org/TR/#xptr`.[5] (In this case, there is a simple correspondence between the XML and the HTML fragment identifier, because both address the fragment using its ID.)

- *The resource must remain available.* Of course, a fragment identifier makes sense only as long as the resource is still available. This brings up the well-known problem of broken links in the Web, and it is independent from specifying fragment identifiers. However, because fragment identifiers are often used with URIs, this issue must be addressed. Resources on the Web often have an astonishingly short life span [Dasen & Wilde 01]; and while some resources disappear (i.e., no longer exist or at least are no longer available via a known URI), others are moved to a new URI without having automatic redirections set up by the Web server operator.

- *The ID must remain the same.* In cases where the fragment identifier uses an ID within the document, it will work correctly only as long as

---

[3]W3C's technical reports page is being served by the Web server with the MIME type `text/html`, so technically it is not an XML resource. However, on inspection (and validation), it can be concluded that the page indeed is XHTML, so it can be regarded as being an XML resource.

[4]Here it is important to notice that XHTML has been specifically designed to be usable by non-XML browsers (such as older HTML browsers). However, as long as there is only limited market pressure to provide XHTML rather than HTML, most content providers will be likely to continue to use HTML.

[5]If this URI does not work in your browser, try `http://www.w3.org/TR/#xptr` instead, which definitely should work. This, however, is not a mistake of the first variant of the URI or of the server but a sign of a badly implemented browser [Dubost+ 01]. At the time of writing, only Internet Explorer handles this case correctly, while Navigator and Opera get a redirect response from the server and then fail to append the fragment identifier to the URI to which they were redirected.

the ID remains valid within the document (and, in the example just given, continues to identify the element representing the XPointer entry within the document). However, since we do not have control over the W3C's document management and identification policy, we have no guarantee that the ID will always be the same and that it will always identify the element we want to reference. The basic dilemma behind this is that the resource (the W3C's Web page) and the reference to it (our fragment identifier) are handled by different entities, which do not necessarily cooperate (or even know each other; for example, even though we know the W3C's Web pages, the W3C probably does not know that we used their ID as an example in this book).

- *The client has to support XPointers.* Even if all previous requirements are satisfied (i.e., the document is XML, it is still available via the URI, and the XPointer can still be interpreted meaningfully), the application processing the URI with the fragment identifier must implement the XPointer standard. At the time of writing, this is not the case for almost all available software, though we hope this will change in the near future. In comparison to XLink and XPath, XPointer is lagging behind in the standardization process; and as long as there is no stable standard, it cannot be implemented.

  The major browsers in their most current versions (at the time of writing, Internet Explorer 5.5, Navigator 6, and Opera 5) all support XML in the sense that they are able to not only download and interpret XML documents, but also to display them using style sheet mechanisms (CSS and/or XSL). There is, however, no support for XPointer currently. Nevertheless, as soon as XPointer reaches recommendation status, we hope to see XPointer support (as well as XLink support) in the next releases of the major browsers.

These are the requirements that must be met when using XPointer. We believe that in the near future XPointer (along with many other XML-based technologies) will become widely supported and a popular technology. For an illustration of how XPointer may not only become useful for hypermedia applications (which are the focus of this book) but also for other relatively simple cases of usage, consider the following scenario:

You find an interesting quote on the Web, possibly in an XHTML resource, that you would like to send to a friend. Instead of copying the quote into an e-mail (which would mean taking the quote out of context) or simply sending the resource's URI (which would make it necessary to somehow indicate exactly which part of the resource you mean), you select the quote with the mouse and then choose the "Generate XPointer" option from your browser's menu, which automatically generates a URI reference that exactly identifies the selected quote. You paste this URI reference into the e-mail and send it to your friend. This way, you have exactly identified the quote that was important to you without taking it out of context. Upon receiving the URI reference, your friend's browser not only requests and displays the resource containing the quote but also automatically highlights the quote identified by the XPointer part of the URI reference.

This example depends on the browser's ability to generate XPointers. Ideally, it would do so in a clever way, because for each subresource there is a multitude of possibilities for creating an XPointer identifying it. We will discuss this important issue in detail later in this chapter (in sections 6.4.3 and 6.4.4), but by now it should be clear that XPointer can provide a lot of value in an XML-based Web.

We now look at the details of XPointer. Section 6.1 discusses the general data model of XPointer, which is a generalization of XPath's data model. After this introductory section, we go into the details of how XPointers may be used as fragment identifiers, described in section 6.2. The next issue is XPointer's extensions to XPath and, in particular, the additional functions that XPointer defines. These functions are discussed in section 6.3.

After this rather formal discussion of XPointer, we then spend some time considering possible usage scenarios and how XPointer may be applied in the best possible way (section 6.4). Finally, even though XPointer is a very new standard, in section 6.5 we briefly describe our view of what XPointer's future may look like.

6.1 GENERAL MODEL

One of the most important aspects of XPointer is that it defines a generalization of the XPath concepts of *nodes, node types,* and *node sets* (as described in section 5.1) to the XPointer concepts of *locations, location types,* and *location sets.*[6] As a reminder, nodes, node types, and node sets in XPath are used to describe concepts that can be identified as nodes in a document's tree representation, as described by the XML Infoset. XPath functionality, such as filtering an axis output by predicate, is generally defined in terms of operations on nodes and node sets (an exception are the string functions, but these are rather limited and always operate on strings within one text node).

XPointer's goal is to define a mechanism for XML fragment identifiers. A very common usage scenario is a user selecting arbitrary document content with a mouse and then wishing to have an XPointer generated that

---

[6]Despite their similar names, these concepts are completely independent from XPath's location paths and location steps and should not be confused with them.

identifies exactly that content (e.g., to use the XPointer for creating a link pointing to that content). Since this selection can span multiple elements and furthermore may start in the middle of the text of one element and end in the middle of another, it is impossible to identify this content with XPath's constructs of nodes or strings. XPointer's solution to this problem is an extension of XPath's data model, described in section 6.1.1. To make the concepts of XPointer's data model easier to understand, we give some examples in section 6.1.2 of how this model maps to real-world scenarios.

6.1.1 XPointer Data Model

XPointer generalizes the concept of XPath nodes to *locations,* and, in essence, this generalization defines each location to be an XPath node, a *point,* or a *range.*[7] The following definitions are taken from the XPointer specification[8] and show how XPath's definition of a NodeType is extended by the concepts point and range:

```
[11] NodeType              ::= 'comment'
                            | 'text'
                            | 'processing-instruction'
                            | 'node'
                            | 'point'
                            | 'range'
```

Based on these definitions, XPointer also defines the *location set* as a generalization of XPath's *node set.* This definition allows XPath node tests to select locations of type point and range from a location set that might include locations of all three types. All locations generated by XPath constructs are nodes, but XPointer constructs can also generate points and ranges. The concepts of points and ranges are defined in the next two sections.

Point

A location of type *point* is defined by a node, called the *container node,* and a non-negative integer, called the *index.* It can represent the location preceding any individual character, or preceding or following any node in the information set constructed from an XML document. Two points are

---

[7]Note that the XPointer concepts of points and ranges directly correspond to the concepts of *positions* and *ranges* as defined by the Document Object Model (DOM) [Kesselman+ 00].

[8]We list XPointer grammar productions only where they help in understanding the concepts behind them. The numbering of the productions has been taken from the XPointer specification [DeRose+ 01a], which should be consulted for a complete and authoritative definition of the XPath grammar. It can be found at http://www.w3.org/TR/xptr.

identical if they have the same container node and index. Each point can be either a *node point* or a *character point,* which are defined as follows:

- *Node point.* If the container node of a point is of a node type that can have child nodes (that is, when the container node is an element node or a root node), then the index is an index into the child nodes, and such a point is called a *node point.* The index of a node point must be greater than or equal to zero and less than or equal to the number of child nodes of the container. An index of zero indicates the point before any child nodes, and a non-zero index n indicates the point immediately after the nth child node.

- *Character point.* When the container node of a point is of a node type that cannot have child nodes (i.e., text nodes, attribute nodes, namespace nodes, comment nodes, and processing instruction nodes), then the index is an index into the characters of the string value of the node. Such a point is called a *character point.* The index of a character point must be greater than or equal to zero and less than or equal to the length of the string value of the node. An index of zero indicates a point immediately before the first character of the string value, and a non-zero index n indicates the point immediately after the nth character of the string value.

Figure 6.2 shows the relationship of container nodes, node points, and character points for an example of an element containing text, then another element (which also contains text), and then some more text.

XPointer's goal is to make XPath's concepts applicable to locations and not only to nodes, and thus the following properties for applying XPath's concepts to points are defined: The `self` and `descendant-or-self` axes of a point contain the point itself. The `parent` axis of a point is a location set containing a single location, the container node. The `ancestor` axis contains the point's container node and its ancestors. The `ancestor-or-self` axis contains the point itself, the point's container node, and its ancestors. The `child`, `descendant`, `preceding-sibling`, `following-sibling`, `preceding`, `following`, `attribute`, and `namespace` axes of points are always empty.

Range

A range is defined by two points, a *startpoint* and an *endpoint.*[9] A range represents all of the XML structure and content between the startpoint and the endpoint. A range whose start- and endpoints are equal is called

---

[9]The start point has to appear before the end point in document order. More discussion about document order and point locations is at the end of this section.

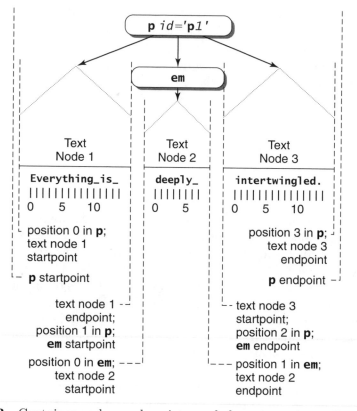

Figure 6.2   Container nodes, node points, and character points.   Reproduced from the XPointer specification [DeRose+ 01a] by kind permission of Steven DeRose, spring 2002.

a *collapsed range*. If the container node of one point of a range is a node of a type other than element, text, or root, then the container node of the other point of the range must be the same node.[10] The axes of a range are identical to the axes of its startpoint.

As a side note, remember that node sets are only one of the object types defined in XPath (the others being boolean, number, and string), and the other XPath object types also exist in XPointer. However, there is one important exception, and this is the result type of a whole XPointer. While an XPath can evaluate to any object type (consider the rather simple XPath 2+3, which evaluates to a number), XPointer requires an XPointer

---

[10]This rule has been defined to make it impossible to create ranges that start within attribute, namespace, comment, or processing instruction nodes and end in a node other than the same node.

to always evaluate to a location set (which is logical, given that there is no way that objects other than location sets could be interpreted as fragment identifiers pointing into documents).

In order to understand some of the functions XPointer provides, it is also essential to introduce the concept of the *covering range*. By definition, a covering range is a range that wholly encompasses a location. This means that the concept of a covering range can be applied to any location, whether it be a node, a point, or a range. Basically, a covering range is the smallest possible range covering a given location. In detail, this is defined as follows:

- For a range location, the covering range is identical to the range.
- For an attribute or namespace location (both node locations), the container node of the start point and end point of the covering range is the attribute or namespace location; the index of the startpoint of the covering range is 0; and the index of the endpoint of the covering range is the length of the string value of the attribute or namespace location.
- For the root location (a node location), the container node of the startpoint and endpoint of the covering range is the root node; the index of the start point of the covering range is 0; and the index of the endpoint of the covering range is the number of children of the root location.
- For a point location, the start- and endpoints of the covering range are the point itself.
- For any other kind of location, the container node of the startpoint and endpoint of the covering range is the parent of the location; the index of the startpoint of the covering range is the number of preceding sibling nodes of the location; and the index of the endpoint is one greater than the index of the startpoint.

In summary, XPointer's extensions to XPath's data model include the extension of the concept of nodes and node sets to that of locations and location sets (with the location being a node, a point, or a range). XPointer also introduces the concept of a covering range to support mapping of locations to ranges. For each location, there is a well-defined covering range.

In addition to these extensions of XPath's data model, XPointer also extends the concept of *document order,* as introduced in section 5.1. In general, the concept is extended not only to arrange nodes in a well-defined order but also to include point and range locations. Figure 6.2 shows how the locations of a document fragment are arranged in XPointer's document order. For defining rules regarding how to determine document order, XPointer introduces the concept of an *immediately preceding node* and then uses it to define how every possible combination of the relevant location types (i.e., nodes, points, and ranges) have to be compared to establish the document order of these locations.

6.1.2 XPointer Data Model Examples

To make these abstract definitions more understandable, we give some examples of how the concepts of locations, points, ranges, and nodes relate to each other. Our scenario is a browser that allows a user to create XPointers by selecting content with a mouse and then using a menu option for generating an XPointer identifying that content.

Marking a Point Within a Document

The simplest use is to mark a point within the document and generate an XPointer for this point (e.g., for creating an XPointer that is attached to an e-mail saying "please insert your text here"). To do this, the browser generates an XPointer that is a point. Depending on where the point has been selected, it is either a node point (if it has been marked within the root node or an element node) or a character point (in all other cases). Depending on how the browser was implemented, different XPointers that refer to the same point could be created. Consider the case where a user selects the point before the first character of a paragraph. Depending on the browser's implementation, this could result in the following:

- a node point into the paragraph's parent element node, identifying the point before the paragraph child,
- a node point with index zero within the paragraph's element node, or
- a character point with index zero within the text node of the paragraph's text.

All these cases make sense. In the first, the point could be used to insert elements before the paragraph element. In the second, the point could be used to insert elements into the paragraph before the first character; while in the third, it could be used to insert characters before the first character within the paragraph's text. It is entirely dependent on the implementation and application how these cases should be treated. Indeed, one possibility would be for the browser to present the user with a choice as to which is the appropriate XPointer.[11]

---

[11] Further complicating things, the browser could base its decision on the document's schema (e.g., the DTD) if available, which could be used to determine whether the paragraph element may have both text and children elements or only text.

Selecting Text Within One Node

Selecting text within one node is the equivalent of selecting two points,[12] the start and the end point of the selection, that lie inside the same node (e.g., the same element, attribute, or comment). From the user's point of view, it may not be apparent whether or not the two points are located within the same node (e.g., if two elements are not visibly separated by any formatting); but for the browser, this is easy to determine. Based on the selection of the user, the browser generates an XPointer defining a range between the selected start and end points. Since in this case the selected text lies within one node, the two points can easily be used to construct an XPointer range, which spans between the two points.

Selecting Text That Spans a Number of Nodes

If the start and the end point lie in different nodes, then the range defined by the two points also spans multiple nodes. According to the range constraints defined by XPointer, this is allowed only if the containing nodes of the startpoint and the endpoint are element, text, or root nodes (in all other cases, the start and endpoint must lie within the same node). A possible selection that spans a number of nodes in the case of an XHTML-like paragraph may select text that is all inside the paragraph but still spans multiple nodes. This may be because in between there are other element nodes (e.g., nodes representing emphasized text or hyperlinks). This situation effectively places the start and the endpoints in different text nodes (making them both children of the same paragraph node).

To further generalize this scenario, the start point and the end point may occur in entirely different subtrees of the document tree, for example, within a paragraph of the first chapter and in a table cell of the third chapter. This still would represent a valid range, spanning from the character point in the text node representing the first chapter's paragraph to the node point in the table row node directly after the selected table cell.

Making Multiple Selections

Even though today's user interfaces in most cases do not support this type of interaction, it would be perfectly reasonable to implement an interface that allows multiple non-contiguous selections. This could be used to create an XPointer that references multiple ranges within the same resource (e.g., attached to an e-mail saying "what do you think about these three statements?"). In a case such as this, it is mainly a question of the design of the user interface as to how multiple selections could be implemented in

---

[12]In XPointer, the startpoint of a range must occur before the endpoint in document order; so if the user makes the selection by first selecting the endpoint, the browser must recognize this and act accordingly.

a user-friendly way. From XPointer's point of view, the multiple selections could be easily combined to yield a single location set.

The preceding scenarios illustrate some typical cases in which XPointer concepts are relevant.[13] So far we have not discussed how exactly the hypothetical browser maps the concepts to actual XPointers, and as a first step toward resolving this issue, we first have to discuss the possible forms of XPointers.

6.2 XPOINTER FORMS

An XPointer is an identification of a part of an XML resource and is mainly intended to be used as a fragment identifier in a URI reference. As such, it must somehow fit into the framework defined for URIs as described in section 3.2. Basically, it must be represented as a printable string that can be used within URI references and exchanged in the same way URIs are exchanged. (To this end, XPointers must obey a number of character-escaping rules, which are not discussed here but are described in detail in section 6.4.1).

XPointer distinguishes three different forms as follows:

```
[1] XPointer              ::= Name
                           | ChildSeq
                           | FullXPtr
```

The first one (a *bare name*) is defined to act mainly as a very concise form and to be backwards compatible with HTML fragment identifiers. This first form is described in section 6.2.1. A second form (a *child sequence*) still uses an abbreviated syntax but allows more flexibility than the first form. It is described in section 6.2.2. Finally, the full form of XPointer is discussed in section 6.2.3. It is the most complex and most powerful XPointer form.

6.2.1 Bare Names

The simplest form of an XPointer is a *bare name*. Basically, it consists of the same name as that provided for the argument of a location step using the id function. This function returns the element that has an attribute

---

[13]Note that our examples assume that the presentation of a document in a browser can be used to identify points in the underlying source document. However, in the case of nontrivial presentations (such as when complex XSL style sheets that map single sections of an XML document to multiple presentation artifacts are used), this correspondence between selections in the presentation and the underlying document may become rather complicated. How this issue could and should be resolved in a general way is at the time of writing still the subject of discussions within the W3C's standardization process for XPointer.

of type ID[14] with the argument's value, so an XPointer bare name does exactly the same thing as an HTML fragment identifier.[15] As an example, the URI reference `http://www.w3.org/TR/#xptr` uses a bare name[16] and may consequently be interpreted as pointing to the element that has an attribute of type ID with the value `xptr`.

There are two reasons XPointer bare names are supported, despite their very limited functionality:

- For reasons of backwards compatibility with HTML and as an easy migration to XHTML without the need to rewrite all fragment identifiers when converting a resource from HTML to XHTML. Otherwise, HTML fragment identifiers become invalid if an HTML resource is converted to XHTML.

- To encourage the use of IDs, which are the most robust mechanism for pointing into XML documents.

XPointer bare names are very easy to understand and use, but they are limited in two ways.

The first limitation is that they may point only to element nodes, because only elements may be identified via ID attributes. The second limitation is that the element to which an XPointer should point must have an attribute of type ID, otherwise it is impossible to point to this element using a bare name. (If the document is under the control of the creator of the XPointer, then an ID may be created by modifying the document, but this is not always an option.)

As an intermediate form of XPointers (between the bare form and full XPointers), we have the child sequence. This form of XPointer, discussed in the next section, is also limited to pointing to element nodes, but it—in contrast to bare names—may point to element nodes that do not carry an attribute of type ID.

6.2.2 Child Sequences

A child sequence is a form of XPointer that selects an element node by navigating through a document's element tree. It resembles an XPath location

---

[14]Note that it is necessary to interpret the DTD to evaluate the type of an attribute.

[15]Except that in HTML, IDs can also be defined using an `<a>` element with a `name` attribute, which, although discouraged, is still widely used because of the lack of browser support for the newer identification mechanism using the `id` attribute defined for virtually every HTML element.

[16]To be more precise, this URI reference's fragment identifier may be regarded only as a bare name XPointer if the W3C's Web server reports an XML-based MIME type for the resource. If it reports an HTML MIME type, as it does at the time of writing, the fragment identifier must be interpreted as an HTML fragment identifier.

path in that it uses a path notation, but it is much more limited in that it can select only elements and uses only the child axis. The syntax for a child sequence is as follows:

```
[2] ChildSeq                  ::= Name? ('/' [1-9] [0-9]* )+
```

An example of a child sequence identifying the same element as the `http://www.w3.org/TR/#xptr` bare name would be `http://www.w3.org/TR/#` `/1/2/17/15/1/1/1`. This is nothing more than a navigation path through the element tree of the XHTML page based on child sequences. It could be spelled out as follows:

- Select the first child of the document root, which is the `<html>` element.
- Select the second child of the `<html>` element, which is the `<body>` element.
- Select the seventeenth child of the `<body>` element, which is a `<dl>` element.
- Select the fifteenth child of the `<dl>` element, which is a `<dt>` element.
- Select the first child of the `<dt>` element, which is a `<b>` element.
- Select the first child of the `<b>` element, which is an `<i>` element.
- Select the first child of the `<i>` element, which is an `<a>` element.

This last `<a>` element is the one carrying the `xptr` ID, which is why the bare name XPointer and the child sequence XPointer select the same element. In this case, we have selected something that is also accessible through an ID. However, what is interesting about the child sequence mechanism is that it would still be possible to select the element even if was not identified through an ID.

Child sequences have a severe disadvantage in that they are very sensitive to document modifications. It is very unlikely that the example just presented will still work after the W3C's page has been modified since the modification is likely to involve inserting or deleting elements preceding the one we want to select, resulting in breaking the intention of the child sequence.[17]

Since child sequences are easy to use but also easy to break, there is a second form of child sequence that uses an element identified by an ID

---

[17]We discuss more about the persistence of XPointers in section 6.4.4. Here it is interesting to note that the child sequence would probably still identify an element after the page has been modified, but most likely not identify the element that we want to identify.

as the starting point rather than using the document root. In this case, the XPointer starts with a bare name but then continues with a child sequence,[18] navigating the document tree starting from the element with the given ID. An example of this kind of child sequence would be `http://www.w3.org/TR/#last-call-list/15/1/1/1`. This would work if the W3C had made the `<dl>` element listing the document in "last call" status accessible through a `last-call-list` ID (which it has not done). This kind of child sequence would make the XPointer more robust to modifications of the document because only changes within the `<dl>` element could possibly break the XPointer.

6.2.3 Full XPointers

Both bare names and child sequences are rather limited in their expressiveness, insofar as they can select only element nodes and also in the way they select these nodes. Therefore, in many cases it is necessary to use more complex XPointers (the so-called full XPointer), which provide a much more flexible way of addressing into a document than bare names or child sequences do. Syntactically, a full XPointer is defined as follows:

```
3] FullXPtr                  ::= XPtrPart (S? XPtrPart)*
4] XPtrPart                  ::= 'xpointer' '(' XPtrExpr ')'
                               | 'xmlns' '(' XPtrNsDecl? ')'
                               | Scheme '(' SchemeSpecificExpr ')'
5] Scheme                    ::= NCName
6] SchemeSpecificExpr        ::= StringWithBalancedParens
7] StringWithBalancedParens  ::= [^()]* ('(' StringWithBalancedParens ')' [^()]*)*
8] XPtrExpr                  ::= Expr
9] XPtrNsDecl                ::= NCName S? '=' S? XPtrNsURI
0] XPtrNsURI                 ::= Char*
```

As an example, now consider the W3C technical reports page. W3C has used IDs to mark individual sections (which are visible as headings and subheadings in Figure 6.1); but unfortunately in XHTML the actual contents of a section are not contained in any specific element. Instead they simply follow a sectioning element, such as the `<h3>` element used for the "Working Drafts in Last Call" section heading. Consequently, using only child sequences, it is impossible to point to the entry for the XPointer working draft entry. This is because the XPointer entry is part of the `<dl>` list following the "Working Drafts in Last Call" heading. So if we want to

---

[18]This is possible because XML rules state that name tokens, the syntax used for IDs, may not contain slash characters, which are used in defining child sequences.

point to the entry for XPointer starting from the heading with the ID, we
have to use a full XPointer as follows:

```
http://www.w3.org/TR/#xpointer(id('last-call')/following::dl[1]/dt[7]//a)
```

Here we mainly exploit the fact that the "Working Drafts in Last Call"
heading is identified by the `last-call` ID. The XPointer part of the URI
reference could be interpreted as follows (commenting on the individual
location steps):

- Select the element having the `last-call` ID. (This is the `<h3>`
  element with the "Working Drafts in Last Call" content.) Here
  we use XPath's `id` function as described in section 5.4.4.
- Select the first definition list (represented by a `<dl>` element)
  following the `<h3>` element. (For an explanation of the XPath
  `following` axis, refer to section 5.2.2.)
- Select the seventh definition term of this list (i.e., the seventh `<dt>`
  child of the `<dl>` element).
- Select the `<a>` element, which is (directly or indirectly) contained
  in the `<dt>` element.

In this example, we see that a normal XPath can be used within an XPointer.
Apart from a few exceptions, XPointer allows unlimited use of XPath's expressiveness. Therefore, it is necessary to know XPath if we are to create
anything more than trivial XPointers (i.e., bare names and child sequences).
Looking at the example just given, note the presence of a special keyword, `xpointer`, which, according to rule 4 from the syntactic definition,
is the specification of a *scheme*. XPointer schemes are an important mechanism for building robust XPointers. According to rule 3 of the syntax,
full XPointers use schemes to define any number of scheme-specific parts.
XPointer specifies that scheme parts must be evaluated left to right, so the
interpretation of the scheme parts is well defined. Currently, there are only
two schemes defined for XPointer (as indicated by rule 4):

- `xpointer` – This is by far the most widely used scheme, and it indicates that the expression that follows (contained in parentheses) is
  an XPointer expression. This scheme has been used in the example
  just given.
- `xmlns` – This second scheme is for the initialization of namespaces.
  In XPath (and, therefore, in XPointer), an expression may contain a
  qualified name (i.e., a name containing a namespace prefix and a local
  name). In order to make the interpretation of qualified names possible,

there must be a mechanism for the initialization of namespaces (i.e., for the assignment of a namespace URI to a namespace prefix). This scheme will be discussed in detail in section 6.4.2.

While these two schemes are the only ones defined in the XPointer specification, it is possible for applications to define their own schemes, which can then be used to access subresources in an application-specific way. This would, however, make the XPointer unusable for any application not supporting the application-specific extension. It is useful to note that the XPointer specification states that interpretation proceeds from left to right and stops once a scheme part that can be successfully interpreted as a locator into the resource has been identified. Consequently, it is possible to concatenate multiple scheme parts, and if the interpretation of a scheme part fails (a so-called *subresource error*[19]), then the interpretation of the XPointer continues with the next scheme part. A simple example for this is the following URI reference:

```
http://www.w3.org/TR/#xpointer(id('xptr'))
    xpointer(/*[1]/*[2]/*[17]/*[15]/*[1]/*[1]/*[1])
```

In this case, the XPointer consists of two scheme parts, both being of the xpointer scheme. If an element with the ID xptr is present in the resource, then the XPointer will locate it.[20] Otherwise, the first scheme part results in a subresource error, and the second part then successfully locates the resource by simply counting element children.[21] Given our example used so far, this XPointer would continue to work even if the ID xptr was removed from the document. However, the XPointer would still break if the ID was removed and the resource's structure was changed in such a way that the "child sequence" no longer identified the element we want to locate.[22]

---

[19]XPointer defines three error types: *syntax errors* for XPointers being syntactically invalid, *resource errors* for XPointers pointing into nonexistent or non-XML resources, and *subresource errors*. Note that XPath allows empty node sets as results and does not regard this situation as an error. However, because XPointer is intended as a specification of document locations, an empty result is an error.

[20]Here it can be seen that a bare name XPointer used in a URI reference such as ...#name is identical to the full form ...#xpointer(id('name')).

[21]In this case, it can be seen that a child sequence XPointer in a URI reference such as ...#/a/b/c is identical to the full form ...#xpointer(/*[a]/*[b]/*[c]). (In this case, the abbreviation mechanisms of XPath are used, otherwise each step would look like child:: *[position()=a], which makes explicit the child sequence positioning.)

[22]It should be noted that given the modification frequency of W3C's technical reports page, the structure of this page is likely to change at least once per week, even though some subtrees (such as the Recommendations section) may remain stable for months.

Formally, as already mentioned, the XPointer specification states that evaluation of XPointer scheme parts must be left to right but also that evaluation of scheme parts must continue if one of the following conditions is met while evaluating a scheme part:

- The scheme is unknown to the application evaluating the XPointer.
- The scheme is not applicable to the media type of the resource.
- The scheme does not locate any subresource present in the resource.[23] This applies to XPointer expressions evaluating to an empty location set (a subresource error).
- If the scheme being interpreted is `xpointer`, the following applies:
    - The string argument in a `string-range` function is not found in the string-value of the location, or the third or fourth argument of the function indicates a string that is beyond the beginning or end of the document.
    - The point returned by the `start-point` function is of type attribute or namespace.

This set of rules for the evaluation of XPointer scheme parts makes it possible to create XPointers with built-in "fault tolerance" (through providing fall-back scheme parts to be used if the original scheme part does not work anymore). In section 6.4.3 we will discuss some interesting examples.

6.3 FUNCTIONS

XPointer is built on top of XPath and extends XPath in several ways. At the most fundamental level, it extends XPath's data model, and this aspect has been covered in section 6.1.1. However, in order to fully exploit this extended data model, XPointer also extends the list of functions provided by XPath. XPath's functions have been described in section 5.4, with an overview provided in Table 5.4. XPointer significantly extends this list of functions. The additional functions provided by XPointer are summarized in Table 6.1.

Before covering the functions in detail, we should note that when XPath was developed it was assumed that the XPath functions would be extended by other specifications. (Indeed, as we have mentioned previously, XPath

---

[23]Note that an XPointer part that uses the `xmlns` scheme never returns a subresource and thus always fails. However, its evaluation has a potential effect on XPointer parts to its right (see section 6.4.2 for more information).

Table 6.1 Overview of XPointer Functions

Function name	Result type	Arguments	Page
end-point	location-set	location-set	157
here	location-set	n/a	158
origin	location-set	n/a	158
range	location-set	location-set	158
range-inside	location-set	location-set	158
range-to	location-set	location-set	159
start-point	location-set	location-set	160
string-range	location-set	location-set, string, number?, number?	160

is more intended as a foundation for other specifications than as a stand-alone standard.) Consequently, the extension of XPath's set of functions is perfectly legal and well defined within the XPath model.

One particularly useful observation about the XPointer functions is that they all accept arguments and produce results using the extended XPointer data model. Furthermore, from the function names it can be concluded that the majority of functions are used for defining ranges. This is not surprising given that ranges are XPointer's most important extension of the XPath data model and are not supported at all by XPath's functions. In the following list, we cover all XPointer functions (supplementing the core XPath functions) in detail:

- end-point – *Returns the end point of a location.*
  Signature: `location-set end-point(location-set)`
  The end-point function accepts a location set as its argument. For each of the locations in this location set, the function adds the end point of the location to the resulting location set, according to the following rules (with x being a location in the argument location set):
  - If x is of type point, the resulting point is x.
  - If x is of type range, the resulting point is the end point of x.
  - If x is of type root or element, the container node of the resulting point is x, and the index is the number of children of x.
  - If x is of type text, comment, or processing instruction, the container node of the resulting point is x, and the index is the length of the string-value of x.
  - If x is of type attribute or namespace, the XPointer part in which the function appears fails.

Thus, the `end-point` function can be used to locate the end point of any location. The complementary function of the `end-point` function is the `start-point` function.

- `here` – *Returns the context of the XPointer.*
  Signature: `location-set here()`
  The `here` function makes it possible to create XPointers relative to the context in which they appear. Since this makes sense only for XPointers within XML resources, an XPointer part containing the `here` function always fails if the XPointer does not appear inside an XML resource.[24] If the containing resource is XML, the `here` function returns a location set with one member: If the XPointer being evaluated appears in a text node inside an element node, the location returned is the element node. Otherwise, the location returned is the node that directly contains the XPointer being evaluated.

- `origin` – *Returns the context of the traversal initiation.*
  Signature: `location-set origin()`
  This function makes sense only in a context where XPointers are used within linking constructs (such as those provided by XLink) and where the processing model is such that the XPointer evaluation is initiated by the traversal of links. If this is the case, the `origin` function returns a location set with one member, which locates the element from which a user or program initiated traversal of the link.
  If the `origin` function is used in a URI reference where a URI is also provided and identifies a containing resource different from the resource from which traversal was initiated, the result is a resource error. It is also a resource error to use the `origin` function in a context where traversal is not occurring.

- `range` – *Returns covering ranges of locations.*
  Signature: `location-set range(location-set)`
  The `range` function returns the covering ranges of all locations in the argument location set. Thus, the result location set of the `range` function always contains a set of range locations, and this set contains, at most, as many range locations as there are locations in the argument location set.[25]

- `range-inside` – *Returns ranges covering the contents of locations.*
  Signature: `location-set range-inside(location-set)`
  The `range-inside` function is similar to the `range` function in that it

---

[24]One possible scenario would be an XPointer being typed into the address bar of a browser, which would not have an XML document as context.

[25]It contains fewer range locations if at least some of the argument locations have the same covering ranges.

also returns ranges covering the locations in the argument location
set. However, the `range-inside` function does not return the covering
ranges for the locations in the argument location set but instead
returns ranges covering the contents of these locations. The following
rules are used to construct the result location set, based on the type
of each location in the argument location set:

- For range locations, the location (i.e., the range) is added to the
  result location set.
- For point locations, the location (i.e., the point) is added to the
  result location set. Consequently, the result location set of the
  `range-inside` function can contain range and point locations.
- For node locations, the location (i.e., the node) is used as the container node of the start and end points of the range location to be
  added to the resulting location set. The index of the start point of
  the range is zero. If the end point is a character point, then its
  index is the length of the string value of the argument node
  location; otherwise it is the number of children of the argument
  node location.

This definition of the `range-inside` function makes sure that
only the contents of locations are added to the result location set.
For example, if the argument location is an element, then the `range-inside` function returns the contents of this element as the result (in
contrast, the `range` function would return the element itself).

- `range-to` – *Returns range from context location to argument location.*
  Signature: `location-set range-to(location-set)`
  This function has a special position among the other functions in that
  it requires a change of the XPath syntax as described in section 5.2.[26]
  In XPointer, rule 4 of XPath's syntax of location paths is changed
  from

```
[4] Step                    ::= AxisSpecifier NodeTest Predicate*
                              | AbbreviatedStep
```

to the following form:

```
[4xptr] Step                ::= AxisSpecifier NodeTest Predicate*
                              | AbbreviatedStep
                              | 'range-to' '(' Expr ')' Predicate*
```

---

[26]This way of incorporating the `range-to` functionality into XPointer is not very elegant;
and in order to avoid similar situations in the future, the XPointer specifications states: "This
change is a single exception for the `range-to` function. It is not a generic change and is not
extensible to other functions. The modified production expresses that a range computation
must be made for each of the nodes in the current node list" [DeRose+ 01a].

This modification of the syntax makes it possible to use the `range-to` function directly as a step of a location path (instead of the situation with other functions, which may be used only within predicates or other expressions). The `range-to` function operates on the context provided by the previous step and produces the context for the following step.

For each location in the context, the `range-to` function returns a range. The start of this range is the start point of the context location, and the end of the range is the end point of the location found by evaluating the expression argument with respect to that context location. Thus, if the context is a location set with more than one location, then for each of these locations, the `range-to` function's argument is evaluated with respect to the location. The result of evaluating the `range-to` function then is the union of all ranges that are the results of these evaluations.

- `start-point` – *Returns the start point of a location.*
  Signature: `location-set start-point(location-set)`
  The `start-point` function accepts a location set as its argument. For each of the locations in this location set, the function adds the start point of the location to the resulting location set, according to the following rules (with x being a location in the argument location set):

  - If x is of type point, the start point is x.
  - If x is of type range, the start point is the start point of x.
  - If x is of type root, element, text, comment, or processing instruction, the container node of the start point is x, and the index is 0.
  - If x is of type attribute or namespace, the XPointer part in which the function appears fails.

  Thus, the `start-point` function can be used to locate the start point of any location. The complementary function of the `start-point` function is the `end-point` function.

- `string-range` – *Matches strings in a location set.*
  Signature: `location-set string-range(location-set, string,`
  `number?, number?)`
  This is one of the most important (and complex) functions provided by XPointer. In many cases, it is necessary not only to use the structure provided by XML (such as elements, attributes, or processing instructions) for identifying resource fragments but also to be able to identify fragments that are text-based. Basically, the `string-range` function enables the identification of strings (or sets of strings) as ranges (or sets of ranges).

For each location in the argument location set, the location's string value (see section 5.1 for the definition of the string value) is searched for the given string.[27] Each non-overlapping match of this string is then added (as a range location) to the resultant location set. If no matching string exists, then the XPointer part (within which the `string-range` function appears) fails.

The optional third and fourth arguments can be used to control the range, which is added to the resulting location set. The third argument specifies from which point, relative to the start of the matched string, the result should be taken. The default value for the third argument is 1, which means the result should be from before the first character matching the search string. The fourth argument specifies the length of the range to be added. The default is the range that extends to the end of the matched string.

These functions can be used to compose XPointers. It should also be noted that most XPath functions can also be used within XPointers. In particular, it can be observed (most easily from looking at Table 6.1) that XPointer's functions are mainly concerned with supporting the concept of locations, which are a construct introduced by XPointer mainly for the purpose of including ranges in the data model.

6.4 USING XPOINTERS

So far we have discussed the specifics of XPointer as a way of identifying resource fragments. In this section, we talk about some of the issues that arise when using XPointers. One of the obvious problems when creating and using XPointers in an environment that is essentially character-based is the issue of character escaping (described in section 6.4.1). Another topic of a similar nature is the question of how to use XPointers with XML Namespaces (discussed in section 6.4.2).

XPointers identify resource fragments by describing ways for locating them inside the resources. As pointed out earlier, this can be done in an endless variety of ways, so composing XPointers is not a mechanical process. Rather, it requires some intelligence in order to compose "good" XPointers. Since XPointer is a new technology, there is not much implementation

---

[27]The string given as `string-range`'s argument is matched literally, which means it is case-sensitive, no regular expressions of any type are possible, and the only normalization that is done is the whitespace handling as defined by XML (which is, in particular, important for line ends). Sophisticated string matching (such as regular expressions) is not supported by XPointer and must be handled at the application level.

experience to build on; but nevertheless in section 6.4.3 we describe some guidelines for composing good XPointers. Finally, in section 6.4.4 we look into the question of what exactly *good* means. In many cases, it will have a lot to do with ensuring XPointer persistence.

6.4.1 XPointer Character Escaping

While composing XPointers is based on the way subresources within XML documents should be identified, they must also be coded in a way that makes it possible to exchange and interpret them unambiguously. XPointers use a character-based notation and are thus easy to compose and read. But several characters within XPointers have special meaning and must therefore be escaped, if they have to be embedded into XPointers. Because of the different standards involved when actually using an XPointer, escaping mechanisms occur on different levels, as follows:

- *XPointer escaping rules.* The XPointer specification defines escaping rules for some special characters. Most importantly, parentheses in XPointer must be balanced. This is because XPointer is built on the assumption that the end of syntactic constructs using parentheses can be found by identifying the balanced parenthesis. Consequently, unbalanced parentheses in XPointers must be escaped, and this is done by prefixing them with the circumflex character, "∧". This makes it necessary to also escape the circumflex character, which is done by escaping it with itself (i.e., the literal circumflex character within an XPointer is written as "∧∧").

- *XML escaping rules.* Very often XPointers will be used within XML documents, and in this case XML's rules for escaping XML special characters must be observed. This means that any characters not representable in the character encoding of the XML document (as well as any characters relevant for XML markup) must be written as character references or as predefined entity references.

- *URI escaping rules.* URI references must adhere to the syntactic rules defined by RFC 2396 [Berners-Lee+ 98], which allows only a limited set of characters. All other characters must be represented using the URI escape mechanism, which represents these characters by a percent sign, "%", followed by two hexadecimal digits.

These character-escaping rules in many cases must be combined when XPointers are used in an XML-based environment. Consequently, character escaping can become quite complicated. The XPointer specification gives

Table 6.2 XPointer Character Escaping (Example 1)

Level	Example
Initial	`xpointer(string-range(//P,"a little hat ^"))`
XPointer	`xpointer(string-range(//P,"a little hat ^^"))`
XML	`xpointer(string-range(//P,&quot;a little hat ^^&quot;))`
URI	`xpointer(string-range(//P,%22a%20little%20hat%20%5E%5E%22))`

Table 6.3 XPointer Character Escaping (Example 2)

Level	Example
Initial and XPointer	`xpointer(id('résumé'))`
XML	`xpointer(id('r&#xE9;sum&#xE9;'))`
URI	`xpointer(id('r%C3%A9sum%C3%A9'))`

some examples of how the different escaping mechanisms affect a given XPointer (reproduced in Tables 6.2 and 6.3).

In the first example (Table 6.2), it is interesting to see that even trivial things such as space characters must be escaped in the URI encoding because spaces are not allowed to appear literally within URIs. In the XML encoding, the double quotes must be escaped only if the XPointer appears within an XML attribute that is delimited with double quotes.

The second example (shown in Table 6.3) shows how to deal with non-ASCII characters. Because XPointer is based on Unicode, the accented letter appears both in the initial and the XPointer form. Based on the assumption that the XML document supports only ASCII, the accented letter must be represented by a character reference to its Unicode code point [Unicode 00]. In the URI encoding, however, the accented character has first to be encoded in UTF-8 [Yergeau 98] before the resulting byte sequence is escaped, so the result looks quite different from the XML escaping.

6.4.2 XPointers and Namespaces

In section 6.2.3, we discussed how XPointer defines the concept of schemes (in fact, each full XPointer is nothing more than a sequence of scheme-specific parts) and that currently only the `xpointer` and the `xmlns` schemes are specified. XPath (and thus, XPointer) makes it possible to use qualified names that have a namespace prefix and a local part. (For a discussion of qualified names and XML Namespaces in general, see section 4.2.) In

XML documents, the namespace prefix can easily be interpreted because, in order for the qualified name to be valid, there must be a namespace declaration associating that prefix with a namespace URI somewhere on an ancestor element.[28] This is no problem since the qualified names in XML are embedded into the context provided by the XML document (in particular, the namespace declarations within this document). An XPointer, however, does not have such a context because it may be used outside any document, simply as part of a URI reference. Consequently, there must be a way to establish the context of namespace declarations for XPointers.

XPointer defines the `xmlns` scheme for declaring namespaces. This is, in a way, very similar to namespace declarations in XML documents. Each `xmlns` scheme part associates one namespace prefix with a namespace URI. However, the syntax is slightly different from the one used in XML. The syntax is defined in rules 9 and 10 of the standard, as shown in section 6.2.3 (and repeated here):

```
[4] XPtrPart            ::= 'xpointer' '(' XPtrExpr ')'
                         |  'xmlns' '(' XPtrNsDecl? ')'
                         |  Scheme '(' SchemeSpecificExpr ')'
[9] XPtrNsDecl          ::= NCName S? '=' S? XPtrNsURI
[10] XPtrNsURI          ::= Char*
```

Thus, whenever an XPointer is used that contains qualified names, it has to contain `xmlns` scheme parts for declaring the prefixes being used in the qualified names, as shown in the following example:

```
...#xmlns(html=http://www.w3.org/1999/xhtml)xpointer(//html:h3[9])
```

It is important to note that the prefix used in the XPointer and the prefix used in the resource need not be the same in order for the XPointer to match. The important part in this case is the namespace URI, so it is necessary only that the URI in the XPointer `xmlns` scheme part and the URI in the XML document (i.e., the namespace declaration using the `xmlns` attribute) are the same.

If two `xmlns` scheme parts within one XPointer declare the same prefix, then the second (i.e., right) declaration overrides the first (i.e., left) one. However, because evaluation of XPointer scheme parts is done stepwise from left to right, an `xpointer` scheme part that appears between the two `xmlns` scheme parts declaring the same prefix will be interpreted using the first declaration.

---

[28]This is with the exception of the `xml` prefix, which is always bound to the namespace URI of the XML Namespaces standard.

6.4.3 How to Compose XPointers

In section 5.5 we described in detail how to use XPath. The same principles apply to XPointer, particularly the key points of "being as specific as possible" and "filtering as early as possible." However, it is important to see the difference in possible application scenarios:

- *XPath and XSLT.* Today, the most frequently used application of XPath is in XSLT. In XSLT, XPaths may be evaluated very often during the processing of a style sheet, so it is important to keep an eye on the efficiency of the XPaths being used. Furthermore, the XSLT author often also controls the XML document (as well as the schema behind it), which makes it easier to compose XPaths that are not compromised by modifications to documents or even the schema.

- *XPath and XPointer.* In XPointer, however, XPath is often used for identifying fragments in resources not under the control of the XPointer's author. On the other hand, XPointers are usually evaluated only once (when locating the fragment within the resource), so efficiency is not a significant issue. Robustness, on the other hand, is very important since the XPointer should continue to work even if the resource that it points into changes.

Consequently, there is a difference between using XPath in the context of XSLT and using it in the context of XPointer. In general, the most important aspect of composing XPointers is robustness, which therefore is discussed separately in section 6.4.4.

As pointed out already, there are countless ways for each given fragment to be identified by an XPointer. We have already demonstrated this with the example of W3C's technical reports Web page at the start of this chapter. Continuing this discussion, we could add that, if, for example, the heading was not identified by the `last-call` ID, it would be possible to locate the heading based on its content,[29] as shown in the following URI:

```
http://www.w3.org/TR#xpointer(//h3[contains(string(.),
   'Working%20Drafts%20in%20Last%20Call')/following::dl[1]/dt[7]//a)
```

However, it would not make much sense to list a huge number of possible XPointers identifying the same resource because this list would never be exhaustive. Furthermore, without knowing the schemas behind the resources and the characteristics of how they are modified, it is hard to actually rate the many variants qualitatively.

---

[29]Because the XPointer is used in a URI reference here, the space characters in the search string must be URI-encoded as `%20` (as described in section 6.4.1).

The main point is that anybody involved in the creation of XPointers (either manually or programmatically) should be aware that this is not a strict science but more of an art form. In particular, any software generating XPointers should be carefully designed in order to generate good XPointers, and doing this is a non-trivial task. The quality criteria depend on the application domain and on how much knowledge there is available about the resources being used. In particular, one criterion that will very often be highly ranked is the persistence of XPointers.

6.4.4 Persistence

As discussed in the introduction to this chapter, the persistence of an XPointer is a serious issue (see also the discussion in section 3.3.2). Even if the resource addressed by a URI is still available, it may have changed, and the XPointer may not work any more, or it may not work as expected. In order to construct robust XPointers (i.e., XPointers that are tolerant against modifications of the resource), it is necessary to follow some guidelines. These guidelines, however, depend on how much is known about the resources being used.

As an example, it is fairly certain that the W3C will keep its overall structure of the technical reports page (see Figure 6.1), and that additions to the individual sections (e.g., "Working Drafts in Last Call") will always be at the start of the section. It would therefore be a reasonable idea to use a section's ID and to then start to count from the end of the list contained within the following:

```
http://www.w3.org/TR#xpointer(id('last-call')/
    following::dl[1]/dt[last()-4]//a)
```

While this approach could (and probably would) work within the "Recommendations" or "Notes" sections (where documents remain), it is less likely to work in the "Working Drafts in Last Call" section where working drafts may change status and may be deleted. By now it should be clear that constructing robust XPointers requires a good deal of knowledge about the resources, which may be impractical or too expensive to acquire.

Using IDs is always a good idea; and as long as there are IDs being used within the resource, it is a good idea to start with an ID and then navigate from there. But again, if the schema of a resource is unknown, then it is not really possible to find out which attributes are used as IDs. (However, it may be possible to make an educated guess, such as looking for attributes with unique values or attributes having the string id as part of their name.)

Besides all these worries about XPointers becoming invalid or incorrect because of resource modifications, it should always be remembered that even though XPointer is the W3C standard for XML fragment identification, it is not the only means of identifying fragments. If, for example, the validity of fragments is very important, then one alternative might be not only to generate XPointers but also to generate information for checking the XPointer's validity. One approach to this might be to use the modification time of the resource at the time the XPointer was generated, or even a digital fingerprint of the resource or subresource (using checksum algorithms such as MD5 [Rivest 92] or SHA [NIST 93]).

Information such as dates or checksums could easily be incorporated into XPointers themselves by using proprietary schemes, which, by definition, would be ignored by applications not knowing or supporting them. That way it would be possible to generate XPointers that would work on all platforms supporting XPointer and that would have the added benefit of being able to be tested for possible modifications of the fragment by platforms supporting the additional XPointer scheme.

6.5 FUTURE DEVELOPMENTS

Of all the W3C specifications relevant to XML linking, XPointer is the standard that has progressed most slowly. There are several reasons. One is that adoption of XPointer has been very slow, and at the time of writing there is only one implementation available. This is not sufficient to act as a catalyst for the W3C standardization process to continue. Some implementors are concerned that XPointer is too complex (in particular, its concept of ranges) and that this keeps vendors from supporting it. There have also been attempts to create profiles of XPointer (which exclude ranges and are therefore much easier to implement); but this would significantly reduce the functionality supported by the core standard, and so far the W3C working group has not agreed to this plan. Unfortunately, XPointer is one of the essential building blocks of the XML linking framework; but as long as the W3C standardization process remains stalled, there will be either little or no progress or some vendors will introduce proprietary solutions to the problem of addressing subresources.

Apart from these more political issues, XPointer is already becoming somewhat outdated by the continuing development of the standards on which it is based—most particularly, XPath. While XPointer is built on top of XPath 1.0, XPath 2.0 [Berglund+ 01], described in section 5.6, is already under development, and it is very possible that it will reach recommendation status earlier than XPointer. Because of the problems with

XPointer standardization, currently no attempts are being made to base XPointer on XPath 2.0.

It is our opinion that it is often better to have a mediocre standard than no standard at all. While XPath and XSLT have demonstrated that even non-perfect standards can provide many benefits (and the opportunity to improve them with their next release), XPointer's development is an example of how the lack of standardization of an essential component of a bigger framework (the XML linking technologies) can stall the development of a very interesting and promising set of technologies and applications.

6.6 CONCLUSIONS

XPointer is the official fragment identifier for XML documents. Using XPointer, it is possible not only to link complete resources but also to create links between parts of resources. XPointer is built on top of XPath, and it extends XPath's model with some new concepts. This chapter describes XPointer in detail and demonstrates to readers how to create their own XPointers. These XPointers may then be used in links, which are described in the following chapter.

7

XML Linking Language

In this section we describe the XML Linking Language (XLink) [DeRose+ 01b], which defines how hyperlinks can be used in an XML-based environment. In section 1.3, we described how linking is done in today's Web. This description is based on the assumption that resources use HTML as their document markup language. However, increasingly XML documents will become available on the Web. There are two possibilities regarding how hyperlinks can be used with XML documents:

- *Application-specific hyperlink definitions.* It is possible to define hyperlinks specifically for certain application areas. One example is XHTML, where the `<a>` element is defined to have the same semantics as HTML's `<A>` element.[1] However, this approach requires XML processors to have built-in knowledge of these specific applications, otherwise they will not recognize the element's hyperlink semantics. Consequently, this approach is not very general and reduces XML's usefulness as a mechanism to freely define and distribute application-specific hypermedia document types.

- *General hyperlink specification mechanism.* In contrast to an application-specific definition of hyperlinks, a general mechanism for using hyperlinks in XML documents can be defined. This is exactly what XLink does. XLink is an application-independent way to use hyperlinks in XML documents, so that an XLink-aware application will be able to recognize and correctly interpret hyperlinks in any XML document, as long as the document uses XLink for its hyperlinks. This works regardless of the actual schema the document is using.

Since XLink defines a general mechanism for embedding hyperlinks in XML documents, it must define a mechanism that enables XLink-specific

---

[1]It should be noted that HTML by definition is case-insensitive, while XHTML accepts only lowercase element and attribute names.

information to be recognized in an XML document. This aspect of XLink is described in section 7.1. XLink makes it possible to specify different types of links using a number of different element types, described in section 7.2. For actually embedding the hyperlink information into XML documents, XLink uses a number of attributes to assign different hyperlink semantics to XML elements, and these attributes are described in detail in section 7.3. Section 7.4 contains explanations of the processing model and conformance requirements that must be satisfied by applications claiming to implement XLink. In section 7.5, we look at how XLinks may be utilized. Finally, section 7.6 describes the future of XLink.

7.1 EMBEDDING LINKS INTO XML DOCUMENTS

XML, as described in section 4.1, is a language for the specification of document types and instances (i.e., documents) of these types. As such, element and attribute names in XML are in no way restricted (except for the syntactic naming rules given by the XML specification) and can be freely chosen by document type authors. However, when XML Namespaces (described in section 4.2) are taken into account, the rules for XML names become a bit more restrictive by dividing names into a namespace prefix and a local part specific to a particular namespace. XLink takes advantage of the XML Namespaces mechanism by defining a namespace of its own. (The official XLink namespace URI is `http://www.w3.org/1999/xlink/namespace/`.) Consequently, any applications implementing XLink must also implement XML Namespaces.

XLink's model of embedding links into XML documents is very simple. XLink defines a number of attributes (described in detail in section 7.3), and these attributes are all in the *global attribute partition* of the XLink namespace (as described in section 4.2). This means that once the XLink namespace has been declared, these attributes can be used on elements from any namespace. The purpose of this is to provide XLink with a way to assign hyperlink semantics to arbitrary elements. The following short XML fragment demonstrates this method of embedding XLink into XML documents:

```
<TypeA xmlns:xlink="http://www.w3.org/1999/xlink/namespace/">
  ....
  <TypeB xlink:type="simple" xlink:href="http://transcluding.com/">
    ....
  </TypeB>
</TypeA>
```

In this example, an arbitrary element (`TypeB`) is employed as an XLink simple link by using two attributes from XLink's namespace on that element. Since, from XML's point of view, the XLink attributes are normal attributes, they have to be declared in the document's DTD. Consequently, the DTD designer must be aware of the fact that XLink is going to be used. However, if DTD designers want to declare elements as being XLink hyperlinks in a more built-in fashion, they can do so by declaring the XLink attributes in the DTD using default values, as shown in the following example:

```
<!ATTLIST TypeA
  xmlns:xlink   CDATA     #FIXED "http://www.w3.org/1999/xlink/namespace/"
>

<!ATTLIST TypeB
  xlink:type    (simple) #FIXED "simple"
  xlink:href    CDATA     #REQUIRED
>

<TypeA>
  ....
    <TypeB xlink:href="http://transcluding.com/">
      ....
    </TypeB>
</TypeA>
```

In this case, the `xmlns:xlink` and `xlink:type` attributes are declared as having fixed values in the DTD, so the attributes do not need to be specified on the element instances. The `xlink:href` attribute is declared as being mandatory and, therefore, must be specified on the element instance. The results of this declaration are that the `TypeB` element type becomes a simple XLink element type by default and that any occurrence of this element has to specify the `xlink:href` attribute for designating the hyperlink's destination (see section 7.5.1 for a more detailed discussion of this technique).

In these examples, we have used the simplest way of specifying hyperlinks with XLink. This method is very similar to HTML's linking mechanisms, but it also has the same restrictions as HTML. However, XLink supports a much more powerful linking model, which is explained in detail in chapter 3 and reviewed in the subsequent section on XLink link types. The basic mechanism of using XLink in the context of XML documents is the same for the simple as well as for the more complex linking situations in XLink.

7.2 LINK TYPES AND ELEMENT TYPES

XLink defines two different types of links, described in section 7.2.1. These conceptual link types utilize certain XML element types (identified by

Table 7.1 Relation Between XLink Link and Element Types

XLink Link Type	Related XLink Element Type(s)
simple	`simple`
extended	`extended`, `locator`, `arc`, `resource`, `title`

XLink attributes) for their implementation. Specifically, the XLink element types, described in section 7.2.2, are different from the conceptual link types supported by XLink. (This can be confusing when starting to learn XLink, because one link often is represented by more than one XML element.) The method of expressing XLink information in XML (i.e., by using XML elements that are interpreted as XLink elements because they contain XLink-conforming attributes) makes it necessary to make some information repeatable by defining specific element types for it. (XML attributes can occur only once on an element, so repeatable information has to be represented by child elements rather than attributes.) Table 7.1 shows how the two concepts relate.

As can be seen, XLink extended links use a number of XLink element types, while XLink simple links use only one. The reason for this is XLink's goal to make the transition from HTML's linking style to XLink easy by providing a mechanism (the simple links) that is very similar to HTML links. In the following two sections, we discuss in detail the link types and the element types.

7.2.1 XLink Link Types

XLink supports two types of links: *simple* and *extended*. While the simple links are modeled after HTML's linking model (making a transition from HTML links to XLink simple links very easy), XLink's extended links are far more powerful and are intended to be used by applications requiring a more elaborate linking model than HTML's. Conceptually, simple links can be viewed as a special case of extended links, but since they use a different syntax, they are regarded as a different type of link. Before we discuss XLink's link types, we will revisit three key concepts introduced in chapter 3.

- *Number of linked resources.* The number of resources included in a link (called the *participating resources*) is one of the key aspects of every link and every link model. While HTML constrains this number to two resources (the local anchor and the remote resource), theoretically this number can be anything between one[2] (being equivalent to an annotation of a resource) and a very large number.

- *Outbound/inbound/out-of-line.* Outbound and inbound links are links in which at least one of the participating resources is part of the link itself (as a starting resource in the case of outbound links, as an ending resource in the case of inbound links). HTML is restricted to outbound links, because the local anchor (which is the starting resource of the link) is defined to be the content of the <A> element. An out-of-line link, however, does not have any of the participating resources as part of the link itself. Therefore, it can be moved around much more easily and, in particular, can be used to create links between resources for which the link creator has no write access.

- *Unidirectional/multidirectional.* Unidirectional links can be traversed only in one direction. For example, HTML links point from the <A> element's occurrence to the remote resource. If links are out-of-line, then they can be used from all participating resources to initiate traversal. Every link that can be used for traversal from more than one of its participating resources is said to be multidirectional.[3] This, however, also includes the possibility that the link itself contains information limiting its possibilities for traversal, for example, the specification that one participating resource of a link can never be used as a target for traversal.

Knowing these basic properties of links, we can now take a closer look at XLink's link types and how they are used within XML documents.

Simple Links

XLink simple links are very similar to the links provided by HTML. Simple links associate two resources[4] with a unidirectional link, and they are always

---

[2] A link having no resources would also be a valid XLink, but it would not make any sense (maybe only as a placeholder).

[3] It is important to recognize that the popular "back" button in today's browsers does not make HTML links multidirectional, since it is a feature of the browser (locally storing a history of previously visited HTML pages) and not of the link itself. Obviously, one cannot initiate traversal in the "back" direction if the current resource has not been the result of a previous traversal (i.e., one cannot use the browser's "back" button if the browser has only just been started).

[4] Note that the XLink recommendation contains a slight contradiction. In one place it states, "A simple link is a link that associates exactly two resources, one local and one remote, with an arc going from the former to the latter," and then in another place it states, "It is not an error for a simple-type element to have no locator (`href`) attribute value. If a value is not provided, the link is simply untraversable. Such a link may still be useful, for example, to associate properties with the resource by means of XLink attributes." In other words, a simple link may be missing the `href` attribute and so have only a single participating resource.

inline. The model of a simple link asserts one local resource (which is part of the link), one remote resource, and a relationship between these two resources that makes it possible to traverse the link from the local resource to the remote resource. Since a simple link is inline, it cannot by definition be multidirectional because traversal can be initiated only from the local resource.

Extended Links

XLink's extended links are more powerful and flexible, and their functionality is a superset of that of XLink's simple links (i.e., all that can be done with a simple link can also be done with an extended link). One generalization of extended links is that they can associate any number of resources, as shown in Figure 7.1. In this figure, the Xlink (represented by the oval) associates five resources, three of which are local resources (indicated by the **resource** attribute value, which will be explained in detail in section 7.3). Consequently, this link is an inline link. The XML representation of this link would include an **extended** type element with three **resource** type and two **locator** type children. Since there are no explicit specifications on how the link may be traversed, traversal is possible from and to all participating resources.

One of the advanced features of XLink is that traversal rules for the participating resources can be specified. These rules define the direction in which an XLink can be traversed. Figure 7.2 shows a scenario where the extended XLink of the previous example has been more specifically defined

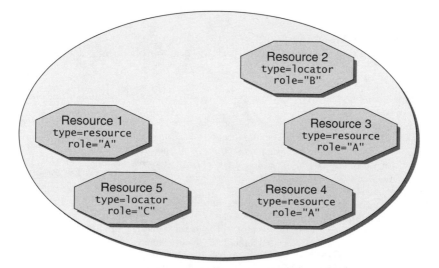

Figure 7.1   Inline extended link

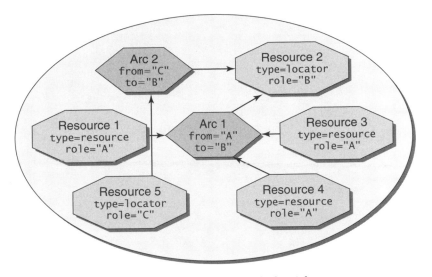

Figure 7.2 Inline extended link with arcs

using two traversal rules.[5] These rules use the `role` attributes of the link's participating resources for specifying the resources between which traversal should be allowed. The XML representation of this link would include an `extended` type element with three `resource` type, two `locator` type, and two `arc` type children. The participating resources of this link are exactly the same as the participating resources of the link in Figure 7.1, but the additional traversal rules define different traversal semantics for this link (for example, it is not possible to traverse this link from Resource 2 to Resource 1 because the traversal rule Arc 1 allows traversal only in the opposite direction).

The previous examples assumed that there are local resources. However, XLink extended links can also be used as out-of-line links, in which case none of the participating resources reside with the link description itself. This scenario is shown in Figure 7.3. In this case, all participating resources are specified as being remote by using the `locator` attribute value. The interesting observation about this link is that it can be created and managed entirely independently from all its participating resources. The XML representation of this link would include an **extended** type element with five **locator** type children. As with our first example of inline links,

---

[5]In Figures 7.1 through 7.4, we have differentiated types of link information graphically. The link itself is represented by a surrounding oval, resources are shown as octagons, and arcs are depicted by hexagons. These entities are conceptually different, but XLink maps them all to XML element types differentiated by special attributes (described in section 7.3).

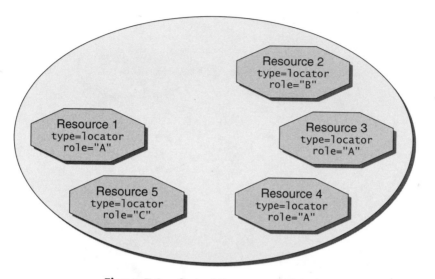

Figure 7.3   Out-of-line extended link

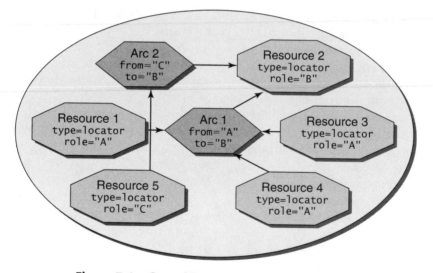

Figure 7.4   Out-of-line extended link with arcs

the first example of out-of-line links does not specify any traversal rules, thereby implicitly allowing the traversal of the link in any direction.

The final example of an extended XLink is an out-of-line link specifying traversal rules, as shown in Figure 7.4. In this example, all participating resources are still specified as being remote; but in addition to the participating resources, the link also specifies rules for the possible traversals.

The XML representation of this link would include an **extended** type element with five **locator** type and two **arc** type children. The rules specified for this example are the same as shown in Figure 7.2, so that these two links are functionally equivalent. However, whereas the link shown in Figure 7.2 has three local participating resources (i.e., resources that are part of the link itself), the link shown in Figure 7.4 does not have any local resources and can therefore be stored and manipulated independently from any of the resources it is linking.

However, this rather conceptual view of XLink's extended links does not explain how extended links are actually expressed in XML. Extended links are described differently from simple links, which are specified using only one XLink element type (the **simple** element type). Specifically, extended links use a number of different element types. In the following section, we take a closer look at XLink's element types.

7.2.2 XLink Element Types

As shown in Table 7.1, XLink represents the two link types using a number of XLink element types. Because these element types make sense only in certain combinations, XLink also defines how XLink element types have to be properly nested. This is shown in Table 7.2, where for each XLink element type it is shown which element types are significant as child elements.

Most importantly, the **extended** element type (shown as an oval throughout the figures in the previous section) represents an extended link but does not directly contain (as an element) all important information. It can therefore be regarded as a container for link information. Much of the information for an extended link is not specified in this element type's attributes but rather in other elements contained in the extended link element. These elements are instances of element types described in the following sections.

Table 7.2 XLink Element Type Relationships

Element Type	Significant Child Element Type(s)	Page
simple	none	173
extended	locator, arc, resource, title	174
locator	title	178
arc	title	178
resource	none	178
title	none	178

Resource

This element type is represented by an octagon in the example figures. In Web terms, a resource is anything that can be addressed via a URI; and typically a link associates several resources. In XLink, resources can be either local or remote. Local resources are specified using the `resource` element type (while remote resources are specified using the `locator` element type). An XLink extended link may contain no local resources (in which case, it is an out-of-line link) but may contain any number of local resources, which all must be specified as `resource` element children of the XLink's `extended` element.

Locators

Remote resources participating in extended links are specified using `locator` elements. In our example figures, these elements are also represented by octagons, because `resource` as well as `locator` elements are used to represents resources. A `locator` element carries almost the same information as a `resource` element with the addition of an attribute for actually locating the resource it represents. This is the most important difference between the `locator` and the `resource` element types: While `locator` elements only represent a resource (essentially by pointing to it), a `resource` element actually contains the resource.

Arcs

A link's most important facets are its resources, but it is also important for applications to be able to specify rules for how link traversal may be used. This is possible using `arc` elements, which specify traversal rules for links. In our figures, these traversal rules are represented by hexagons. Traversal rules specify which resources of a link are starting resources (i.e., from which resources traversal may be initiated) and which resources are ending resources (i.e., resources that may be traversed to). Additionally, it is possible to specify how this traversal of arcs should be done (see section 7.3.4 for details) and how these arcs should be interpreted (see section 7.3.3 for details).

Any resource may be a starting as well as an ending resource, and it is possible to define XLink arcs using arc elements that specify a class of arcs (for an example see Figures 7.2 and 7.4, where the Arc 1 element identifies three starting resources and one ending resource, resulting effectively in three arcs). If no arc is specified for an extended link, it is assumed that traversal may go from any resource of the link to any other resource.

Titles

Titles are specified with the `title` element type. They can be used in different contexts, as shown in Table 7.2. In principle, `title` elements can be used in all contexts where the `title` attribute (as described in section 7.3.3) can be used (see Table 7.3 for a list of elements),[6] and the purpose of a `title` element is to enable applications to use more complex title content (i.e., XML text with arbitrarily complex structures) than the simple string content possible with the `title` attribute. Whether titles are specified using attributes or elements is entirely up to the link author. The following list shows which XLink element types a `title` element may be a child of:

- *Child of an* `extended` *element.* In this case, the `title` element contains the title of the extended link (as discussed in the "Extended Links" section earlier in this chapter). This title does not describe any individual property of the link, but the link as a whole.
- *Child of a* `locator` *element.* It is possible to describe the title of remote resources (discussed earlier in the "Locators" section) using a `title` element as a child of the `locator` element representing the remote resource.[7]
- *Child of an* `arc` *element.* Arcs between a link's resources (discussed earlier in the "Arcs" section) can also be described with `title` elements containing the arcs' titles. As is the case with all occurrences of `title` elements, it is up to the link creator to decide whether `title` attributes or `title` elements should be used.

Table 7.3 Attribute Use Patterns for XLink Element Types

Attribute Name	simple	extended	locator	arc	resource	title	Page
arcrole	○			○			183
actuate	○			○			184
from				○			188
href	○		●				182
label			○		○		188
role	○	○	○		○		182
show	○			○			185
title	○	○	○		○		183
to				○			188
type	●	●	●	●	●	●	180

---

[6]The only exception to this is the `simple` element type, which may have a `title` attribute, but not a `title` element type child.

[7]It is not possible to use `title` element type children for the `resource` element (see the "Resource" section on the preceding page). The reason for this asymmetry between remote and local resources is not clear from the XLink specification.

It is important to note that in all cases it is perfectly legal for multiple `title` elements to appear as children of the same parent XLink element, which may be very useful for internationalization and localization purposes. How an XLink application chooses which `title` element to display is outside the scope of the XLink specification, but one obvious approach would be to use XML's `xml:lang` attribute, which identifies languages of element attributes and content by using language tags as defined by Internet RFC 3066 [Alvestrand 01] (see section 7.5.1 for an example).

7.3 ATTRIBUTES

In the previous section, we presented the XLink link types (conceptually, as well as their mapping onto element types); while in section 7.1, we described the basic mechanism of embedding XLinks into XML documents. Now we discuss how to combine these two issues, describing how different aspects of various types of XLinks can be specified in XML documents using particular attributes of the XLink element types.

XLink uses attributes for embedding the link formation in XML documents. XLink defines ten attributes, grouped into five different categories: element type attribute (`type`), locator attribute (`href`), semantic attributes (`role`, `arcrole`, `title`), behavior attributes (`actuate`, `show`), and traversal attributes (`label`, `from`, `to`). These attributes are shown in Table 7.3. In this table, a "•" sign indicates a mandatory attribute,[8] while a "o" sign indicates attributes that are optional. If an attribute occurs on an element but is neither mandatory nor optional for this element type, then it does not convey any XLink semantics.

7.3.1 Element Type Attribute

XLink uses attributes to embed links into XML documents, and one of these, the `type` attribute, assigns XLink semantics to the element on which it appears. It is a very important attribute because it defines which other XLink attributes can be used on a particular element (according to the rules summarized in Table 7.3).

type
The `type` attribute determines the XML Linking Language element type of the element that it appears on. Because of the fact that there is a predefined

---

[8]It is easy to understand why the `type` attribute is mandatory for all XLink element types—because it has to be present to specify the element's type. Without the `type` attribute, it wouldn't be possible to specify an element as being of a certain XLink element type.

set of XLink element types, the `type` attribute may have only the following values:

- `simple` – This value defines an element as being an XLink simple link. Simple links provide the easiest way to use XLink and are very similar in nature to the links provided by HTML. Simple links are described in detail in the "Simple Links" section earlier in this chapter. One important aspect of simple links is that all information relevant for the link is specified in attributes of the simple link element.

- `extended` – XLink extended links are more complex to use than simple links, but are also more powerful. The "Extended Links" section describes their possible uses. It is important to note that most of the information necessary for an extended link is not specified in attributes of the extended link's element but in attributes of other child XLink elements contained in the extended link element.

- `locator`, `arc`, `resource`, `title` – These values are used to assign XLink semantics to elements according to the element types described earlier in the "XLink Element Types" section. These element types may appear only as direct or indirect children of `extended` type elements (according to the relationship shown in Table 7.2).

- `none` – This value can be used to declare explicitly that an element does not have any XLink-specific semantics, so that any attributes appearing on the element or any XLink elements appearing within the element do not have any XLink semantics.

Obviously, the `type` attribute has to be mandatory for all XLink element types because it is the only way an XLink application can identify XLink element types in an XML document.

7.3.2 Locator Attribute

Links connect resources, and therefore one of the most important aspects of a link is the actual identification of these resources. In XLink, resources can be either local (implicitly for simple links, or explicitly by using `resource` type elements as described in the "Resource" section earlier in this chapter) or remote. Remote resources may occur in simple as well as in extended links; and in both cases the same attribute is used, the `href` attribute. In the case of simple links, it is used directly on the `simple` type element (it is optional on `simple` type elements because they may be links with only the local resource); and in the case of extended links, it is used on `locator` type elements (it is mandatory on `locator` type elements because their only purpose is to locate remote resources by reference).

href

This attribute has the same name as the corresponding attribute in HTML's link element, and it serves the same purpose. It is a reference identifying a remote resource; and because XLink is part of the Web architecture, resources must always be identified using a URI reference as described in section 3.2. If the URI points into a resource (i.e., contains a fragment identifier) and this resource is an XML document, then the fragment identifier must be an XPointer.

The href attribute is the only way to locate remote resources in XLink, and there is no mechanism for making additional assertions about these resources. If applications are interested in additional functionality—for example, for ensuring link integrity, such as with checksums, cache identifiers, or anything else—it is possible to specify this information in additional attributes specific to the application and not in XLink's namespace.

7.3.3 Semantic Attributes

Not only do links associate resources, but this association also has some meaning. This meaning is, however, application-specific—in other words, there is no predefined set of "link meanings" in XLink. For example, a link for the book you are currently reading may associate resources such as the authors' personal Web pages, the publisher's Web site, a number of online stores selling the book, several Web pages with reviews of the book, and, of course, the book's own Web site. While XLink makes it possible to create such a link, there is no standardized way to describe the actual semantics of the linked resources. XLink follows the path of many Web technologies and defines a way in which semantic information may be specified but does not define a given set of semantics.

Semantics are specified using URI references. Both attributes (role and arcrole), which carry semantic information that can be interpreted by applications, must be URI references. This reference identifies a resource that describes the intended semantics, but XLink makes no assumption about the actual resource format. In addition to the two machine-readable semantic attributes, there is one that is intended to present semantics in a human-readable way (title). The following XLink attributes can be used to specify semantic information:

role

This attribute describes the role that an item plays. It may be used to describe the role of a link (appearing on a simple or extended element) or the role of a resource (appearing on a locator or resource element). Even though the role attribute has the same name for link (simple/extended) and resource (locator/resource) elements, notice that it serves different purposes. In the first case, it describes the role of the complete link (e.g., that a particular link is describing a book); while in the latter case, it specifies the role of a particular resource within the link (i.e., the "book" link may associate resources describing people, publishers, magazines, and the book itself).

arcrole

While the `role` attribute describes the roles of a link and a resource within a link, the `arcrole` attribute describes the role of an arc. In XLink, arcs are represented either by `arc` elements or, implicitly, by a `simple` element; and consequently these are the two element types that may carry an `arcrole` attribute.

In our previous example of the link describing this book, the arcs connecting the various resources of the link may carry `arcrole` attributes that define a "person" resource as being the author of a "book" resource. One resource—for example, a publisher—may have different arcs with different roles attached. For example, the book's publisher may have two arcs going from the "book" resource to the "publisher" resource—one with an `arcrole` attribute for the book's publication; the other with an `arcrole` attribute indicating that the publisher is also running an online store selling the book.

There is one special case of an `arcrole` attribute defined in the XLink specification. This is the special case of a linkbase, where the arc identifies a linkbase for a particular resource. This case is discussed in detail in section 7.5.3.

title

While the `role` and the `arcrole` attributes are meant to carry machine-readable role descriptions, the `title` attribute is intended to contain human-readable information about the element on which it appears. It is allowed for all elements that identify links and/or resources (i.e., `simple`, `extended`, `locator`, and `resource` elements).

In XML, attributes can carry only character data—in other words, it is not possible to use structured XML information as an attribute value. If link authors want to create titles that are more than simple character strings (e.g., structured titles or titles in different languages for internationalization purposes), they can instead use the `title` element type (or even use both a `title` attribute and a `title` element), as described in the "Titles" section earlier in this chapter.

XLink's semantic attributes provide a mechanism for link authors to associate semantic information with links or, more specifically, with a link as a whole, its resources, or its arcs. The semantics are entirely application-dependent. XLink's only requires them to be expressed as URI references.

The actual resources behind these references are in no way prescribed or restricted by XLink. Furthermore, if link authors feel that XLink's `role` and `arcrole` attributes are not sufficient for a particular application, they are free to supplement links with their own, non-XLink, semantic information.

7.3.4 Behavior Attributes

A link describes an association between several resources. Generally, applications are expected to do something with links, and as described in section 1.3.2, even today's restricted linking technologies result in varying behaviors, depending on what kind of link is encountered when displaying a Web page (for example, `<A>` links are visually formatted and users may traverse them by clicking on them, while `<IMG>` links are automatically traversed by the browser to embed the image into the formatted Web page). It is not possible to describe all possible behaviors of applications in advance (for example, style sheet processing also uses links, but the actual process of applying a style sheet is much too complex to be described in a generic way), but XLink defines a restricted two-dimensional vocabulary of how applications should behave when traversing a link. Because traversal always implies an arc (links may be traversed only in the ways prescribed by the link's arcs), both attributes may be used only on `arc` or `simple` elements (the latter implicitly defining an arc between the local and the remote resource). The two attributes are described in the following sections.

actuate

If an application encounters a link with arcs leading from a starting resource currently being presented to ending resources located elsewhere (for example, a different XML document), it is important to determine the application's behavior. The `actuate` attribute describes the desired timing of link traversal and can have the following values:

- `onLoad` – This value instructs the application to traverse to the ending resource immediately on loading the starting resource (i.e., to perform automatic initial processing). This effect is well-known from HTML's mechanism for using images, as follows:

  `<IMG SRC="http://www.w3.org/Icons/w3c_main" ALT="W3C Logo">`

  In this example, the browser traverses the link when formatting the HTML page. Even if the HTML page contains more than one `<IMG>` element, the browser loads all images, because HTML defines this behavior as being the default for images. (It can be turned off in most browsers by disabling the automatic image loading.)

- onRequest – In many cases, links are not to be followed automatically, but are traversed on request, for example, by user interactions. In case of requested traversal, the application must make sure that a starting resource (i.e., anchor) can be identified (in most browsers, this is achieved by different formatting, for example, underlining and/or color) and that the user can trigger traversal through some kind of interface (in most browsers, a simple mouse click initiates link traversal). HTML's links are a good example for this behavior, as follows:

```
<A HREF="http://transcluding.com">...</A>
```

A link like this will display the <A> element's content, formatted in a way that identifies it as a link, and if the user points and clicks on it with the pointer, the browser will traverse the link—in other words, load the target document.

- other – The two predefined values for the **actuate** attribute probably cover many application areas, but it is possible that some applications may want to specify alternative (or additional) semantics. XLink therefore supports an **other** value for the **actuate** attribute, which instructs the XLink processor to look for application-specific markup further describing the expected behavior for link traversal.

- none – If a link author explicitly wants to specify no specific actuation semantics for the traversal to the ending resource, this can be done using the **none** value, which also implies that there is no markup that is application-specific from which any behavior could be determined.

show

The **show** attribute describes how the result of the link traversal should be presented. The values supported by XLink are as follows:

- new – This value indicates that the resource resulting from the traversal should be presented in a new presentation context, for example, a new window. The most popular example for this behavior can be easily expressed in HTML:

```
<A HREF="http://transcluding.com" TARGET="_blank">...</A>
```

A browser traversing this link will open a new window with the target page in it, while the page containing the link will still be visible in its original window.

- replace – In this case, the presentation context containing the start-ing resource (i.e., the resource from which traversal was initiated) should be replaced by the ending resource. This is the default behavior of HTML links as shown in the following example:

```
<A HREF="http://transcluding.com">...</A>
```

A second, more explicitly coded variant is as shown:

```
<A HREF="http://transcluding.com" TARGET="_self">...</A>
```

Clicking on a link like this will instruct the browser to load the target page into the same window as the link, effectively replacing the resource containing the link with the new resource.[9]

Consequently, a traversal based on `actuate="onLoad"` and `show="replace"` attributes will have an effect similar to automatic forwarding to the presentation context of the ending resource. However, if there is more than one starting resource specifying this behavior, the application behavior is unconstrained by the XLink specification.

- embed – In this case, the application is instructed to embed the ending resource into the presentation context of the starting resource, with the exact behavior of embedding being application-dependent. HTML also has an example for this case:

```
<IMG SRC="http://www.w3.org/Icons/w3c_main" ALT="W3C Logo">
```

The browser typically embeds the referenced image into the formatted document (unless image loading is turned off in the browser). XLink's `embed` value implies that the starting resource is replaced by the ending resource.[10] In almost all cases, this is different from the `replace` value, which replaces the entire presentation context containing the starting resource.[11]

The `embed` value combined with an `actuate="onLoad"` attribute can be used to implement transclusion. XLink does not define how an application should display embedded content, but a reasonable

---

[9]It is important to note that in this case not only is the starting resource of the link replaced (this would be only the `<A>` element's content) but also the complete presentation context of this resource (i.e., the whole Web page).

[10]Because the `<IMG>` element is always empty, it is not important or is it even apparent that the starting resource (i.e., the `<IMG>` element's empty content) is replaced by the ending resource.

[11]Consequently, if the starting resource is the whole document, then `replace` and `embed` will have the same effect.

implementation should identify the embedded content as coming from another resource and should also provide a way for the user to view the embedded content in its original context.

- **other** – Embedding and replacing in many cases may be sufficient to describe the behavior of links that are used only for creating interlinked presentations. However, links may also imply some kind of processing or other behavior, such as that resulting from HTML's style sheet mechanism:

```
<LINK REL="stylesheet" TYPE="text/css" HREF="general.css">
```

In this case, the browser should not traverse the link to somehow display the ending resource of the link, but instead should retrieve the ending resource (the CSS style sheet) and use it to style the starting resource. This kind of behavior is highly application-specific, and XLink therefore supports an **other** value for the **show** attribute, which instructs the XLink processor to look for markup that is application-specific further describing the expected behavior on link traversal.

- **none** – If a link author explicitly wants to associate no specific behavior with the traversal to the ending resource, this can be done using the **none** value, which also implies that there is no application-specific markup from which any behavior can be determined.

If the starting and/or the ending resource of a link traversal consists of multiple non-contiguous locations, then application behavior is unconstrained. However, application designers either should make sure that resources are always contiguous, or should specify what they expect applications to do in case of non-contiguous locations.

Even though it is fairly simple to explain XLink's behavior attributes using analogies to HTML, the issues get much more complicated when thinking of more complex presentation models such as XML documents formatted by XSL style sheets. In this case, it is easily possible for one contiguous starting resource in the underlying XML document to appear several times in the formatted result (for example, a heading appearing in the table of contents as well as the content itself),[12] and a reasonable application behavior in cases such as this is hard to define. The W3C has noticed this problem and is currently working on a presentation model for XLink [Walsh 01], which we discuss in section 8.1.1.

---

[12]Note that this case is different from non-contiguous resources, which are explicitly excluded from the **show** attribute's behavior in the XLink specification.

7.3.5 Traversal Attributes

XLink's traversal attributes are used to make the actual connection between a link's arcs (represented by `arc` elements) and a link's resources (represented by `locator` and/or `resource` elements). The mechanism for this is very easy to understand—resources can be labeled with names, and arcs use these names. XLink supports the following attributes:

`label`
This attribute can be used to label resources and may therefore appear on `locator` and/or `resource` elements. Its value must be a valid namespace-compliant XML name. It is not required to be unique within a link (i.e., there can be several resources within one link having the same label).

`from`
The `from` attribute may appear on an `arc` element and specifies the name of the starting resource. There must be at least one resource having a label with that name.

`to`
Complementary to the `from` attribute, the `to` attribute also appears on `arc` elements and specifies the name of the ending resource. There must be at least one resource having a label with that name.

XLink's concept of arcs is described in the "Arcs" section earlier in this chapter. The most important aspect to keep in mind is that one `arc` element can define more than one arc, which is the case if the `from` and/or `to` attribute specify labels that appear on more than one of the link's resources.

7.4 INTERPRETATION OF XLINKS

XLink is a specification that defines a generic way for expressing link information in XML. As such, it is built on top of XML and associated standards, which need to be observed by any application processing XLinks. The next section summarizes the processing requirements that must be met when working with XLink. Furthermore, XLink defines conformance criteria that go beyond the requirements of the underlying XML standards, and section 7.4.2 describes these conformance requirements.

7.4.1 Processing

XLink is built on top of the Extensible Markup Language, and consequently, XML and some of its important companion standards are essential for correctly processing XLinks. In particular, the following standards must be observed:

- *XML* [Bray+ 00] (see section 4.1) – XML is the foundation of XLink, which specifies information in terms of XML elements and attributes. Consequently, XML defines how elements and attributes are used syntactically within an XML document.

- *XML Namespaces* [Bray+ 99] (see section 4.2) – XLink directly uses XML Namespaces by defining a namespace of its own and expressing all information as attributes within this namespace. For applications to be able to correctly and unambiguously identify XLink information within an XML document, the XML document not only has to be well formed but also has to be compliant with the XML Namespace specification.

- *XML Base* [Marsh 01] (see section 4.3) – Given that XLink is used for linking between resources, it obviously has a strong reliance on references to resources, and these references may be absolute or relative. In the case of relative references, they must be interpreted according to the rules defined by XML Base, which makes it necessary for XLink applications to implement XML Base.

- *URI* [Berners-Lee+ 98; Hinden+ 99] (see section 3.2) – References to resources are always given as URI references, and any application interpreting these references must do so according to the relevant specifications. This does not mean that an XLink application will always be able to retrieve all referenced resources (for example, if a URI reference specifies a scheme not supported by the processing application, then this resource cannot be retrieved), but at least it must be able to correctly process and interpret these references.

Even though XLink specifies all attributes in XML syntax, the standard explicitly states that it is not necessary for XLink applications to work only with XML syntax. If XLink applications instead are set up to work with XML's data model (the XML Infoset [Cowan & Tobin 01], as described in section 4.5), they are allowed to do so. Consequently, it is possible to implement XLink applications that operate on XML Infoset information items and thus never generate or use XML syntax. In this case, XLink's XML syntax would serve only as an exchange syntax and export format to other XLink applications, while internally XLink would be used as a data model.

7.4.2 Conformance

The processing requirements described in the previous section make sure that XLink applications always work with XML syntax and that certain rules, such as how to interpret relative URI references, are followed. However, XLink also defines constraints not covered by the standards listed in the previous section. These constraints must also be followed by XLink applications. XLink describes conformance on a per-element basis, stating that an XML element conforms to XLink if the following are true:

1. It has a `type` attribute from the XLink namespace whose value is one of `simple`, `extended`, `locator`, `arc`, `resource`, `title`, or `none`.

2. It adheres to the conformance constraints imposed by the chosen XLink element type, as shown in Tables 7.2 and 7.3. While XLink defines that extraneous (i.e., neither mandatory nor optional) elements or attributes are simply ignored (i.e., they do not carry any XLink semantics), it is an error if mandatory elements or attributes are not present.

Applications conform to XLink if they process XML documents or XML Infosets containing conforming XLink elements and observe all rules defined by XLink, for example, the requirement that `from` and `to` attributes of the `arc` elements must use names that appear on at least one of the link's resources.

7.5 USAGE

So far, we have described how XLink can be used to define linking information for XML environments. However, even though this is the foundation on which future XML linking applications will be built, it is also important to have some guidelines for using XLink in an effective way. In this section, we cover some topics that are not essential for XLink from a standards point of view, but that can be very helpful for applying XLink in real-world scenarios.

In particular, in section 7.5.1 we discuss techniques for declaring XLink elements and attributes in schema definitions. Because XLink may be extended for special scenarios where its features are not sufficient, in section 7.5.2 we describe how extensions of XLink can be implemented in schema definitions. Finally, in section 7.5.3 we describe how XLink can be used as the foundation for linkbases and how future applications may use XLink as an export format for huge collections of link information.

7.5.1 XLink Element and Attribute Declaration

XLink defines a number of attributes for embedding link information into XML documents, but it does not make any assumptions about the schema being used for the documents containing XLinks. It is perfectly legal for

XML documents containing XLink information to have no schema at all, in which case they would be well-formed documents (as opposed to valid documents). However, in many cases it is advisable to define schemas when working with XLink, because validating a document may be a useful step in detecting errors as early as possible.

Because XLink makes no assumptions about schemas, it is the author's choice alone as to which schema language to use. The two most popular candidates are DTDs, as defined in the XML specification itself, and XML Schema [Biron & Malhotra 01; Thompson+ 01]. Although we limit our discussion to DTDs (for the sake of brevity), the same principles that we describe for defining DTDs for XLink content also apply to XML Schema (and to any other schema language for XML).

As we have discussed, XLink information is carried only by attributes, even though the `type` attribute also introduces a way to assign XLink semantics to elements. Most applications will probably combine their own data model (which will be entirely application-specific) with XLink's data model to make their data model XLink-enabled. The advantage of this approach is to be able to use existing software for creating, modifying, managing, and presenting XLinks within XML documents. In most cases, application designers will probably want to assign XLink semantics to some of their elements, thus making them links in the XLink sense. This can easily be achieved by defining `#FIXED` attributes for the elements that should have XLink semantics. Consider the following:

```
<!ELEMENT simple ANY >
<!ATTLIST simple
  xmlns:xlink     CDATA        #FIXED "http://www.w3.org/1999/xlink"
  xlink:type      ( simple )   #FIXED "simple"
  xlink:href      CDATA        #REQUIRED
  xlink:role      CDATA        #IMPLIED
  xlink:arcrole   CDATA        #IMPLIED
  xlink:title     CDATA        #IMPLIED
  xlink:show      ( new
                  | replace
                  | embed
                  | other
                  | none )     #IMPLIED
  xlink:actuate   ( onLoad
                  | onRequest
                  | other
                  | none )     #IMPLIED >
```

In this example, the `simple` element type has fixed attributes that declare the namespace[13] and the element's XLink element type (in this case,

---

[13]If the element is always used in the same document type, then the namespace could simply be declared once on the document element.

it is declared to be a simple link). The other attributes declared for the `simple` element type represent the relevant XLink attributes, as shown in Table 7.3. It should be noted that for some attributes (`title`, `show`, and `actuate`), the allowed values can be specified in the DTD; while for other attributes (`href`, `role`, and `arcrole`), the DTD declaration is too permissive, so that further constraints at the application level are necessary to make sure that the element not only is valid XML but also conforms to XLink.[14] This is a general pattern, showing that some of XLink's constraints can be reflected in a schema while others have to be checked on the application level (i.e., by the application processing the XLinks).

Similar DTD declarations can be made for extended links and the XLink element types associated with them. The XLink specification contains an example of such a declaration.

Two things, which are described next, should always be kept in mind when creating schema definitions for XLink elements and attributes:

1. No schema language today is sufficiently powerful to formally declare all conformance constraints defined by XLink. Different schema languages have different levels of support (for example, URIs have to be declared as simple `CDATA` in DTDs, while XML Schema supports the `anyURI` datatype), though some level of checking on the application level will always be necessary. There are two things to consider:

   - Use a schema language that is as powerful as possible, so that as much checking as possible can be done on the schema level.
   - Use a validation tool that includes XLink support. We currently do not know any XML parser that also validates XLink (or any XLink parser that can be easily put on top of an XML parser); but with the increased support for XLink, software like this will certainly appear.

   Note the following for DTDs as well as for XML Schema: Defining things in a declarative way is always better than writing code, so care should be taken to avoid as much as possible checking that needs to be coded within applications.

2. Even though XLink defines conformance constraints that ensure links can always be interpreted in a meaningful way, applications may

---

[14]In this case, XML Schema would provide an easy way to already declare the attributes with the appropriate syntactic constraints by using the `anyURI` datatype. Consequently, when XML Schema instead of DTDs is used, applications can rely on stronger validation and thus can be kept smaller and less complex.

choose to be more restrictive and define more constraints. The following are examples:

- For internationalization purposes, applications may choose to generally disallow `title` attributes and instead require as many `title` elements to be present as there are languages to be supported. This requirement could be implemented in a number of different ways, including the following:

```
<!ELEMENT locator  ( title-en, title-de, title* ) >
<!ELEMENT title-en ANY >
<!ATTLIST title-en
  xml:lang         CDATA       #FIXED "en"
  xlink:type       ( title )   #FIXED "title" >
<!ELEMENT title-de ANY >
<!ATTLIST title-de
  xml:lang         CDATA       #FIXED "de"
  xlink:type       ( title )   #FIXED "title" >
<!ELEMENT title    ANY >
<!ATTLIST title
  xml:lang         CDATA       #REQUIRED
  xlink:type       ( title )   #FIXED "title" >
```

In this example, titles for locators would always have to be present in English and German and would be optional in other languages.

- Applications may restrict local resources to certain types of information and may provide elements to make sure that the local resources always have the expected form, as follows:

```
<!ELEMENT book (title, subtitle, isbn?) >
<!ATTLIST book
  xlink:type    ( resource )   #FIXED "resource" >
  xlink:role    CDATA          #FIXED "http://roles.org/book"
  xlink:title   CDATA          #REQUIRED
  xlink:label   NMTOKEN        #REQUIRED >
```

In this example, the type as well as the role of the element is fixed, which makes every **book** element an element that is an XLink resource and that plays the role described by the URI reference supplied as the **role** attribute value. The children of the **book** element contain information further describing the book.

This general technique of constraining the XLink application's linking declarations (by designing the schema to specifically use particular attribute values) can make XLink application development much easier. In particular, the more limitations declaratively specified in the schema, the less work has to be done in the application.

This discussion of what to keep in mind when declaring XLink document types concludes our examination of how to define and use elements and attributes for XLink applications. We have limited our discussion to DTDs, but the general principles are applicable to other schema languages as well. A W3C note [Maler+ 00] is available that specifically discusses how to use XLink in existing document types, but it is limited to XML Schema.

7.5.2 Extending XLink

XLink defines a format for representing links in XML, but it is not the only possible way to define links, and it does not define all possible aspects of link information. For example, an application might want not only to create links to remote resources but also to store these resources in a cache, so that the cached copy is still available if the remote resource itself is unavailable. There are many problems to be solved if caching is to be implemented, and the approach we take here certainly is too simple to be used in practice. It is merely intended to illustrate the issue of how to extend XLink.

A cached resource could be treated as a separate resource and associated with the original resource via a link using a special `arcrole` value indicating that one end of the arc is any resource, while the other end is the cached copy. However, from a modeling point of view, this might be overly cumbersome and create too many links. Also, since a cached copy always is associated with a resource, it could be argued that the caching information should be made part of the remote resource's locator, as follows:

```
<!ELEMENT locator    ( title* ) >
<!ATTLIST locator
   xlink:type        ( locator )   #FIXED "locator"
   xlink:href        CDATA         #REQUIRED
   xlink:role        CDATA         #IMPLIED
   xlink:title       CDATA         #IMPLIED
   xlink:label       NMTOKEN       #REQUIRED
   cache-id          NMTOKEN       #REQUIRED
   cache-timestamp   NMTOKEN       #REQUIRED >
```

In this case, the locator element's declaration is extended by two attributes (which are not from the XLink namespace) describing the caching information for the resource represented by the locator. A locator element like this could be interpreted by the application implementing the caching strategy, which could access the cached copy. However, it could also be used by any other XLink application, which would ignore the caching information (because the attributes are not from the XLink namespace), but could provide normal access to the remote resource.

This example demonstrates how we can add additional information to suit applications' needs that go beyond XLink's capabilities but that may still benefit from the linking foundations laid by XLink. Another typical example would be to extend the locator element with checksum information so that applications could easily check whether the remote resource had been changed since the checksum was generated. Again, applications supporting the checksum information would benefit from the possibility of detecting changes in remote resources; while basic XLink applications, although failing to notice whether the resource had been changed, could still use the locators.

7.5.3 Using XLink for Linkbases

One of XLink's most interesting features is its ability to create out-of-line links—links that have only remote resources. A collection of out-of-line links is called a *linkbase,* and XLink provides one mechanism for representing this. Linkbases are not a concept introduced by XLink; and even though every linkbase will include XLink concepts, it is not necessarily limited to them. Consequently, linkbases can be built on top of XLink's model but can also extend XLink where appropriate to make them more useful (such as including cache information or checksums, as discussed before in section 7.5.2).

As described in section 7.3.3, the `arcrole` attribute contains semantic information (in the form of an URI reference) about the arc between two resources. XLink defines one special value for this attribute[15] (`http://www.w3.org/1999/xlink/properties/linkbase`), which indicates that the ending resource is a linkbase for the starting resource. Applications processing this kind of arc are expected to retrieve the linkbase (an XML document containing a collection of XLinks) and extract all links from it that are relevant to the starting resource.

The linkbase as a collection of links is an interesting concept that has been widely studied. Linkbases can be used to change the perspective on content and link handling [Wilde & Lowe 00]. In Figure 7.5 we show how information providers can use the concept of linkbases (shown at the storage

---

[15]This is the only predefined value for semantic attributes in the XLink specification, and the resource behind that URI demonstrates that the specification of semantics often is given only in prose and not in some machine-readable format.

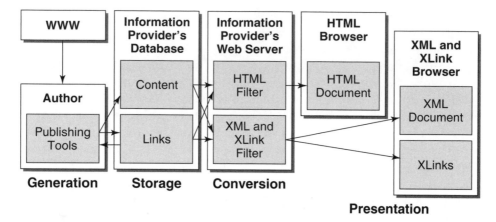

Figure 7.5   XLink and linkbases

level) to create a web of information resources that can be dynamically assembled for presentation. This web is assembled in four stages:

- *Generation.* Authoring tools normally are very content-centric— in other words, they concentrate on the task of creating content. However, when creating content (such as writing articles), authors usually use other interlinked resources (such as Web pages), and authoring tools could be specifically designed to support authors in capturing these interrelationships in the form of links.

- *Storage.* Authoring tools that support capturing link information would require that we not only store the content generated by authors but also store the linking information. On a conceptual level, it is not important exactly how content and links are being stored—whether they use XML-based formats, databases, or other means of storage. The important issue is that we store links separately from content while also ensuring that the content model and the link data model are integrated.

- *Conversion.* While the content is stored in a database or a content management system, the links are kept in a separate linkbase. When we make this information available (in Figure 7.5 this is through a Web server, though many other possibilities also exist), it is necessary to convert the information to a form that can be utilized by appropriate presentation tools.

- *Presentation.* Presentation can be based on very different technologies; but since our focus is highly interlinked information, we assume the use of various Web-based technologies, such as HTML or XML/XLink. The conversion step can be used to adapt the information to any form necessary, probably using some transformation process such as XSLT.

Even though XLink can be used directly at the presentation level (assuming the browser is XLink-compliant), this is not necessarily required. For example, XLink may simply be used as an exchange format for linking information. Prior to presentation, the XLinks are converted to some form of presentation linking (such as the links in HTML). It would make sense to align the system's internal link data model with XLink if it is foreseeable that XLink will be a popular export format, but that would not be necessary.

Further refining the concept of content management and linkbases, it becomes apparent that where we have a large volume of link information, not only do we need to have an effective form of storage (i.e., a linkbase), but we also need appropriate metadata that describes the links. This is where topic maps [ISO 00; Pepper & Moore 01] come into play. Topic maps are a form of semantic net, and they make it possible not only to express semantic information about resources (such as that one resource describes a particular person and another describes a particular city) but also to associate these information items (for example, this particular person has been born in this particular city). This makes it possible to organize the link information much better than by simply collecting links because more semantic information can be captured.

A simple example can be visited at `http://wildesweb.com/glossary/`, which is a glossary of Web-related terms. The glossary itself is stored as one XML document with a data model similar to topic maps. Starting from this XML document, an XSLT style sheet is applied to generate a set of highly interlinked HTML pages and also a printable version, which is available as a PDF document.[16] Even though this is a small example, it shows the basic steps illustrated in Figure 7.5. At the time of writing, no XML/XLink presentation is available because no browser fully supports these formats, but it would be very easy to extend the conversion process with another XSLT style sheet generating XML/XLink from the original XML document. This glossary example also demonstrates that link information can become very important and that services may exist in the future that offer only linkbase access but no content of their own.

One problem currently unsolved in the linkbase scenario is the access to linkbases. Technically, an XLink processor is required to retrieve the complete linkbase and then use only the links relevant to the resource

---

[16]The printable version is generated by transforming the XML document into LaTeX (also using an XSLT style sheet) and then producing a PDF document by using the `pdflatex` program.

currently being processed. This obviously is not a reasonable strategy for large linkbases (primarily due to performance considerations), so it is necessary to have a protocol that enables XLink processors to query a linkbase for certain links (e.g., to request all links in which a certain Web page participates as a starting resource). However, this problem is currently unsolved. We hope that in the future standards will emerge that specify how to query XLink linkbases.

7.6 THE FUTURE OF XLINK

XLink is a very new standard, and software products supporting it are only just starting to appear (see section 8.2 for some examples). However, compared to its companion standard, XPointer, XLink is generally accepted; and we hope that future versions of popular software (such as Web browsers) will offer full XLink support. However, even though XLink and XPointer technically are independent, they complement each other; and we hope that the disruptions in XPointer's development will not also stop XLink's success. This remains to be seen; but regardless of their support in popular software, the lessons learned from XPointer and XLink can already be used to implement much better content management systems than are available today.

One political question about XLink's success is also very interesting: Since XLink's new features (in particular, transclusion and out-of-line links) somehow blur the line between different resources, people and companies may have problems with some of XLink's applications and copyright issues. Even HTML with its limited linking abilities has caused a large number of lawsuits against "illegal links" ("deep linking" is one such example, "framing" is another), and XLink opens new doors in this direction, making copyright infringements more likely than today. How companies (and, in particular, software producers) deal with that problem will be one of the main factors governing the fate of XLink.

7.7 CONCLUSIONS

XLink is the language for embedding link information in XML documents. XLink generalizes and extends HTML's linking model and enables users to create complex links. This chapter describes XLink in detail and builds on the foundations laid in chapter 3. XLink will provide the structural fabric of the XML-enabled Web, and the goal of this chapter is to familiarize readers with all the advanced concepts supported by XLink, such as multi-ended links, third-party links, and linkbases.

Part III

Application
Weaving the Web We Want

8

Authoring Aspects

Up until now, the focus of the book has been on the concepts associated with more sophisticated linking and the emerging technologies that support these concepts. We have largely overlooked how these concepts and technologies might be applied for actual systems within the current Web environment. For example, how do we utilize, in practice, the concepts of out-of-line links and linkbases to support the separation of linking from resources and hence to improve the maintainability of our applications? Investigating issues such as these is the purpose of the next two chapters.

In this chapter, we investigate the authoring of applications to take advantage of XLink and XPointer, as part of the broader XML framework. Specifically, we look at some general issues affecting how we author and use XLink, then we investigate the tools, applications, and environments beginning to emerge. Finally, we consider authoring issues related to how these applications can be most effectively utilized. In the following chapter, we then consider some of the issues that need to be addressed in moving from the current Web environment to the new environment.

8.1 PRACTICAL ISSUES

We begin by considering a number of practical issues that impact how we use XLink and XPointer. Many of these issues relate to the fact that these technologies are still rather immature and hence they are still evolving and changing. Tool support is also rather fragmented. In brief, the key issues we will be discussing can be divided into technological issues (such as the problems introduced by the lack of presentation semantics) and developmental issues (such as the challenges of more complex authoring resulting from a more complex linking model).

8.1.1 Lack of Presentation Semantics

The XLink and XPointer recommendations do not provide any indication of how the resultant links (or anchors) should be presented. This in itself is not necessarily inappropriate—HTML does not, for example, specify how a link should be presented. The usual mechanism of underlining the link is simply a convention that has evolved, initially because of decisions made by browser designers. This is a presentation and formatting issue and is likely to be at least partially addressed by XSL-FO as it evolves. Indeed, we may even see usage conventions emerge in much the same way as they did for HTML links.[1]

The real problem however arises a level above this with the presentation semantics (as distinct from presentation formats). For example, in XLink it is possible to define an arc that has as a destination an XPointer that refers to a location set with multiple locations. XLink does not define how this is to be interpreted. Should the locations be merged sequentially? And if so, in what order? Should the components be uniquely identifiable in the resultant resource (i.e., should a user be able see that the result is actually a composite or should it be seamless)? Similar issues are raised with other forms of linking, such as multisource links and resources that are the source of multiple arcs.

We could resolve these issues at the formatting level or even within the browser, but this raises several concerns. First, it means that we potentially end up with different semantics depending on where and how we view the link. Further, the author's intention will often be link-specific, so it is our belief that the appropriate place to resolve many of these issues is within the link specification (or a normative companion document). Without this mechanism we run the risk of authors manipulating their link specifications to achieve a desired presentation and corrupting the link as a result.

We will illustrate this with an example. In the first case, we wish to create a link that has an arc from a term within a document (say, "transclusion") to a collection of definitions of the term. We could simply create multiple arcs; but this doesn't reflect the semantics of what we wish to express, which is that there is one arc to a composite resource containing definitions that should always be presented together (because doing so provides a comparison we wish to preserve). We do, however, wish the reader to realize that the resource is actually a composite and to be able to identify the various components.

Contrast this example with a situation where we create a link that has an arc from a bank customer's name to a composite resource that contains the details of all their account names and balances (located in

---

[1]However, the issue of XML linking and style is much more complex than HTML's simple linking model, in particular due to the fact that XLink often links XML documents, which in many cases are presented not as plain XML but as styled results of a transformation process such as XSL. Investigation of how this combination of linking and transformation should be handled has only just begun [Walsh 01].

independent locations). In a case such as this, the user need not know that the arc destination is a composite. XLink has no mechanism for expressing the difference between these two examples. At present, issues such as these would be dealt with on an ad hoc basis through proprietary or non-standard attributes added to the link and arc specifications.

8.1.2 Unclear Processing Model

The processing model associated with XLink is still somewhat unclear (work on this issue has started within the W3C [Walsh 01], but it will take some time until there is a consensus on how it should be resolved). This confusion is especially with respect to the interactions between XML, XSL, and XLink. This makes the processing of XML files somewhat awkward. Probably the most complex aspect is that XSL processing can occur on either the server-side or the client-side, but clients always retrieve complete resources and interpret fragments locally (and XPointers identify fragments).

This problem may be a little unclear, so we will explore an example. Consider initially a situation where we have a collection of XML resources (without XLinks) being accessed through a browser. The XML resources can have associated XSLT style sheets used to transform the XML resource for presentation.[2]

This transformation of the XML resources by the XSLT style sheet can occur either in the client (the browser retrieves both the XML resource and the style sheet, performs the transformation, and presents the result) or at the server (the server receives the request for the XML resource, performs the transformation, and returns the resultant resource). Client-side transformation can be important for supporting user-specified presentation formats. Server-side transformations can be important when attempting to support server-based customization or if the browser is not capable of performing the transformation itself.

The problem with the processing model can be seen initially in link traversal.[3] Say we have an arc to `http://aaa.com/b.xml#xpointer(//this/that)`. With this situation, there are two possible processing sequences. In the first, we retrieve the file `b.xml`, transform it by a suitable style sheet, and then apply the XPointer to extract the relevant fragment (presumably for presentation). The second possibility is that we retrieve the

---

[2]This transformation is, at present, typically into HTML or XHTML. In the future, it will be more likely to be into a document using the XSL-FO formatting vocabulary.

[3]Strictly speaking, this is not a problem with links and arc traversal at all. We would encounter this problem with any URI that refers to XML resources and contains a fragment identifier. It is, however, likely to be most evident when we start creating complex linking structures.

resource, apply the fragment identifier to extract the relevant subresource, and then apply a style sheet to this subresource. The two different processing sequences can potentially result in quite different information being presented.

It could be argued that the second scenario is more appropriate, since the arc destination (as expressed by the URI) appears to indicate that we wish to obtain just the fragment specified and then to present this as appropriate. This, however, creates difficulties when (as is often the case) the XSLT-based transformation occurs on the server, before the resource is even returned to the browser where the fragment identifier can be interpreted. But the first scenario may also become hard to deal with if the subresource identified by the XPointer is affected by the style sheet in a non-trivial way (e.g., it could appear in several places in the styled result, or it could not appear at all if the style sheet simply ignores the subresource). Confusing, to say the least!

The situation becomes even less clear when we start dealing with complex links. For example, consider the situation where we have an arc with multiple destinations. How do we process this? One possibility would be for the browser to retrieve the resources, then extract the relevant fragments if appropriate, merge these in some way (as we discussed in the previous section, how this is done is not specified), and then apply an appropriate style sheet. But where and how is this style sheet specified? An alternative would be to retrieve each resource, process it using the relevant style sheets—potentially into a presentation format—and then extract the relevant sections as defined by the fragment identifiers and merge the preformatted information.

One key reason clarification of this processing model is important is that without this clarification we do not know whether the fragment identifiers are applying to the raw XML resources or to the resources after they have been transformed. The identification of subresources is likely to be different depending on from which resource we are extracting the fragment—the resource prior to or the resource after the transformation.

We can circumvent this issue to a small extent by ensuring that the fragment identifiers are designed robustly—such as by specifying the fragment using IDs that survive through the transformation process. This is, however, a rather inadequate solution. We also have a raft of additional problems associated with linkbases. At what point are external linkbases retrieved, analyzed, and integrated with the document? The XSL formatting may well have been constructed in the absence of any knowledge about (third-party) linkbases and so may not contain any relevant formatting for these links. Can we include another XSL document that specifies how to format these third-party links? How do we specify this? Or do we just leave it up to the browser to determine the link presentation independent of any

XSL-specified formatting? And if we do that, then why include any link formatting at all in XSL-FO?

Without clear directions on how these issues will be resolved and given that at the time of writing none of the mainstream browsers support XPointers as fragment identifiers, we simply have to work around these problems. Essentially, we utilize XLinks solely as a server-side representation and use customized server-side processing of the XML files and the associated links. The XLinks simply never make it to the browser—except possibly as simple embedded single-source, single-destination links. This approach unfortunately makes true transclusion an impossibility, because transclusion by definition can be achieved only if the client is able to support it by making content from different resources available within one presentation context.[4] However, while clients do not support transclusion, we can still start to create content according to this model.

If we decide that we absolutely must have more complex client-side links, then (given that we cannot let XPointer-based fragment identifiers become visible to the browser, as it will essentially ignore them) we could use a workaround such as the following: We do some server-side processing of requested XML files to modify any included links so that they refer to a server side process and pass this process the XPointer so that it could deal with the links as appropriate. In other words, we modify

```
http://aaa.com/b.xml#xpointer(//this/that)
```

so that instead it is

```
http://aaa.com/linkproc?resource=b.xml&xpfrag=//this/that
```

Then a script (called *linkbase,* which could be implemented in the scripting or programming language of choice) could retrieve the requested XML file, extract the relevant fragment, embed it into a suitable XML document, and return it to the browser. Note, however, that this is rather inadequate, given that this obviously stops the browser from locally applying the fragment identifier and hence from providing a clear context for the fragment.

One final comment is worth making. Despite the problems with the processing model, at least the *link data model* behind the presentation is

---

[4]This also raises a number of legal issues. Transclusion itself will be the subject of many legal controversies, as indicated by the problems around the limited transclusion features supported by today's Web: frames and inline images (for an extensive and regularly updated list of relevant material, see `http://www.jura.uni-tuebingen.de/~s-bes1/lcp.html`). However, simulating transclusion by assembling resources on the server side, possibly including material from third-party resources, will certainly be regarded as copyright infringement.

now well defined, so that it is possible to create content according to that data model. As the presentation semantics and the processing model become clearer, the content will become increasingly useful and increasingly accessible using standard tools.

8.1.3 Tool Support

As with all new and evolving technologies, the tool support for XLink and XPointer is currently somewhat fragmented. This is likely to continue to be true during a transition period. At present, no mainstream browsers directly support XLink or XPointer. There are various tools for processing XLinks, but implementations of XPointer are rather sparse. The tools that do exist (such as *libxml*) are yet to be effectively integrated with XML environments.

This creates difficulties in a number of different areas. First, the tools we use to directly manage the XML-based content typically do not have any explicit support for XLinks. Given that XLinks are essentially represented simply as a series of suitable attributes and subelements within an XML document, we can code these by hand. It would be much simpler, however, if the tools that we used to enter XML data allowed us to do things such as selecting a location within an XML document and from this generate an XLink (or even add an XLink to a separate linkbase). In the absence of such functionality, we are constrained, at present, to manual generation of XLinks.

A second problem is with the subsequent processing of XLinks. A number of tools are beginning to emerge that allow XLinks to be processed. A typical functionality would be to specify a linkbase and then have the links processed and used to modify the source XML documents. At the time of writing, however, there were no tools that yet support the full XLink and XPointer specifications.

One view that minimizes the impact of the lack of tool support is if we regard XLink, XPointer, and XPath as foundation back-end technologies that can be used as a base for the design of quality hypermedia linking applications. In effect, XLink and XPointer can be seen as exchange formats, not necessarily as the data model actually used within applications. Since XLink and XPointer are much richer than the current standard within applications (HTML), this approach makes a lot of sense by providing us with a rich and powerful data model for linking.

8.1.4 Loss of Context

XLink provides the ability to transclude content, for example,

```
<simplelink href="bloggs.xml" show="embed" actuate="onLoad"/>
```

This simple link incorporates content from one source directly into another source. Using links in this way means that it becomes much easier to take information out of one context and place it in an entirely different context. This raises both usability issues (it becomes much easier for users to misunderstand content) and legal issues (we have the potential for infringement of copyright, for example).

Consider the first of these two problems. XPointer allows us to specify arbitrary fragments of XML documents. As such, we can create "virtual" documents composed of fragments from other sources. Indeed, depending on the presentation semantics adopted (which, as we just discussed, are still not clear), it may not even be evident that the various components were ever obtained from different sources. This can be a valuable design approach—allowing us to reuse content in quite rich ways. It does, however, also create potential problems with developers unwittingly (or even intentionally in some cases!) removing content from a context that ensured a specific interpretation.

XLink and XPointer do not provide any support for addressing this (nor should they). Rather, it is an issue developers who utilize these technologies need to be aware of and need to take into account in developing and managing content. However, we very much hope that future tools supporting XLink and XPointer will make context available to users, so that a subresource embedded into a resource may be viewed in this new context but also may be traced back to its origin by using a "view subresource in original context" menu option provided by the browsing tool. This would be in the true spirit of transclusion, where content may be used in a different context but should never be separated from its original context.

8.1.5 Legal Issues

Associated with the ability to transclude content are a number of legal considerations. To illustrate this, consider the problems associated with the following possibilities:

- The ability to include fragments of someone else's XML content directly in your own document (potentially with no indication that the content came from some other source), for example, including a paragraph from an online version of this book in your student essay.
- The ability to add links from third-party content to your own analysis (or someone else's information) that reflect on that content, for example, a link from a companies software product information to your bug reports on that product.

- The ability to provide alternative link destinations for pre-existing links within third-party content, for example, adding your own company's products to the link destinations within a competitor's online catalog.

Some of these issues were hinted at by the difficulties introduced by the use of frames within HTML, where it was possible to create an HTML frameset that included your own content alongside the content from another site. This situation has already resulted in a number of high-profile court cases. XLink is likely to be much more problematic, given that the "inclusion" is much more seamless than it is when frames are used. Surprisingly though, this problem has never become a substantial issue for resources other than text. In HTML, it is possible to link to images, style sheets, scripts, applets, and other kinds of external resources, but there seems to be little problem with these media. It may be that these resources depend too substantially on their intended original usage to be widely useful in some other context—a salient lesson for anyone contemplating transclusion of content.

It is also interesting to note that Xanadu (the original source of the concept of transclusion [Nelson 93]) solves this problem by introducing the concept of "transcopyright," and includes a concept for a mechanism for dealing with this by ensuring that the original context remains available and by using micropayments for the use of content. These mechanisms are still, however, a distant hope for the current implementators of XML, XLink, and XPointer.

The effective resolution of this issue is probably going to depend on the browser vendors. It is in browsers where it should be made clear to users that content comes from different sources. This, however, needs to be done in such a way that it does not clutter the interface with copyright notices and unnecessary contextualization—a tough design problem.

8.1.6 More Complex Authoring

XLink and XPointer obviously result in more complex information structures—albeit ones that should result in more effective and usable applications, and more powerful management of the underlying content. Nevertheless, these more complex structures naturally mean more complex authoring and therefore a greater burden on the developers.

As the Web matures and moves from the novelty stage to being a mature tool with which we have built up some experience, it becomes clearer that there is a dearth of high-quality hypermedia. By *quality* hypermedia, we mean hypermedia that has structured the various information viewpoints in a way that is appropriate to the users and developers goals and that is richly linked in a way that actively supports the satisfaction of multiple (and often conflicting) information needs. Many Web sites provide sophisticated linking, but rarely does this have the degree of richness that takes it to the level where it becomes almost transparent to the user. Consider, for example, an online catalog where in a page containing information on a book the user could click on the author's name and retrieve information on the author or a list of other books by the author (depending on the context, or maybe they could choose). You could click on the publisher and choose whether you wanted information on the publisher or a list of similar books by the same publisher. You could click on the price and get a cost breakdown or maybe a list of books in a similar price range. You could select a word from the title, and it would link to a dictionary entry, and so forth. In other words, the linking is rich, intuitive, and appropriate. Most Web sites are very link-poor in comparison to what can, at least in theory, be achieved.

One of the reasons why good hypermedia is so rare is that it is extremely difficult and expensive to author.[5] The introduction of XLink and XPointer make this both easier and more difficult. It is easier in that we can create rich generic linkbases that provide useful links throughout a site as well as create more powerful links. It is harder insofar as we have a more complex set of linking options available to us. Creating hypermedia is, and always should be, a creative process rather than a purely mechanical one.

8.2 EMERGING SUPPORT FOR XLINK AND XPOINTER

If we consider the authoring issues we have discussed in the previous section, then it would be easy to conclude it is all just too hard. Why should we bother? Can't we just ignore this new linking technology and continue to create applications in the same way we have been doing for HTML (except, of course, that XML itself provides some useful functionality)?

Well, yes, we could—but this overlooks the whole point of XLink and XPointer, which is that they provide a mechanism for creating richer, more usable, and more effective applications. Yes, it will be more difficult to create these applications, especially in the short term until more effective tools become available. The potential gains, however, will be substantial (at least when we are building interactive and information-rich applications).

So, we can begin by considering the limited support for XLink and XPointer that is beginning to emerge. We can break this down into support

---

[5]Another reason is that many commercial Web sites are extremely self-serving in the sense that they never link to anything else but themselves. This, however, is mainly motivated by strategic reasons rather than technical or organizational limitations.

at various levels: support within existing browsers, support within code libraries, and hand-coded support. Before we launch into a discussion of these areas, it is important to note that this is a rapidly evolving field. In the following sections we discuss emerging support and then continue on to look at tool support. We will, however, be limited to looking at the support and tools that exist at the time of writing. While we try to look a little into the future, it would be a good idea to have a look at more up-to-date sources of information, such as the following:

- W3C: `http://www.w3.org/XML/Linking`
- XML Cover Pages: `http://www.oasis-open.org/cover/xll.html`

8.2.1 Support in Existing Browsers

At the time of writing, none of the current versions of the mainstream browsers provide anywhere near full support for XLink or XPointer. Microsoft's Internet Explorer, version 6 uses the Microsoft XML implementation (MSXML) to support XML-related functionality. While MSXML4 supports the evaluation of XPath expressions, this is limited to their use within fragment identifiers and in the processing of XSLT style sheets. MSXML4 does not, however, provide support for XPointer or XLink.

Netscape Navigator, version 6 provides its XML support through its Gecko browser engine. This includes support only for simple links, using the syntax from the March 1998 working draft of XLink (which is now somewhat outdated). In other words, it is possible to include only links such as the following:

```
<title xml:link="simple" show="replace"
      href="http://aa.bb.cc/a_file.xml">
   A title
</title>
```

Just as an aside, in the latest version of XLink, this would be written as follows:

```
<title xlink:type="simple" xlink:show="replace"
      xlink:href="http://aa.bb.cc/a_file.xml">
   A title
</title>
```

The most recent Opera browser, version 6, does not appear to support XLink or XPointer at all. The W3C's Amaya authoring tool and browser provides support for simple links and uses XLink and XPointer as part of its collaborative annotation application (XLink for representing the connection between document and annotation, and XPointer for describing where an annotation should be attached to a document) but is yet to provide more general support for XLink and XPointer.

Apart from the mainstream browsers, a number of other tools support the browsing of XML documents. For example, the InDelv client (version 6.0 at the time of writing) provides support for native viewing of XML documents. InDelv's support for XLink and XPointer is rather incomplete and based on older versions of the specifications. For example, InDelv provides partial support for XPointers, but various features—such as the `here()` and `origin()` functions—have yet to be implemented. The only XLink support is for simple links with an `actuate` attribute with a value of `auto`, a `show` attribute equal to `parsed`, and an `href` attribute equal to a valid URI (these are referred to as "auto" links).

It is interesting to note that the developers of InDelv state (in their online documentation):

> XLink is only used to support auto links in this software. This is because all other links are visible to the user and must be presented accordingly. The presentation of links is better handled by XSL formatting objects given the current state of the technology. It is expected that more work will be done by the W3C to combine XLink and XSL in a way that leverages both completely.... You must map the linking element to a simple-link format object, just as you would with any other XSL hyperlink. Auto links, which never display to the user, are supported using the XLink syntax.

In other words, this explicitly recognizes the problem just discussed regarding a lack of clarity in handling link presentation semantics.

8.2.2 Parsers and Code Libraries

It is probably at the level of XML parsers and supporting code libraries that the best support for XLink and XPointer exists (possibly because developers can concentrate on functionality rather than on integration into a complex software product).

A number of tools exist for processing XML resources containing XLinks. For example, XTooX[6] is an open source XLink processor that supports XLink linkbases. Basically, it converts extended, out-of-line links into inline links, taking as input a linkbase and outputting modified XML files. Because the implementors could not find an XPointer implementation they could use, XTooX supports only XPath for the identification of subresources within XML resources.

---

[6]See `http://www.xlinkit.com/xtoox/index.html`.

Similarly, X2X[7] is an XLink engine that supports out-of-line extended links and linkbases. As with XTooX, XML resources are processed to dynamically insert links when requested, though the links are stored in a database rather than flat files. X2X also uses an XPath-based syntax (extended by proprietary functions) to address XML subresources.

Another examples of available libraries is the Gnome XML Library libxml,[8] which implements XPointer, XML Base, XSLT, and XInclude.

Other tools—such as xlinkit.com[9]—focus on supporting the creation of XLinks. Xlinkit provides an environment for specifying rules for relationships between resources (using an XML-based rule language) and then generates XLinks based on these rules. XPath Visualiser[10] is a simple but effective tool that provides a visual presentation of an evaluated XPath expression, which is useful in constructing XPaths and therefore in constructing a restricted set of XPointers.

8.2.3 Hand-Coded Support

In the absence of direct tool support, it is still possible to build systems that make effective use of XLink and XPointer. Specifically, by hand-coding support in various ways, it is possible manage XLinks. For example, it is relatively straightforward to write XSLT style sheets that recognize elements that incorporate XLink attributes. These elements can be used to transform, as appropriate, out-of-line links into simple links that can then be recognized by a conventional browser (or even further transformed into HTML <A> elements).

Alternatively, there are various commercial-grade SGML tools available that support processing of XML resources. For example, OmniMark facilitates the processing of XML files through suitable scripting and pattern matching (using a proprietary transformation language). As with the use of XSLT, it is possible to write OmniMark "programs" that identify link elements and transform these as appropriate. A number of similar SGML tools exist (see `http://xml.coverpages.org/publicSW.html` for a list of public SGML software).

A typical use of this approach might be to use XML and XLink to represent the content at the server back-end and then to use a suitable Web server extension to support preprocessing of requested XML files. When an XML file is requested, all linkbases are searched and used to map the out-of-line links into simple links that can be embedded directly into the XML

---

[7]See `http://www.stepuk.com/products/prod_X2X.asp`.
[8]See `http://xmlsoft.org/`.
[9]See `http://www.xlinkit.com/`.
[10]See `http://www.vbxml.com/downloads/default.asp?id=visualiser`.

content before it is returned to the client (or further processed using suitable style sheets).

8.3 DEVELOPMENT TOOLS

We intended to discuss the various development tools that support the authoring and management of XLinks. For example, development tools could be used to support fragment identification, link authoring, linkbase management, and so forth.

Unfortunately, at the time of writing, we are not aware of any major XML development tools that support XLink and/or XPointer (though many provide support for generating XPath expressions for fragments of XML documents), so we don't really have anything to write about yet! It is unclear when the first major browser will fully support XLink, and XPointer still is in the process of being standardized; so we are waiting for XML linking to be widely supported. Therefore, you will need to monitor the relevant XML Web sites.

8.4 AUTHORING APPROACHES

Let us turn our attention to the process whereby we create richly linked applications. In other words, if we are going to create XML-based applications that make appropriate use of XLinks, then we need to consider aspects such as how to identify appropriate links and when this should be done, distributed control over links and linkbases, and accessibility and usability design issues.

8.4.1 Identifying Things to Link

An issue that we have alluded to a number of times is that identifying and creating "good" links can be very hard. This is one of the reasons why most Web sites are rather "link-poor" (at least relative to what could be achieved through high-quality design).

So how *do* we locate appropriate links within our content? To answer this, we will break the problem apart into a number of smaller issues. Specifically, when do we locate links? How does this fit into the design process? How do we do this without confusing the structure of the site?

As a way of starting to answer some of these questions, let us consider an analogy that should be familiar to most readers—the use of bookmarks within a Web browser. Most people try to organize bookmarks in some way—usually by aggregating them into specific folders and subfolders.[11] If

---

[11]Bookmark folders was a feature that was not present in the older versions of browsers but is now supported by most browsers.

we put too many bookmarks into one folder, then they start to become difficult to find and so lose much of their value. The whole point of a bookmark is that it is an easy-to-locate shortcut.

Links can be viewed in a similar vein. We need to be judicious in our selection of links. Too few links and it becomes difficult to locate a path toward the information that satisfies a specific need. Too many links and the choices available make it increasingly difficult to identify the correct link. The situation is similar to search engines, where finding matching Web pages is no longer the real challenge (a response of "your search returned 230,000 matches" is not likely to be particularly useful). Rather, the key is being able to rank them in a useful manner, so that users will find the really useful links (i.e., search results) within the first couple of returned results.

The key to effective design of links lies in understanding two things: the nature of the underlying content and the objectives of the users. Both of these tend to be (or at least should be) modeled and understood early in the design process. Once these are known, it becomes possible to develop a set of rules that can guide in the selection of suitable links.

Consider, for example, the following situation. We are designing an e-commerce Web system that provides online purchasing of products, detailed product descriptions, product support, and so forth. A typical linking rule (derivable from a usage scenario where users are browsing the catalog to locate items to purchase) would be that products should be linked to similar products.

Developing linking rules is, however, not sufficient. We also need to understand the context in which these links may be useful. This highlights an interesting point. Consider normal HTML links: the link is embedded into the HTML code and is therefore an integral part of the content. With XLink, we can separate the links into a separate linkbase, and we can therefore choose to use or ignore them as appropriate. A key aspect of the design process is deciding in which contexts certain links should be available.

For example, we can identify numerous cases where the product information would be incorporated into different viewpoints (possibly through a suitable XSLT transformation of the raw XML content about the product). Two key viewpoints would be the product details available when a user is browsing the catalog and the product information combined with support documentation for the product. In the first case, we may wish to include the links to related products. In the second case, these links would simply be distracting to the user. Achieving this type of functionality is relatively straightforward, simply requiring specification of which linkbases are to be used when generating the different viewpoints.

So, the upshot of this is that understanding the content interrelationships is important to identifying potential links to the model, and that understanding user objectives is important in determining the circumstances under which these links should be used. There are various techniques that can be used to support the former aspect. For example, the Object-Oriented Hypermedia Design Model (OOHDM) [Schwabe & Rossi 95; Schwabe+ 96] and the Web Markup Language (WebML) [Ceri+ 00] both provide mechanisms for modeling the information domain and identifying potential links. The understanding of user objectives can be supported by approaches such as usage-centered design [Constantine & Lockwood 99].

8.4.2 Controlling Linking and Ensuring Link Integrity

Apart from the ability to identify suitable links and then to select the appropriate contexts in which they should be used, it is also important to be able to control their use. To understand this a little more clearly, consider the potential role that linkbases can play. It is possible for anyone to create a linkbase (stored on his or her own server) that defines links over content of other content providers and over which they have no control. Further, keep in mind that this includes not only links that support navigation from content but also transcluding links (i.e., those using the XLink attributes `show="embed"` and `actuate="onLoad"`). In other words, users are able to transclude arbitrary sections of any content available on the Web into their documents. This has implications for persistence and the responsibilities regarding maintaining availability of the content and consistency of the structure.

Basically, we need to clearly separate the issues of creating linkbases for content under your own control (which makes an integrated development environment a necessity) and creating linkbases of references to external content. In the latter case, we have to deal with the fact that the external content may change or disappear. In effect, this means that if our application includes links that refer to external content, then we need to ensure we have in place mechanisms that monitor this external content for changes.

Many current content management systems already contain modules for checking external links regularly. This method could be applied to linkbases as well—though the mechanisms may need to be hand-coded until support is included in available tools. Possible mechanisms include checking resources for availability only or checking for changes in the resources using modification dates or `ETags` as provided by HTTP.

As an example of a typical approach targeted at resource fragments, we could develop mechanisms for creating and checking fragment digital fingerprints (e.g., MD5 [Rivest 92]) computed and stored by the linkbase. Basically, the process would be to obtain the resource, then compute the location set to which a specific XPointer refers, and finally calculate the fingerprint for this location set. This fingerprint can subsequently be stored and rechecked as appropriate (periodically or on demand).

8.4.3 Link Semantics

The preceding discussions have implied that links can be selectively utilized in various ways. To do this effectively, we need to be able to associate semantic information with links. This can be readily achieved by using the role, arcrole, and title attributes. For example, consider the following XML file containing descriptions of various products:

products.xml

```
<?xml version="1.0" encoding="UTF-8"?>
<catalog>
  <product id='23428'>
    <title>ABC Microwave Oven - Model 34X</title>
    <description>great oven!</description>
  </product>
  <product id='75386'>
    <title>XYZ Microwave Oven - Model TRL7</title>
    <description>even better model! incredible!</description>
  </product>
  <product id='11111'>
    <title>QRS Microwave Oven - Model SDF</title>
    <description>the ultimate in oven construction!</description>
  </product>
  <product id='99999'>
    <title>QRS Convection Oven - Model LKJG</title>
    <description>you won't believe how good this oven is!</description>
  </product>
</catalog>
```

We can then define a series of XLinks for this content. In the following file, we have two different types of links. The first is links that associate products with similarities, and the second is links that associate a product with its manufacturer.

links.xml

```
<?xml version="1.0" encoding="UTF-8"?>
<links xmlns:xlink="http://www.w3.org/1999/xlink/namespace/">

  <link xlink:type="extended" xlink:role="product-manufacturer">
    <loc xlink:type="locator"
        xlink:href="products.xml#xpointer(id('23428'))"
        xlink:label="item"/>
    <loc xlink:type="locator"
        xlink:href="manufacturers.xml#xpointer(id('ABC'))"
        xlink:label="madeby"/>
    <go xlink:type="arc"
        xlink:from="item"
        xlink:to="madeby"/>
  </link>
```

```
<link xlink:type="extended" xlink:role="similar-products">
  <loc xlink:type="locator"
      xlink:href="products.xml#xpointer(id('23428'))"/>
  <loc xlink:type="locator"
      xlink:href="products.xml#xpointer(id('75386'))"/>
  <loc xlink:type="locator"
      xlink:href="products.xml#xpointer(id('11111'))"/>
</link>

<link xlink:type="extended" xlink:role="similar-products">
  <loc xlink:type="locator"
      xlink:href="products.xml#xpointer(id('99999'))"/>
  <loc xlink:type="locator"
      xlink:href="products.xml#xpointer(id('11111'))"/>
</link>

</links>
```

The interesting thing to note in this linkbase is that we have associated with each link a suitable `role` that can then be used to support various different uses of the link. Consider the following (somewhat simplistic) XSLT style sheet:

products.xsl

```
<?xml version="1.0" encoding="UTF-8"?>
<xsl:stylesheet version="1.0"
    xmlns:xsl="http://www.w3.org/1999/XSL/Transform"
    xmlns:xlink="http://www.w3.org/1999/xlink/namespace/">

<xsl:output method="html"/>

<xsl:template match="product">
  <xsl:variable name="prod-id" select="@id"/>
  <h1><xsl:value-of select="title"/></h1>
  <p> ... </p>

  <h3>Other similar products</h3>
  <!--
    select all similar products where
        - they are different from the current product
        - there is a link that
            - has the correct role (i.e., product similarity)
            - includes the similar product
            - includes the current product
  -->

  <xsl:for-each select="document('products1.xml')/catalog/product">
    <xsl:variable name="this-prod-id" select="@id"/>

    <xsl:if test="($this-prod-id != $prod-id) and
        document('links1.xml')/links/link
          [@xlink:role='similar-products']
```

```
                [loc/@xlink:href[substring(substring-after(string(),
                        '#xpointer(id('), 2, 5)=$prod-id]]
                [loc/@xlink:href[substring(substring-after(string(),
                        '#xpointer(id('), 2, 5)=$this-prod-id]]">
            <xsl:value-of select="title"/><br/>
        </xsl:if>
    </xsl:for-each>

    <hr/>
</xsl:template>

</xsl:stylesheet>
```

This transforms an XML `product` element into an HTML page that describes a particular product. The transformation includes a suitable set of XSLT expressions to determine all products linked to the selected product but restricts this to those links that have an appropriate role. The key elements of the selection process are as follows:

- `document('products1.xml')/catalog/product` – This creates a set of all products (the "candidates") so that we can determine if any are linked to the current product.
- `document('links1.xml')/links/link` – We check each link to see if it connects the current product with the candidate product.
- `[@xlink:role='similar-products']` – This is a key point: we restrict the links to those that have an appropriate role.
- `[loc/@xlink:href[substring(substring-after(string(), '#xpointer(id('),2,5)=$prod-id]]` – This somewhat unwieldly XPath predicate is simply a temporary hack to cope with the fact that XPointers are not currently handled by any tools. It strips out the ID part of the XPointer and compares it to the ID of the product in order to see if the product is participating in that particular link.
- `[loc/@xlink:href[substring(substring-after(string(), '#xpointer(id('),2,5)=$this-prod-id]]` – This continues the previous step by checking to see if the candidate product is participating in the link.

We output the title of each product that is validly linked to the current product. This is an example of using XSLT to transform a set of XML resources and an associated linkbase into a form that is usable with current browsers (i.e., independent from XLink/XPointer support on the client side).

So, we can now use link roles to define (rather simplistically) the semantics of a link. The next level up from this is to increase the level of sophistication of the semantic information that we attach to a link. One way of doing this would be to use the `role` attribute to define a resource that specifies more complex information about the link. This could, for example, be done using Resource Description Framework (RDF) as a basis for specifying information about the link.

Theoretically, any meta-data can be expressed in RDF. We can therefore use the `role` attribute to specify an RDF file that contains appropriate meta-data about the link. This is, however, probably overkill for all but a very small number of applications.

8.4.4 Accessibility and Usability

One final issue that impacts on our approach to designing and authoring links in XML-based systems is the problem of accessibility and usability. The W3C has a Web Accessibility Initiative (WAI)[12] group concentrating on how to make Web content easily accessible, and this group has already published specifications for creating content [Chisholm+ 99, 00, 01], user agent design guidelines [Jacobs+ 01a, 00b], and authoring tool design guidelines [Treviranus+ 00a, 00b]. These documents, however, concentrate on the current state of affairs on the Web; and even though there is lot of room for improvement with the current state of accessibility and usability on the Web, the new technologies discussed in this book open up a whole new set of opportunities.

In general, creating usable and accessible content is not limited to specific technologies, and there is a good deal of material available about usability engineering, for example on `http://useit.com`, the Web site of accessibility expert Jakob Nielsen [Nielsen+ 99a, 99b]. However, starting from current Web technologies, it becomes clear that there are even more challenges in a fully XLink/XPointer-enabled Web, as follows:

- *Number of links.* If links are created from external linkbases rather than being embedded in the resource itself, the number of links within a single resource may become quite large. In particular, the number of links for a single resource depends on the linkbases consulted when presenting the resource. It thus becomes essential not to present all links but only the links most relevant to the user. Choosing a small but good subset of the available links will become essential for not overloading users.

- *Placement of links.* While it is impossible to create overlapping links in HTML, this can very easily happen when assembling links for a resource from different linkbases. Overlapping links may make sense in some cases, but in general they will be hard to justify and, more

---

[12]See `http://www.w3.org/WAI/`.

important, very hard to properly visualize within a client. The number of links is important to the issue of link placement, but the choice of links for linkbases is even more important.

- *Origin of links.* Since links may come from a number of sources (for example, in a fully XLink-enabled browser, users will be able to specify their own linkbases, from which the browser then fetches links and inserts them into the resources), it is important to be able to distinguish between links that were part of the resource itself, and links from (possibly multiple) external linkbases.

- *Origin of resources.* Transclusion makes it possible to dynamically assemble resources for presentation. However, this also means that one presentation may in fact contain fragments from various resources. Users must be able to distinguish between content coming from different resources. Furthermore, users should be able to look at transcluded content in its original context, maintaining the true spirit of transclusion.

While all these requirements can be fulfilled by adding information to the presentation, it is certainly a challenge to not clutter the interface with information, overloading users and thus making browsing the Web more difficult than it is today. Client designers may choose to not make all information about a link permanently visible. But, in the case of transcluded content, for example, this could easily lead to serious problems with the content's copyright.

So far there are no implementations available that solve all these problems, and it will take some time until a really good client implementing all the nice features of XLink/XPointer becomes available. There are some promising ideas, however, about how parts of the problem could be solved, for example, by using techniques such as the *link lens* [Stanyer & Procter 99] (based on the *magic lens* [Stone+ 94] model) for presenting link information.

8.5 CONCLUSIONS

This chapter goes into the specifics of how XML's linking technologies can and should be used to create and manage content. Even though universal XLink/XPointer support by browsers will take some time to be realized, XLink's potential can already be leveraged by using it for content management. In the same way as XML is used today for generating HTML, WML, or PDF output, XLink/XPointer can be used to generate richly interlinked Web content.

9

Transitioning to a New Model

When moving from *traditional* Web hypermedia to the new models of linking discussed in this book, not only do we need to design new strategies for authoring content, but we also need to implement appropriate transition strategies. In this chapter, we therefore consider approaches to migrating from a conventional model of Web content and link management to a model that utilizes the more sophisticated techniques discussed so far in this book.

For example, in many cases we will have legacy content that we wish to convert into a form that uses a separated database/linkbase storage model. We will look at how this might be accomplished. Another transition issue is the coexistence of old and new Web pages, requiring a server to decide dynamically which content to serve. We describe how such a server may be set up and which Web technologies (HTTP content negotiation [Holtman & Mutz 98] and CC/PP [Klyne+ 01]) may be used to enable the server to adapt dynamically to client requests.

Before focusing on the specifics of making the transition to this new model, and the consequences for information providers and the system architectures they are using, it is worthwhile to outline at a broad level what steps should be taken to get to a new model of handling hypermedia:

- *First, determine whether the potential changes to a new model provide sufficient additional benefits to justify the costs*. It is unlikely to be useful for small, unstructured applications such as newspaper columns or articles. Conversely, it potentially provides significant benefits for large structured applications such as online catalogs, where the complexity of interrelations between resources is likely to be very high (both in structure and in volume).

- *If the benefits do make it worthwhile, then it is of utmost importance to develop suitable information models*. XLink and XPointer will provide good starting points but nothing more. As has been discussed in the previous chapter, even if XLink and XPointer are used internally (which is not a requirement for transitioning to a new model), there is still quite some work to do regarding how to handle aspects such as link semantics, rules for their usage, and their limitations.

- *The resulting information model needs to be mapped onto specific implementation models, data formats, and technologies.* Furthermore, questions of interoperability with partner, clients, and legacy applications have to be resolved.

It is important to keep in mind that finding people who can develop these models and mappings and then implement them will not be easy. However, for any company considering itself knowledge- or information-based, the effort is likely to be worthwhile. Quality control is essential, especially during the process of designing the information model, because any errors occurring during this phase will have serious consequences for the entire lifetime of the resulting architecture (which is probably at least several years).

We begin this chapter by looking at the various issues that influence the approach that might be taken when transitioning to "new" Web hypermedia models. We then consider in more detail the actual strategies: development of a hybrid system to support both models, development of a completely new system, and so forth. Finally, we consider approaches to the migration of existing content to the new model.

9.1 ALTERNATIVE APPROACHES

While in this book we often speak of Web technologies and refer to typical Web scenarios such as content provided by a server and requested by clients using conventional Web browsers, we do not want to limit the applications of XML and its hypermedia mechanisms to Web scenarios only. In many cases, it is possible to use the technologies presented and discussed in this book without ever making anything publicly available on the Web. Information architects and designers of information systems might be inspired to apply some of the technologies for the XML-based Web to different application scenarios, and it is therefore important to recognize XML, XLink, and XPointer not only as Web technologies, but also as catalysts for a paradigm shift within the information management domain.

9.1.1 Issues

There are a number of issues that influence the approach we might take to negotiating the transition (i.e., the transition either from old Web technologies or from non-Web technologies to the approaches described in this book). Key factors include the quantity of existing content, the format used to represent existing content, existing infrastructure, potential benefits from adopting a more sophisticated linking model, available skills, technology stability, and the sophistication of the users.

Before we work through this list in more detail, we wish to emphasize that it does not make sense even to be considering using more sophisticated linking unless it can be shown that the potential benefits (in terms of improved business functionality or user experience) outweigh the likely costs (of more complex authoring minus potential cost savings in content maintenance).

Let us begin by considering the quantity of existing content. If we have a limited amount of existing content, then it may be feasible to manually migrate this content into an alternative form (specifically, XML) and add appropriate XLinks. With larger volumes of information, it naturally becomes impractical to do this manually, and we need to investigate ways of automating the conversion (discussed in section 9.4). Also note that irrespective of the motivations described in this book for migrating content to XML, many organizations simply choose to do this migration because of the improved content management that XML facilitates (especially with respect to flexible use of the content).

The form of the legacy content is related to the quantity of content to be managed. Specifically, content that has a high degree of structural complexity becomes more difficult to convert. To illustrate this, consider a large collection of legacy information stored in HTML format. This is likely to be harder to convert than an equivalent body of content stored in a database (which is likely to already be well structured according to a suitable database schema).[1]

The existing infrastructure will also affect the ability of an organization to migrate to an XML/XLink system. Specifically, if the organization already has a development environment that supports sophisticated content management (based on a semantically rich information model), then it will be easier to make the transition. However, in many cases legacy content has been authored directly in HTML (rather than being generated from a semantically richer source), so that it is hard (and expensive) to retrofit the semantics to the existing content.

Given the complexity of the systems being developed and limitations of the underlying technology, as well as the rapid pace of change (in particular in the light of the fact that XLink and XPointer are very new technologies), the poor availability of suitable skills is likely to affect an organization's

---

[1]The main problem here is that HTML content usually is linked, but the links do not carry any semantics, so that it is hard to automatically convert the linking information into semantically meaningful associations between individual resources.

decisions as to when, how, and to what extent to adopt more sophisticated content management approaches.

Similarly, the stability of the technology is a major issue. At the time of writing, many of the aspects of the technology are still quite unstable, and useful development tools and environments are still embryonic. As such, there will be a trade-off between the benefits to be gained and the difficulty in coping with the unstable technology. In some cases, it may make sense to delay implementation until the technology has stabilized to a greater degree and more effective tools have become available. However, it is important to stress the fact that even though it may be too early to adopt a fully XLink/XPointer-based architecture, the content/link separation may be something to consider, even if the eventual implementation is based on means other than XLink and XPointer.

9.1.2 Alternatives

Apart from all these issues, how do we actually make the transition? Before we can answer this, we need to distinguish carefully between what we might call *internal transition* and *external transition*.

- Internal transition relates to how we migrate the internal mechanisms we used for representing and managing content (for example, the internal data model, the data formats, data structures, transformation methods for import/export, etc).

- External transition relates to how we migrate to alternative approaches for accessing and utilizing information (for example, the way content is presented to the user).

Although interrelated, these two aspects can be treated relatively independently. In each case, we can look at different approaches: Big Bang migration of all content (i.e., do it all at once); incremental transition with dual systems (i.e., have two systems running in parallel); or hybrid systems with suitable content selection (i.e., migrate different parts at different times). As an example, we could make no change to the external view of the content but adopt a hybrid approach for the internal content management.

In general, a Big Bang transition is likely to have a lower total cost (since we are not developing and maintaining intermediate solutions) but will also present the greatest risk. An incremental transition using dual systems running in parallel will allow the development and exploration of initial prototypes and the development of suitable skills and expertise with the technology, hence reducing the risk, but is likely to result in a somewhat fragmented system. Typically, hybrid systems tend to favor compromises and cost more in the long run but will be cheaper in the beginning.

Given the four broad strategies (no change, Big Bang, incremental transition with dual systems, and incremental development with a hybrid system) and the ability to apply these to both internal and external views, we have, in effect, sixteen possibilities (though, in effect, at least one of these—no internal change and no external change—can be ignored). The next sections consider some of the more relevant of these possibilities.

Internal: Big Bang – External: Big Bang

In this case, the entire system is migrated at once—both the internal representations and management of the content, and the external delivery and presentation of the content. Although this is ultimately desirable to avoid legacy system overhead, currently it presents several problems. The most critical is that the external tools and browsers do not yet support effective utilization of content in the forms described in this book.

Internal: Big Bang – External: No Change

This approach is a little more interesting. We modify the way the content is represented and managed internally but provide mechanisms for mapping the content back into the same form as current systems. A simple example would be to use XML and XLink internally but adapt the server so that the content is mapped back into HTML (potentially through the use of XSLT) prior to delivery to the client. This would be appropriate for systems that did not have large amounts of content and/or were not highly mission-critical.

Internal: Dual System – External: No Change

Similar to the previous scenario, but rather than doing a complete conversion in one attempt, we develop a second system to run in parallel with the original and incrementally migrate the content. We then develop mechanisms that allow the fusion of the two approaches. This approach is more appropriate for systems already storing a lot of data and for systems where the Big Bang approach is too risky.

Internal: Hybrid – External: No Change

Again, similar to the previous scenario, but rather than developing multiple systems, we develop a hybrid internal system where some content is managed as XML while other content is managed in a legacy form, with suitable integration measures between the two. This approach allows us to progressively develop expertise and explore possible solutions. It is possibly the most appropriate for large, complex mission-critical systems.

Internal: Hybrid – External: Hybrid

Is there any mid-point between having a Big Bang change to the external view and no change to the external view? Certainly, there is. Again, we can create a hybrid solution. This is possible to do in several ways. For example, we can use content negotiation so that the system can deliver either XML/XLink content or HTML content depending on the client's capabilities. Alternatively, we can deliver XML/XLink content but embed it into HTML pages with suitable scripting to manage the required presentation and navigation semantics.

After this short look at some of the possible combinations, let us move on to examining some of the possible transition strategies in more detail.

9.2 EXAMPLE STRATEGIES

To illustrate the possible approaches, we consider two key strategies, demonstrating how they can be used to transition to a richer approach to managing and representing content.

9.2.1 Internal Hybrid, External No Change

In this approach, we use a hybrid model internally, but retain the same external model. In other words, we adopt multiple internal data models and ensure that they are suitably integrated and that the externally delivered (and possibly externally provided) data adheres to conventional models (such as HTML or XHTML).

Put very simply, a typical architecture would be a conventional server with suitable extensions for filtering and translating new content but also for delivering existing content where it has not yet been migrated. We would have content in multiple forms—at least HTML and other traditional forms (such as server-side scripting), as well as content that is progressively migrated to XML/XLink. This has several implications. The first is that we need to be able to map the new content (e.g., XML/XLink) into the old delivery formats (e.g., HTML/XHTML), including developing suitable link semantics. The second is that we need to understand how to integrate the old and new internal formats.

The integration of content becomes particularly difficult when we have content within the same domain but represented in different forms. Consider the following situation: We are developing an online shopping site and have considerable data on the available products. Rather than migrating all the content across into a new form, we elect to adopt a hybrid approach and do the migration incrementally. There will therefore be a considerable period of time when we have part of the catalog represented in a traditional form (probably stored in a database and mapped to HTML using appropriate scripting languages such as ASP or PHP). Another portion of the catalog will be represented as XML content and will be richly linked and cross-referenced using XLink. This raises a couple of interesting points:

- Can we cross-link the XML content with the database content in any meaningful way, and if so, then how do we actually do this?
- How do we merge the internally disjoint data content sets in a way that makes them appear seamless to a user of the system?

The first question is not easy to answer. In general, it is a difficult task to integrate two data models in a way that does not result in too many restrictions. Abiteboul and colleagues [Abiteboul+ 99] discuss the differences between the relational data model (which often, but not always, is the foundation for legacy data) and XML's data model, and it becomes apparent that the two models are not always easy to integrate. The following questions arise:

- *Can relational data be represented in XML?* This question is surprisingly easy to answer. Given that relational modeling basically models all information in tables, which may have dependencies, a (very naive) way of representing relational data in XML might look like this:

```
<!ELEMENT  data    (table*) >
<!ELEMENT  table   (row*) >
<!ELEMENT  row     (column*) >
<!ELEMENT  column  ANY >
```

  This, of course, is a very simple first approach, but it illustrates the basic idea. Further refining this approach, we could use ID/IDREF/IDREFS attributes to model dependencies between individual columns, and we could also implement additional mechanisms making sure that all rows of one table have the same number of columns.[2] There is much more work to be done before such a model can be used in practice; but it is important to notice that from the modeling point of view, it is easily possible to represent the structure behind relational data using XML.

- *Can XML data be represented in a relational way?* Unfortunately, it is not as easy as the other way around. XML has been derived from

---

[2]This could also be achieved by introducing an individual element for each column of a table, with the content model of the row listing all these elements explicitly.

SGML, which has its roots in the world of documents rather than relational data. Thus, one of the strengths of XML is its ability to represent semistructured data.[3] The relational model, however, focuses on strongly structured data (i.e., tables), which makes it rather difficult to define a general model of mapping XML to relational structures. There are simple ways of mapping XML documents to relational structures, such as creating one table for all nodes of the XML tree (in most cases, elements) and then creating another table for the relationships between the nodes, effectively representing the edges of the tree. While this process works in principle, it produces a representation of the XML document that is very hard to manage. (For example, how could an XPath-based query be efficiently executed on this kind of representation?)

As we can see, there is irregularity between the two data models; and while it is rather simple to represent relational data in XML, it can be quite challenging to find a reasonable relational representation of an XML schema. The reason for this is the difference in heritage. While the relational data model comes from a background of structuring and querying methods for large sets of strongly structured data, XML has its roots in the field of markup languages for documents, which traditionally are geared more toward flexible and semistructured models, because document authors should have the possibility to create a large diversity of documents based on the same schema.

So, does this mean that XML and relational data models cannot or should not be combined? Fortunately, we are discussing a transition from the strongly structured (relational) to the semistructured (XML) model, so that transitioning from the first to the second is not really a problem. As long as we make sure that we have a defined way of migrating the strongly structured content to the semistructured new model, the transition process can be implemented fairly easily.

There is an interesting issue about how we support the ongoing migration of content from the old data model across to the new. One possible approach is to treat the existing data (i.e., the data represented in the old data model) as read-only data. It may be used, but it may not be modified.

---

[3]*Semistructured data* is any data that has structure (such as XML documents) but in an irregular and—at the time of modeling—unpredictable way. For example, a book clearly is structured information; but the number of chapters, the number of sections within chapters, and the number of subsections within the sections are not already known when the general model of a book is defined. Put another way, strongly structured data can be represented as balanced trees, while semistructured data is an irregular tree. This irregularity is one of the strengths of semistructured data because in many applications the exact structure of the information to be stored is not known in advance.

Similarly, no new content may be created using the old model. Whenever existing content needs to be updated or modified or we need to create new content, we must do so using the new data model. That way it is guaranteed that any modifications are made based only on the new data model. This approach has two main advantages:

- *Transition occurs on an as-needed basis.* Only when content is modified or created do we require the new model. Legacy content is still stored using the old model, and therefore it is not necessary to transform a large amount of data at any time. The transition process can be regarded as an ongoing process, which may be slowed or accelerated according to available resources.

- *The old data model needs to be compatible only with the new one.* If the old data model is never used for creating or modifying content, then all we need is a mapping from the old data model to the new data model. What we do not need is a mapping from the new data model to the old data model, because we will never need to make such a transition. This makes the data-modeling phase much easier, because mapping a new (and probably semantically richer) data model to the old one can be challenging.[4]

If we choose an approach of internally using a hybrid model while ensuring that the external representation remains unchanged (at least at the time of the internal transition), we need to be able to answer the question of how to integrate the hybrid system in a way that enables the same access methods as before. Seen from a layer point of view, this approach means to insert a new layer (the new data model) between the old system and the access methods. The only way of reasonably managing the access to the hybrid data in a consistent way is through an integration layer, which is accessed by clients and which manages the hybrid system underneath. This approach is known as Enterprise Application Integration (EAI) [Rowell 01; Ruh+ 00]; and even though in most cases the goals behind EAI systems are a bit different from what we are discussing, the basic idea is the same.

This idea of EAI as an interesting approach for handling disparate data sources can be applied for all approaches that do not depend on a unique internal representation, which means that it is applicable to the following scenario as well.

---

[4]In some cases, it may be not very hard to do this mapping from the new model to the old model; but during the transformation probably some semantics would be lost, which is something that absolutely needs to be avoided when thinking about an information architecture.

9.2.2 Internal Hybrid, External Hybrid

In the approach just described, all externally delivered content is mapped back into a conventional form (e.g., HTML or XHTML), probably through an integration layer that provides a consistent view of the hybrid data sources. We can go one step further and create not only a hybrid system internally, but also one that is externally hybrid. In this case, we assume that there are clients that support only conventional HTML and/or XHTML pages, as well as clients supporting XML and XLink. Since a client fully supporting XLink enables a more advanced presentation of content, supporting an externally hybrid model can be a viable approach.

There are several ways we can do this. Probably the simplest is to use some form of content negotiation (discussed in section 9.3) to allow the server to make a decision about the form in which the content should be delivered. If the client requesting the content does not support XLink, then the content is mapped back to HTML or XHTML. If the client does support XLink, then richer content can be made available. Alternatively, if there is no support for XLink but the client does support suitable client-side functionality, then the content can be delivered as XML and XLink but coupled with suitable scripting to perform the interpretation and content mapping on the client side.[5]

Even though one may be tempted to implement the internally and externally hybrid approach through a vertical separation, it is highly advisable to use an integration layer even in this approach. This layer unifies the hybrid internal data models, making it much easier to define different mappings from this layer to the hybrid formats to be supported for client access.

Building this integration layer proves to be the central task for all possible strategies, because it is the entity representing the new data model of the whole architecture. In the same way as XML often is used as a hub for data exchange, this integration layer is the hub for the interface between possibly multiple internal and external data formats. It is therefore essential to make the design of this integration layer the core task of the transition process, in particular because this integration layer (i.e., the data model and the functionality it provides) will be the only path through which data is accessed.[6]

---

[5]A typical example for this is Microsoft's Internet Explorer, which supports XSLT and therefore can be used to transform any XML-based content on the client side.

[6]As discussed already, in some cases it may be a reasonable strategy to incorporate functionality in the integration layer, which makes it impossible to have write access to data in legacy systems, thus forcing users to migrate content whenever it is modified.

9.3 CONTENT NEGOTIATION

The example strategies presented in the previous section show that the internal data model ideally should be completely independent from the externally presented data model. Of course, there must be mappings between the two, but these mappings should be clearly separated from the models themselves. This allows the addition of new internal data models (for example, if other legacy data has to be included) or new external data models (for example, if a new partner in a content syndication scenario has to be served) without the need to change anything within the system beyond a new mapping.

In general, a Web-based application scenario should adapt to its clients. Today, a common approach is to author content that can be used by as many clients as possible, but the growing diversity of clients causes a basic dilemma:

- *Content should be as sophisticated as possible.* Sophistication requires specialization; and therefore the more sophisticated the features used by the client are, the more requirements have to be fulfilled by the client (well known as the "this site is best viewed with Internet Explorer 5.5 or higher, Shockwave, and a true color monitor with a resolution of at least 1024 by 768" syndrome). Even though sophistication is positive for the users who can make use of it, it is frustrating for other users.

- *Content should be as widely usable as possible.* The most basic content also should be the most versatile content. For example, HTML pages strictly adhering to the 3.2 version of the standard [Raggett 97] can be viewed by essentially all browsers today. However, many of the advanced features of newer HTML versions and/or scripting are not available.

There is a tension between content sophistication and usability, and this will increase as the diversity of clients grows. While the vast majority of Web users today use a computer with a decent-sized color screen, the number of users with various kinds of devices, varying from mobile phones through palm-top computers to regular desktop models, will undoubtedly increase. It will become much more important to be able to serve all these users (and better than by just saying "come again once you are using another device"), and therefore *content negotiation*—the ability to serve content adapted to each client's capabilities—will become much more important than it is today.

HTTP [Fielding+ 99], the Web's transfer protocol, supports content negotiation [Holtman & Mutz 98] and, consequently, could be used for satisfying at least the most basic content negotiation requirements. Surprisingly, most Web sites today, by far, do not support even that basic level of content negotiation, for example, for selecting between languages. Most major browsers send the language preference set by their user to the server so that the server can automatically select which language to serve. However, many Web sites still rely on the user making this selection explicitly, which is an unnecessary barrier to getting to the content of the site.

HTTP supports only rather simple content negotiation. Klyne, who carried out a detailed requirements analysis, showed that content negotiation can be done in a more powerful way [Klyne 99]. W3C's Composite Capability/Preference Profiles (CC/PP) [Klyne+ 01; Nilsson 00; Nilsson+ 00] is a general framework for how clients may communicate not only their capabilities (such as the display size or the available input devices), but also their preferences (such as the language) to the server, which then can use this information to serve the request in a way that is most appropriate for this particular client.

Content negotiation, when taken to its extremes, means that each response is generated individually so that no two responses will ever carry the exact same content. This view of content negotiation may go a little too far and may be inappropriate (at least in most circumstances), but starting from today's "best viewed with..." Web, there is a good deal of room for improvement.

Of course, if a server is designed for a closed user group (for example, an intranet Web server), then it is possible and legitimate to make certain assumptions about the clients. It may, for example, be the company policy to use a certain browser, and either people not using that browser are simply rejected by the server or at least they must live with the fact that the pages might not work as expected.

After this rather general discussion of content negotiation, we describe a simple example of how content negotiation may work in the case of a data model based on XLink or similar concepts (with the most important feature being that links may associate any number of resources). In the following list, we show the different ways content may be processed before delivering it to the client. We assume that some content negotiation mechanism makes it possible to detect the level of support for the supported content formats:

- *XLink-capable client.* In this case, the content can be delivered in XML/XLink form directly to the client. Assuming that the internal model of the system is very close to XML and XLink, this is a very easy task.

- *HTML-capable client with scripting capabilities.* In this case, XML and XLink have to be transformed into HTML. However, because scripting is supported, the delivered content can be augmented with scripting code that simulates an advanced linking model. This technique has been described by Oberholzer and Wilde [Oberholzer & Wilde 02]. Since it is difficult to write scripting that is both portable and robust, this approach may also require differentiation between clients and the subsequent delivery of scripting code adapted to the specific platform.

- *Basic HTML client (no scripting supported).* If the client does not support scripting, then the sophisticated linking model has to be somehow transformed to simple HTML. Possible strategies here include the selection of the "best" resource for every link or the generation of separate "link pages" (as implemented by the Webcosm [Davis+ 92; Hall+ 96] system). This latter approach has the advantage of not losing any information but makes following a link a lengthy two-step process.

These are only some ideas about how content negotiation could be used. When using content negotiation, it is usually desirable to provide maximum support for those platforms that are most popular; while for less popular platforms it may not make sense to implement individual content representations.

An important point about content negotiation is that it is very flexible. When a new client becomes popular enough to warrant providing it with specifically created content, then all that has to be done is to define a mapping between the system's data format and the format required by the new client[7] and then to update the configuration of the content negotiation mechanism so that the mapping is applied every time a request from this new client is received.

9.4 MIGRATION OF CONTENT

So far we have concentrated on the side of the process where the content is delivered to some client for presentation. However, generally speaking, a client may also be used as an editor, which not only presents the content but also enables users to make modifications to it. These modifications have to find their way back into the system, and this needs to be be considered when designing the integration layer we introduced in section 9.2.

Generally, the integration layer not only has to provide functionality for reading the data but also must support write operations. Because the

---

[7]Naturally, this mapping can range from a very simple XSLT program that can be created in a couple of days to more sophisticated mappings, which might be much more expensive to develop and implement.

integration layer is the platform that implements the data model of the new system, it is very important to make sure no inconsistencies can be introduced by other systems modifying data through means other than the integration layer. These considerations are most important for hybrid systems, where several underlying data models are accessed by the integration layer. In a system set up with a Big Bang approach (i.e., which has only one internal data model), life is much easier with respect to migration issues.

In a hybrid system, the integration layer should include all the logic that is necessary to make sure that the migration strategy is adhered to in the following areas:

- *Read access to data.* In the case of read access to data, the integration layer can simply serve the data from the appropriate source; and since it is not being modified, it is not important to differentiate between new and old data.

- *Creation of data.* When new data is created, the integration layer must ensure that it adheres to the new data model.

- *Modification of data in the new system.* Modifying data is not a problem as long as the data is part of the new data model already. In that case, it can simply be modified without any special treatment.

- *Modification of data in the old system.* If data from the old data model has to be modified, the integration layer ideally should enforce the strategy of removing the data from the old model and recreating it in the new model (with the updates submitted by the client). Depending on the data models, this process might be more or less complicated; and it may even require human intervention.[8] Using this strategy, the integration layer itself guarantees that the migration is a continually progressing process.

Naturally, it is also possible to think of a strategy that re-creates all content at once (the internal Big Bang approach discussed in section 9.1.2). This approach is viable if it is possible to create filters that automatically convert the content from the old data model to the new one. However, very often it becomes apparent that older data models are not as semantically rich as is necessary for a fully automated conversion,[9] in which case assisted

---

[8]For example, if the old data model supports untyped links only, then re-creating links in the new data model may require the assignment of types to the links, such as "informative link" or whatever is appropriate in the application context.

[9]Popular examples are HTML for the Web content world, which very often is not authored in a way that makes it possible to recover the semantics behind the structure, and Word for the document world, which also very often is not used in a way that makes automatic conversion easy.

processes, with manual support for the conversion, become a possibility. These conversion strategies often yield high-quality results but also are very expensive—possibly prohibitively so for very large amounts of data.

9.5 BUILDING NEW SITES

If a system is designed from scratch, then life becomes much easier, since there are no migration issues for existing content. Furthermore, it is possible to design a data model that reflects all the advanced linking concepts discussed throughout this book. However, it is important to keep in mind that XML as well as XLink are primarily exchange formats, not necessarily internal data formats of content management systems. Therefore, the process of defining an application-specific data model should, on the one hand, concentrate on what is important in the application domain but, on the other hand, try to make sure there is a reasonable way of mapping internal data to exchange formats such as XML and XLink.

When building a new site, one of the most important things to keep in mind is meta-data (i.e., data describing data, and in this particular case, data describing the site's content). While capturing data (such as text, images, or similar media) is usually very straightforward, capturing meta-data, which is equally important in terms of ensuring that the data is as useful as possible, is often overlooked. While meta-data is not dealt with in detail in this book, it is the primary source from which associations between individual pieces of information can be inferred and thus can hardly be overrated when thinking about hypermedia. Adrienne Tannenbaum presents many topics relevant to meta-data [Tannenbaum 01].

Even if it is agreed that data models should have strong support for meta-data in order to make the information as useful as possible, this still does not prescribe how to do the actual modeling. Information modeling is a complex and controversial subject, and what method to choose is a question not only of the application domain but also of personal taste and experiences. A rather old method, the Entity-Relationship Model [Chen 76], has a long track record but is geared more toward the eventual creation of relational models than semistructured data. The Unified Modeling Language (UML) [OMG 01] also is a well-established modeling language, but its focus is more on software systems than information models. Although there are approaches to mapping UML models onto XML schema, none of these has yet become well established.

Rather than using a rather abstract method, it is also possible to specify an information model directly in XML Schema [Thompson+ 01]. XML Schema is a much better schema language for XML than DTDs, so it may be worthwhile to make the extra effort to learn XML Schema.

When a new site is built, meta-data should be included in the design of the data model because only meta-data makes it possible to generate new views for data, to infer facts that are hidden in the associations between individual resources, and to use the information in a semantically rich way. However, creating meta-data is expensive and requires expertise; so great care should be taken to include meta-data only in the data model that can and will be generated during the site's lifetime. Meta-data containing wrong information is almost useless (and hard to detect once it finds its way into the system!); so the secret of successful meta-data handling is to keep only as much as necessary, while in parallel ensuring a very high level of quality of meta-data being captured.

9.6 CONCLUSIONS

XLink and XPointer are new standards. Few organizations will, however, be developing a new system from scratch. Rather, it is much more likely that they will be progressively migrating existing systems. This means that, for most developers, transition strategies for content are very important because legacy content must still be made available, even if new technologies are adopted. Consequently, this chapter presents and discusses transition strategies in a structured way. Internal and external views are described, enabling users to adopt the transition strategy that can be implemented with a minimum of risk and a maximum of benefits.

Epilogue

XML is an exciting new way to work with information. As with every tool for structured information, it is essential that the model behind it is suitable for the required applications. XML in this sense is very similar to database systems, which also heavily depend on the data model and how it is mapped to the database's mechanisms. Our goal with this book has been twofold. First, we have attempted to show that hypermedia is a very powerful way to represent complex information and that XML and the associated technologies XLink and XPointer are an appropriate way to implement hypermedia concepts. Second, we have shown that the Web as it is today would benefit substantially from supporting the advanced linking mechanisms of XLink and XPointer. We believe that in the near future browsers will start to be not only XML-capable, but also XLink/XPointer-capable clients.

The dual goals of this book are reflected in our attitude toward actually using XLink and XPointer. Even if the development of XLink and XPointer support is slower than we would hope, information providers can still benefit from the concepts and technologies described in this book by applying them internally and then transforming them into more simple representations for the outside world.

It is notoriously difficult to predict the success of specific technologies. We believe that XLink and XPointer are technically sound and are capable of introducing new ways of representing information that would lead to a whole new level of linked resources on the Web. However, the technical quality often is not the only criterion influencing a technology's success; and even though other factors such as lobbying and commercial interests are well known, there still is a lot of uncertainty regarding the future of XLink and XPointer, as demonstrated by the following (rather extreme) examples:

- *Surprisingly successful.* The Short Message Service (SMS) of the GSM mobile communications standard is successful in a way that was not anticipated by anybody [ETSI 99]. Even though the SMS service is as basic as a communications service can get these days (you can transmit only 160 characters, and they have to be typed on a less-than-ideal numeric keypad), it has inspired new ways of communicating and also is a major source of revenue for mobile carriers.

- *Disappointing market acceptance.* On the other hand, the Wireless Application Protocol (WAP) was heavily marketed as the next big wave for mobile communications and yet has been a clear failure. WAP still exists, and the migration from WAP 1.1/1.2 [WAP 99] to WAP 2.0 [WAP 01], which leaves not much more than the name,[1] may help to increase market figures. But the mismatch between the marketing noise around WAP and its acquired user base demonstrates that not everything can be sold to people.

Thus, it can be seen that market success can be hard to predict. In particular, market success is not necessarily related to the marketing efforts for a specific technology. Furthermore, a technology is not always used in the way expected by its creators. A very good example of this is XML itself. Even though XML is successful as a Web technology, its biggest success story is its universal acceptance as a data format in B2B scenarios. XML seems to be increasingly accepted as the standard way to exchange structured data, a kind of ASN.1 [ITU 97] for the Internet.

Based on the very different, but also very interesting, success stories of SMS, WAP, and XML, we must accept that there is a lot of uncertainty when thinking about the possible development of a technology. Not surprisingly, we believe that the Web could greatly benefit from the advanced hypermedia features of XLink and XPointer; but so far, the support of these standards in products has been a bit disappointing.

One of the reasons why XLink's deployment on the Web may be problematic is the question of intellectual property rights. XLink's transclusion features not only support very exciting applications but also introduce new ways content may be used illegally. HTML already is the topic of copyright lawsuits all over the world (the most common cases being *framing*[2] and *deep linking*[3]). Browsers that fully support XLink's transclusion features would certainly introduce new forms of content misuse. Copyright laws are

---

[1]Basically, the whole "wireless is different" attitude of the WAP 1.x standards (resulting in a large number of slight variations of standard technologies, just enough to make them incompatible with the actual standards) is now gone, and WAP 2.0 uses standard Internet and Web technologies such as TCP/IP and XHTML.

[2]Integrating someone else's Web page into your own HTML frame set by referencing it in one of the `<FRAME>` elements.

[3]Using links "into" someone else's Web site instead of pointing to the entry page.

different in different countries, but important examples such as the U.S. Digital Millennium Copyright Act (DMCA) demonstrate that it may already be illegal to simply provide the technology that could be used to circumvent copyright protection.[4]

We hope that XLink and XPointer will soon be supported by major browsers. New application scenarios, such as independent linkbase providers offering expertise (i.e., a well-maintained linkbase) in certain areas, would open up new business opportunities and new ways to explore the Web. The vision of the Web as an open hypermedia system certainly is exciting. While we wait for this vision to become a reality, the lessons learned from XLink and XPointer can already be used by information providers to better handle their information internally.

This is the most important lesson to be learned from this book: No matter what kind of clients are available, it is always a good idea to make the internal data model as versatile and as powerful as possible. W3C also has identified this as a central point for the future development of the Web, as demonstrated by documents discussing device independence [Ritz+ 01] and by an entire activity devoted to that area, the Device Independence Activity.[5] So no matter when XLink and XPointer will appear in widely used clients, using them today can already provide substantial benefits, with the added value of being ready for the support of XLink clients as soon as they become available.

---

[4]This assumes that it is used to circumvent an *effective* technological copyright protection.
[5]See `http://www.w3.org/2001/di/`.

References

[Abiteboul+ 99] Abiteboul, Serge, Peter Buneman, and Dan Suciu. *Data on the Web: From Relations to Semistructured Data and XML.* Morgan Kaufmann, San Francisco, 1999.

[Adler+ 01] Adler, Sharon, Anders Berglund, Jeff Caruso, Stephen Deach, Paul Grosso, Eduardo Gutentag, R. Alexander Milowski, Scott Parnell, Jeremy Richman, and Stephen Zilles. "Extensible Stylesheet Language (XSL) Version 1.0." World Wide Web Consortium Recommendation, REC-xsl-20011015, October 2001.

[Adobe 00] Adobe Systems, Inc. *PDF Reference: Version 1.3, Second Edition.* Addison-Wesley, Boston, 2000.

[Altheim+ 01] Altheim, Murray, Frank Boumphrey, Sam Dooley, Shane McCarron, Sebastian Schnitzenbaumer, and Ted Wugofski. "Modularization of XHTML." World Wide Web Consortium Proposed Recommendation, PR-xhtml-modularization-20010222, February 2001.

[Altheim & McCarron 00] Altheim, Murray, and Shane McCarron. "Building XHTML Modules." World Wide Web Consortium Working Draft, WD-xhtml-building-20000105, January 2000.

[Altheim & McCarron 01] Altheim, Murray, and Shane McCarron. "XHTML 1.1— Module-based XHTML." World Wide Web Consortium Recommendation, REC-xhtml11-20010531, May 2001.

[Alvestrand 01] Alvestrand, Harald Tveit. "Tags for the Identification of Languages." Internet best current practice RFC 3066, January 2001.

[Apparao+ 98] Apparao, Vidur, Steven Byrne, Mike Champion, Scott Isaacs, Ian Jacobs, Arnaud Le Hors, Gavin Thomas Nicol, Jonathan Robie, Robert Sutor, Chris Wilson, and Lauren Wood. "Document Object Model (DOM) Level 1 Specification." World Wide Web Consortium Recommendation, REC-DOM-Level-1-19981001, October 1998.

[Apple 89] Apple Computer. *HyperCard Stack Design Guidelines*, 1989.

[Beckett 01] Beckett, Dave. "Refactoring RDF/XML Syntax (Revised)." World Wide Web Consortium Working Draft, WD-rdf-syntax-grammar-20011218, December 2001.

[Berglund+ 01] Berglund, Anders, Scott Boag, Don Chamberlin, Mary F. Fernández, Michael Kay, Jonathan Robie, and Jérôme Siméon. "XML Path Language (XPath) 2.0." World Wide Web Consortium Working Draft, WD-xpath20-20011220, December 2001.

[Berners-Lee 92] Berners-Lee, Tim. "The World Wide Web." In *Proceedings of the 3rd Joint European Networking Conference*. Innsbruck, Austria, May 1992.

[Berners-Lee+ 94] Berners-Lee, Tim, Larry Masinter, and Mark McCahill. "Uniform Resource Locators (URL)." Internet proposed standard RFC 1738, December 1994.

[Berners-Lee+ 98] Berners-Lee, Tim, Roy T. Fielding, and Larry Masinter. "Uniform Resource Identifiers (URI): Generic Syntax." Internet draft standard RFC 2396, August 1998.

[Berners-Lee+ 99] Berners-Lee, Tim, Mark Fischetti, and Michael Dertouzos. *Weaving the Web*. HarperCollins, San Francisco, 1999.

[Biron & Malhotra 01] Biron, Paul V., and Ashok Malhotra. "XML Schema Part 2: Datatypes." World Wide Web Consortium Recommendation, REC-xmlschema-2-20010502, May 2001.

[Boag+ 01] Boag, Scott, Don Chamberlin, Mary F. Fernández, Daniela Florescu, Jonathan Robie, Jérôme Siméon, and Mugur Stefanescu. "XQuery: A Query Language for XML." World Wide Web Consortium Working Draft, WD-xquery-20011220, December 2001.

[Borenstein & Freed 92] Borenstein, Nathaniel S., and Ned Freed. "MIME (Multipurpose Internet Mail Extensions): Mechanisms for Specifying and Describing the Format of Internet Message Bodies." Internet informational RFC 1341, June 1992.

[Bos+ 98] Bos, Bert, Håkon Wium Lie, Chris Lilley, and Ian Jacobs. "CSS2 Specification." World Wide Web Consortium Recommendation, REC-CSS2-19980512, May 1998.

[Boyer 01] Boyer, John. "Canonical XML Version 1.0." World Wide Web Consortium Recommendation, REC-xml-c14n-20010315, March 2001.

[Braden 89a] Braden, Robert. "Requirements for Internet Hosts—Application and Support." Internet standard RFC 1123, October 1989.

[Braden 89b] Braden, Robert. "Requirements for Internet Hosts—Communication Layer." Internet standard RFC 1122, October 1989.

[Bray+ 98] Bray, Tim, Jean Paoli, and C. M. Sperberg-McQueen. "Extensible Markup Language (XML) 1.0." World Wide Web Consortium Recommendation, REC-xml-19980210, February 1998.

[Bray+ 99] Bray, Tim, Dave Hollander, and Andrew Layman. "Namespaces in XML." World Wide Web Consortium Recommendation, REC-xml-names-19990114, January 1999.

[Bray+ 00] Bray, Tim, Jean Paoli, C. M. Sperberg-McQueen, and Eve Maler. "Extensible Markup Language (XML) 1.0 (Second Edition)." World Wide Web Consortium, REC-xml-20001006, October 2000.

[Brickley & Guha 00] Brickley, Dan and R. V. Guha. "Resource Description Framework (RDF) Schema Specification." World Wide Web Consortium Candidate Recommendation, CR-rdf-schema-20000327, March 2000.

[Bush 45] Bush, Vannevar. "As We May Think." *Atlantic Monthly* 176(1): 101–108, 1945.

[Carlisle+ 01] Carlisle, David, Patrick Ion, Robert Miner, and Nico Poppelier. Mathematical Markup Language (MathML) Version 2.0. World Wide Web Consortium Recommendation, REC-MathML2-20010221, February 2001.

[Ceri+ 00] Ceri, Stefano, Piero Fraternali, and Aldo Bongio. Web Modeling Language (WebML): A modeling language for designing Web sites. In *Proceedings of the Ninth International World Wide Web Conference,* Elsevier, Amsterdam, 2000.

[Chamberlin+ 01] Chamberlin, Don, Peter Fankhauser, Massimo Marchiori, and Jonathan Robie. "XML Query Requirements." World Wide Web Consortium Working Draft, WD-xmlquery-req-20010215, February 2001.

[Chen 76] Chen, Peter Pin-Shan. "The Entity-Relationship Model—Toward a Unified View of Data." *ACM Transactions on Database Systems* 1(1):9–36, 1976.

[Chisholm+ 99] Chisholm, Wendy, Gregg Vanderheiden, and Ian Jacobs. "Web Content Accessibility Guidelines 1.0." World Wide Web Consortium Recommendation, WAI-WEBCONTENT-19990505, May 1999.

[Chisholm+ 00] Chisholm, Wendy, Gregg Vanderheiden, and Ian Jacobs. "Techniques for Web Content Accessibility Guidelines 1.0." World Wide Web Consortium Note, NOTE-WCAG10-TECHS-20001106, November 2000.

[Chisholm+ 01] Chisholm, Wendy, Jason White, and Gregg Vanderheiden. "Web Content Accessibility Guidelines 2.0." World Wide Web Consortium Working Draft, WD-WCAG20-20010824, August 2001.

[Clark 99a] Clark, James. "Associating Stylesheets with XML Documents." World Wide Web Consortium Recommendation, REC-xml-stylesheet-19990629, June 1999.

[Clark 99b] Clark, James. "XSL Transformations (XSLT) Version 1.0." World Wide Web Consortium Recommendation, REC-xslt-19991116, November 1999.

[Clark 01] Clark, James. "XSL Transformations (XSLT) Version 1.1." World Wide Web Consortium Working Draft, WD-xslt11-20010824, August 2001.

[Clark & DeRose 99] Clark, James, and Steven J. DeRose. "XML Path Language (XPath) Version 1.0." World Wide Web Consortium Recommendation, REC-xpath-19991116, November 1999.

[Coates+ 01] Coates, Tony, Dan Connolly, Diana Dack, Leslie L. Daigle, Ray Denenberg, Martin J. Dürst, Paul Grosso, Sandro Hawke, Renato Iannella, Graham Klyne, Larry Masinter, Michael Mealling, Mark Needleman, and Norman Walsh. "URIs, URLs, and URNs: Clarifications and Recommendations 1.0." World Wide Web Consortium Note, NOTE-uri-clarification-20010921, September 2001.

[Comer 00] Comer, Douglas E. *The Internet Book, Third Edition.* Prentice-Hall, Englewood Cliffs, N.J., 2000.

[Connolly+ 97] Connolly, Dan, Rohit Khare, and Adam Rifkin. "The Evolution of Web Documents: The Ascent of XML." *World Wide Web Journal* 2(4): 119–128, 1997.

[Constantine & Lockwood 99] Constantine, Larry L., and Lucy A. D. Lockwood. *Software for Use.* Addison-Wesley, Reading, Mass., 1999.

[Cowan 01] Cowan, John. "XML 1.1." World Wide Web Consortium Working Draft, WD-xml11-20011213, December 2001.

[Cowan & Tobin 01] Cowan, John, and Richard Tobin. "XML Information Set." World Wide Web Consortium Recommendation, REC-xml-infoset-20011024, October 2001.

[Daniel 00] Daniel, Ron. "Harvesting RDF Statements from XLinks." World Wide Web Consortium Note, NOTE-xlink2rdf-20000929, September 2000.

[Dasen & Wilde 01] Dasen, Marcel, and Erik Wilde. "Keeping Web Indices Up-to-Date. In *Poster Proceedings of the Tenth International World Wide Web Conference,* pp. 202–203. Elsevier, Hong Kong, May 2001.

[Davis+ 92] Davis, Hugh C., Wendy Hall, Ian Heath, Gary J. Hill, and Robert J. Wilkins. "Towards an Integrated Information Environment with Open Hypermedia Systems." In *Proceedings of the Fourth ACM Conference on Hypertext,* pp. 181–190. ACM Press, Milano, Italy, November 1992.

[DeRose+ 01a] DeRose, Steven J., Eve Maler, and Ron Daniel. "XML Pointer Language (XPointer), Version 1.0." World Wide Web Consortium Candidate Recommendation, CR-xptr-20010911, September 2001.

[DeRose+ 01b] DeRose, Steven J., Eve Maler, and David Orchard. "XML Linking Language (XLink), Version 1.0." World Wide Web Consortium Recommendation, REC-xlink-20010627, June 2001.

[Dubost+ 01] Dubost, Karl, Hugo Haas, and Ian Jacobs. "Common User Agent Problems." World Wide Web Consortium Note, NOTE-cuap-20010206, February 2001.

[DuCharme 98] DuCharme, Bob. *XML: The Annotated Specification.* Prentice-Hall, Upper Saddle River, N.J., 1998.

[Ellerman 98] Ellerman, Castedo. "Channel Definition Format (CDF)—Version 1.01." Technical report, Microsoft Corporation, Redmond, Wash, April 1998.

[Engelbart 88] Engelbart, Doug. "The Augmented Knowledge Workshop." In Adele Goldberg, ed., *History of Personal Workstations,* pp. 187–236. ACM Press, New York, 1988.

[ECMA 99] European Computer Manufacturers Association (ECMA). "ECMA-Script Language Specification." Standard ECMA-262, December 1999.

[ETSI 99] European Telecommunications Standards Institute (ETSI). "Digital Cellular Telecommunications System (Phase 2+); Technical Realization of the Short Message Service (SMS); Point-to-Point (PP)." ETSI TS 100 901, GSM 03.40 (version 7.3.0 Release 1998), November 1999.

[Fallside 01] Fallside, David C. "XML Schema Part 0: Primer." World Wide Web Consortium Recommendation, REC-xmlschema-0-20010502, May 2001.

[Ferraiolo 01] Ferraiolo, Jon. "Scalable Vector Graphics (SVG) 1.0 Specification." World Wide Web Consortium Recommendation, REC-SVG-20010904, September 2001.

[Fielding 95] Fielding, Roy T. "Relative Uniform Resource Locators." Internet proposed standard RFC 1808, June 1995.

[Fielding+ 99] Fielding, Roy T., Jim Gettys, Jeffrey C. Mogul, Henrik Frystyk Nielsen, Larry Masinter, Paul J. Leach, and Tim Berners-Lee. "Hypertext Transfer Protocol—HTTP/1.1." Internet proposed standard RFC 2616, June 1999.

[Franks+ 99] Franks, John, Phillip M. Hallam-Baker, Jeffery L. Hostetler, Scott D. Lawrence, Paul J. Leach, Ari Luotonen, and Lawrence C. Stewart. "HTTP Authentication: Basic and Digest Access Authentication." Internet proposed standard RFC 2617, June 1999.

[Friedl 97] Friedl, Jeffrey E. F. *Mastering Regular Expressions.* O'Reilly & Associates, Sebastopol, Calif., 1997.

[Fung 00] Fung, Khun Yee. *XSLT: Working with XML and HTML.* Addison-Wesley, Boston, 2000.

[Halasz+ 87] Halasz, F., T. Moran, and R. Trigg. "NoteCard in a Nutshell." In *Proceedings of ACM CHI+GI '87 Conference,* pp. 45–52, Toronto, 1987.

[Hall+ 96] Hall, Wendy, Hugh C. Davis, and Gerard Hutchings. *Rethinking Hypermedia: The Microcosm Approach.* Kluwer, Boston, 1996.

[Halsall 96] Halsall, Fred. *Data Communications, Computer Networks and Open Systems, Fourth Edition.* Addison-Wesley, Wokingham, England, 1996.

[Hardman+ 93] Hardman, Lynda, Dick Bulterman, and G. van Rossum. "The Amsterdam Hypermedia Model: Extending Hypertext to Support Real Multimedia." *Hypermedia Journal* 5:47–69, 1993.

[Hinden+ 99] Hinden, Robert M., Brian E. Carpenter, and Larry Masinter. "Format for Literal IPv6 Addresses in URLs." Internet proposed standard RFC 2732, December 1999.

[Holtman & Mutz 98] Holtman, Koen, and Andrew H. Mutz. "Transparent Content Negotiation in HTTP." Internet experimental RFC 2295, March 1998.

[Hoschka 98] Hoschka, Philipp. "Synchronized Multimedia Integration Language (SMIL) 1.0 Specification." World Wide Web Consortium Recommendation, REC-smil-19980615, June 1998.

[IEEE 85] Institute of Electrical and Electronics Engineers (IEEE). "IEEE Standard for Binary Floating-Point Arithmetic." IEEE Std. 754-1985, 1985.

[ISO 86] International Organization for Standardization (ISO). "Information Processing—Text and Office Systems—Standard Generalized Markup Language (SGML)." ISO 8879, 1986.

[ISO 93] International Organization for Standardization (ISO). "Information Technology—Universal Multiple-Octet Coded Character Set (UCS)." ISO/IEC 10646, 1993.

[ISO 96] International Organization for Standardization (ISO). "Information Technology—Processing Languages—Document Style Semantics and Specification Language (DSSSL)." ISO/IEC 10179, 1996.

[ISO 00] International Organization for Standardization (ISO). "Information Technology—SGML Applications—Topic Maps." ISO/IEC 13250, 2000.

[ITU 97] International Telecommunication Union (ITU). "Information Technology—Abstract Syntax Notation One (ASN.1): Specification of Basic Notation." ITU-T Recommendation X.680, December 1997.

[ITU 99] International Telecommunication Union (ITU). "Splitterless Asymmetric Digital Subscriber Line (ADSL) Transceivers." ITU-T Recommendation G.992.2, June 1999.

[Ion & Miner 99] Ion, Patrick, and Robert Miner. "Mathematical Markup Language (MathML) 1.01 Specification." World Wide Web Consortium Recommendation, REC-MathML-19990707, July 1999.

[Jacobs+ 01a] Jacobs, Ian, Jon Gunderson, and Eric Hansen. "Techniques for User Agent Accessibility Guidelines 1.0." World Wide Web Consortium Working Draft, WD-UAAG10-TECHS-20010912, September 2001.

[Jacobs+ 01b] Jacobs, Ian, Jon Gunderson, and Eric Hansen. "User Agent Accessibility Guidelines 1.0." World Wide Web Consortium Candidate Recommendation, CR-UAAG10-20010912, September 2001.

[Kay 00] Kay, Michael. *XSLT Programmer's Reference*. WROX Press, Chicago, 2000.

[Kay 01a] Kay, Michael. "XSL Transformations (XSLT) Version 2.0." World Wide Web Consortium Working Draft, WD-xslt20-20011220, December 2001.

[Kay 01b] Kay, Michael. *XSLT 1.1 Programmer's Reference*. WROX Press, Chicago, 2001.

[Kesselman+ 00] Kesselman, Joe, Jonathan Robie, Mike Champion, Peter Sharpe, Vidur Apparao, and Lauren Wood. "Document Object Model (DOM) Level 2 Traversal and Range Specification." World Wide Web Consortium Recommendation, REC-DOM-Level-2-Traversal-Range-20001113, November 2000.

[Klyne 99] Klyne, Graham. "Protocol-Independent Content Negotiation Framework." Internet informational RFC 2703, September 1999.

[Klyne+ 01] Klyne, Graham, Franklin Reynolds, Chris Woodrow, and Hidetaka Ohto. "Composite Capability/Preference Profiles (CC/PP): Structure and Vocabularies." World Wide Web Consortium Working Draft, WD-CCPP-struct-vocab-20010315, March 2001.

[Knuth 86] Knuth, Donald Ervin. *The TEXbook*. Addison-Wesley, Reading, Mass., 1986.

[Kristol & Montulli 00] Kristol, David M., and Lou Montulli. "HTTP State Management Mechanism." Internet proposed standard RFC 2965, October 2000.

[Lagoze 96] Lagoze, Carl. "A Container Architecture for Diverse Sets of Metadata." *D-Lib Magazine* 2(7), July 1996.

[Lamport 94] Lamport, Leslie. *LaTeX: A Document Preparation System, Second Edition*. Addison-Wesley, Reading, Mass., 1994.

[Lassila & Swick 99] Lassila, Ora, and Ralph R. Swick. "Resource Description Framework (RDF) Model and Syntax Specification." World Wide Web Consortium Recommendation, REC-rdf-syntax-19990222, February 1999.

[Lease 00] Lease, Karen. "External Entities and Alternatives." In *Proceedings of XML Europe 2000,* June 12–16, Paris.

[Le Hors+ 02] Le Hors, Arnaud, Philippe Le Hégaret, Gavin Thomas Nicol, Lauren Wood, Mike Champion, and Steven Byrne. "Document Object Model (DOM) Level 3 Core Specification." World Wide Web Consortium Working Draft, WD-DOM-Level-3-Core-20020114, January 2002.

[Lie & Bos 99] Lie, Håkon Wium, and Bert Bos. "Cascading Style Sheets, Level 1." World Wide Web Consortium Recommendation, REC-CSS1-19990111, January 1999.

[Lowe & Hall 99] Lowe, David, and Wendy Hall. *Hypermedia and the Web: An Engineering Approach.* John Wiley & Sons, Chichester, England, 1999.

[Maler+ 00] Maler, Eve, Daniel Veillard, and Henry S. Thompson. "XLink Markup Name Control." World Wide Web Consortium Note, NOTE-xlink-naming-20001220, December 2000.

[Marsh 01] Marsh, Jonathan. "XML Base." World Wide Web Consortium Recommendation, REC-xmlbase-20010627, June 2001.

[Marsh & Orchard 01] Marsh, Jonathan, and David Orchard. "XML Inclusions (XInclude) Version 1.0." World Wide Web Consortium Working Draft, WD-xinclude-20010516, May 2001.

[Marshall+ 94] Marshall, C. C., F. M. Shipman, and J. H. Coombs. "VIKI: Spatial Hypertext Supporting Emergent Structure." In *Proceedings of ACM ECHT '94,* pp. 13–23, Edinburgh, Scotland, Sept. 18–23, 1994.

[Maurer 96] Maurer, Hermann. *HyperWave—The Next Generation Web Solution.* Addison-Wesley, Reading, Mass., 1996.

[Mockapetris 87a] Mockapetris, P. "Domain Names—Concepts and Facilities." Internet standard RFC 1034, November 1987.

[Mockapetris 87b] Mockapetris, P. "Domain Names—Implementation and Specification." Internet standard RFC 1035, November 1987.

[Moore & Freed 00] Moore, Keith, and Ned Freed. "Use of HTTP State Management Mechanism." Internet best current practice RFC 2964, October 2000.

[Murata+ 01] Murata, Makoto, Simon St. Laurent, and Dan Kohn. "XML Media Types." Internet proposed standard RFC 3023, January 2001.

[NIST 93] National Institute of Standards and Technology (NIST). "Secure Hash Standard (SHS)." FIPS Publication 180, May 1993.

[Nelson 67] Nelson, Theodor Holm. "Getting It Out of Our System." In G. Schechter, ed., *Information Retrieval: A Critical Review.* Thomson Books, Washington, D.C., 1967.

[Nelson 93] Nelson, Theodor Holm. *World Enough.* Mindful Press, Sausalito, Calif., 1993.

[Nelson 95] Nelson, Theodor Holm. "The Heart of Connection: Hypermedia Unified by Transclusion." *Communications of the ACM* 38(8): 1–33, 1995.

[Nielsen 99a] Nielsen, Jakob. *Designing Web Usability: The Practice of Simplicity.* New Riders, Indianapolis, 1999.

[Nielsen 99b] Nielsen, Jakob. "User Interface Directions for the Web." *Communications of the ACM* 42(1): 65–72, 1999.

[Nilsson 00] Nilsson, Mikael. "Composite Capability/Preference Profiles: Terminology and Abbreviations." World Wide Web Consortium Working Draft, WD-CCPP-ta-20000721, July 2000.

[Nilsson+ 00] Nilsson, Mikael, Johan Hjelm, and Hidetaka Ohto. "Composite Capability/Preference Profiles: Requirements and Architecture." World Wide Web Consortium Working Draft, WD-CCPP-ra-20000721, July 2000.

[Novoselsky & Karun 00] Novoselsky, A., and K. Karun. "XSLTVM—An XSLT Virtual Machine." In *Proceedings of XML Europe 2000*, June 12–16, Paris.

[Oberholzer & Wilde 02] Oberholzer, Glenn, and Erik Wilde. "Extended Link Visualization with DHTML: The Web as an Open Hypermedia System." Technical Report TIK-Report No. 125, Computer Engineering and Networks Laboratory, Swiss Federal Institute of Technology, Zürich, January 2002.

[OMG 01] Object Management Group (OMG), *OMG Unified Modeling Language Specification Version 1.4,* Framingham, Mass., September 2001.

[Pemberton 00] Pemberton, Steven. "XHTML 1.0: The Extensible HyperText Markup Language." World Wide Web Consortium Recommendation, REC-xhtml1-20000126, January 2000.

[Pepper & Moore 01] Pepper, Steve, and Graham Moore. "XML Topic Maps (XTM) 1.0." TopicMaps.org, Specification xtm1-20010806, August 2001.

[Peterson & Davie 99] Peterson, Larry L., and Bruce S. Davie. *Computer Networks: A Systems Approach, Second Edition.* Morgan Kaufmann, San Francisco, 1999.

[Plzak+ 99] Plzak, Raymond, Amy T. Wells, and Ed Krol. "FYI on Questions and Answers—Answers to Commonly Asked 'New Internet User' Questions." Internet informational RFC 2664, August 1999.

[Postel 81a] Postel, Jon B. "Internet Protocol." Internet standard RFC 791, September 1981.

[Postel 81b] Postel, Jon B. "Transmission Control Protocol." Internet standard RFC 793, September 1981.

[Proc XML 00] *Proceedings of XML Europe 2000*, June 12–16, 2000, Paris.

[Raggett 97] Raggett, Dave. "HTML 3.2 Reference Specification." World Wide Web Consortium Recommendation, REC-html32, January 1997.

[Raggett+ 99] Raggett, Dave, Arnaud Le Hors, and Ian Jacobs. "HTML 4.01 Specification." World Wide Web Consortium Recommendation, REC-html401-19991224, December 1999.

[Ritz+ 01] Ritz, Shlomit, Stéphane Maes, and Lalitha Suryanarayana. "Device Independence Principles." World Wide Web Consortium Working Draft, WD-di-princ-20010918, September 2001.

[Rivest 92] Rivest, Ronald L. "The MD5 Message-Digest Algorithm." Internet informational RFC 1321, April 1992.

[Robertson+ 81] Robertson, C., D. McCracken, and A. Newell. "The ZOG Approach to Man-Machine Communication." *International Journal of Man-Machine Studies* 14: 461–488, 1981.

[Rowell 01] Rowell, Michael. *Understanding EAI: Enterprise Application Integration.* Sams, Indianapolis, 2001.

[Ruh+ 00] Ruh, William A., Francis X. Maginnis, and William J. Brown. *Enterprise Application Integration: A Wiley Tech Brief.* John Wiley & Sons, Chichester, England, 2000.

[Schulzrinne+ 96] Schulzrinne, Henning, Stephen L. Casner, Ron Frederick, and Van Jacobson. "RTP: A Transport Protocol for Real-Time Applications." Internet proposed standard RFC 1889, January 1996.

[Schwabe & Rossi 95] Schwabe, Daniel, and Gustavo Rossi. "The Object-Oriented Hypermedia Design Model." *Communications of the ACM* 38(8): 45–46, 1995.

[Schwabe+ 96] Schwabe, Daniel, Gustavo Rossi, and Simone D. J. Barbosa. "Systematic Hypermedia Application Design with OOHDM." In *Proceedings of the 1996 ACM Conference on Hypertext,* pp. 116–128. ACM Press, Washington, D.C., March 1996.

[Shafer+ 96] Shafer, Keith, Stuart L. Weibel, Erik Jul, and Jon Fausey. "Introduction to Persistent Uniform Resource Locators." In *Proceedings of International Networking Conference INET'96,* pp. BFC-1–BFC-9, Montreal, June 1996.

[Shneiderman 87] Shneiderman, Ben. "User Interface Design for the Hypertics Elec tronic Encyclopedia." In *Proceedings of the 1987 ACM Conference on Hypertext,* pp. 189–194. ACM Press, Chapel Hill, N.C., November 1987.

[Shneiderman & Kearsley 89] Shneiderman, Ben, and Greg Kearsley. *Hypertext Hands-On!: An Introduction to a New Way of Organizing and Accessing Information.* Addison-Wesley, Reading, Mass., 1989.

[Simpson 94] Simpson, William Allen. "The Point-to-Point Protocol (PPP)." Internet standard RFC 1661, July 1994.

[Stallings 99] Stallings, William. *Data and Computer Communications, Sixth Edition.* Prentice-Hall, Englewood Cliffs, N.J., 1999.

[Stanyer & Procter 99] Stanyer, Dominic, and Rob Procter. "Improving Web Usability with the Link Lens." In *Proceedings of the Eighth International World Wide Web Conference,* pp. 455–466. Elsevier, Toronto, May 1999.

[Stone+ 94] Stone, Maureen C., Ken Fishkin, and Eric A. Bier. "The Movable Filter as a User Interface Tool." In *CHI '94: Proceedings of the ACM Conference on Human Factors and Computing Systems,* pp. 306–312. ACM Press, Boston, April 1994.

[Tanenbaum 96] Tanenbaum, Andrew S. *Computer Networks, Third Edition.* Prentice-Hall, Englewood Cliffs, N.J., 1996.

[Tannenbaum 01] Tannenbaum, Adrienne. *Metadata Solutions: Using Metamodels, Repositories, XML, and Enterprise Portals to Generate Information on Demand.* Addison-Wesley, Boston, 2001.

[Thompson+ 01] Thompson, Henry S., David Beech, Murray Maloney, and Noah Mendelsohn. "XML Schema Part 1: Structures." World Wide Web Consortium Recommendation, REC-xmlschema-1-20010502, May 2001.

[Treviranus+ 00a] Treviranus, Jutta, Jan Richards, Ian Jacobs, and Charles McCathieNevile. "Authoring Tool Accessibility Guidelines 1.0." World Wide Web Consortium Recommendation, REC-ATAG10-20000203, February 2000.

[Treviranus+ 00b] Treviranus, Jutta, Jan Richards, Ian Jacobs, and Charles McCathieNevile. "Techniques for Authoring Tool Accessibility Guidelines 1.0." World Wide Web Consortium Note, NOTE-ATAG10-TECHS-20000203, February 2000.

[Unicode 00] Unicode Consortium. *The Unicode Standard: Version 3.0.* Addison-Wesley, Boston, 2000.

[Wall+ 00] Wall, Larry, Tom Christiansen, and Jon Orwant. *Programming Perl, Third Edition.* O'Reilly & Associates, Sebastopol, Calif., 2000.

[Walsh 01] Walsh, Norman. "XML Linking and Style." World Wide Web Consortium Note, NOTE-xml-link-style-20010605, June 2001.

[WAP 99] WAP Forum. "Wireless Application Protocol." WAP white paper, June 1999.

[WAP 01] WAP Forum. "Wireless Application Protocol—WAP 2.0 Technical White Paper," August 2001.

[Weibel+ 98] Weibel, Stuart L., John A. Kunze, Carl Lagoze, and Misha Wolf. "Dublin Core Metadata for Resource Discovery." Internet informational RFC 2413, September 1998.

[Wilde 98] Wilde, Erik. *Wilde's WWW—Technical Foundations of the World Wide Web.* Springer-Verlag, Berlin, 1998.

[Wilde & Lowe 00] Wilde, Erik, and David Lowe. "From Content-Centered Publishing to a Link-Based View of Information Resources." In *Proceedings of the 33rd Hawaii International Conference on System Sciences,* IEEE Computer Society Press, Maui, Hawaii, January 2000.

[Wood+ 00a] Wood, Lauren, Arnaud Le Hors, Vidur Apparao, Steven Byrne, Mike Champion, Scott Isaacs, Ian Jacobs, Gavin Thomas Nicol, Jonathan Robie, Robert Sutor, and Chris Wilson. "Document Object Model (DOM) Level 1 Specification (Second Edition)." World Wide Web Consortium Working Draft, WD-DOM-Level-1-20000929, September 2000.

[Wood+ 00b] Wood, Lauren, Arnaud Le Hors, Vidur Apparao, Laurence Cable, Mike Champion, Joe Kesselman, Philippe Le Hégaret, Tom Pixley, Jonathan Robie, Peter Sharpe, and Chris Wilson. "Document Object Model (DOM) Level 2 Specification." World Wide Web Consortium Candidate Recommendation, CR-DOM-Level-2-20000510, May 2000.

[W3C 95] World Wide Web Consortium (W3C). *Hypertext Terms,* April 1995.

[Yankelovich+ 85] Yankelovich, N., N. Meyrowitz, and N. Van Dam. "Reading and Writing the Electronic Book." *IEEE Computer* 18(10): 15–30, 1985.

[Yergeau 98] Yergeau, François. "UTF-8, A Transformation Format of ISO 10646." Internet proposed standard RFC 2279, January 1998.

[Zakon 97] Zakon, Robert H. "Hobbes' Internet Timeline." Internet informational RFC 2235, November 1997.

Index

A

Abbreviations, XPath, 106, *118*–120
Absolute location paths, 104
Absolute URIs, 101
Access control, 20
Accessibility issues, in XML-based
    systems, 219–220
actuate = "onLoad" attribute, 47
Actuate value, in XLink, 184–185
Adaptive hypertext systems, 25
ADSL. *See* Asymmetric digital
    subscriber line
<A> element, 185
<a> element, 9, 18, 39, 154, 169
<A> links, 184
AHM. *See* Amsterdam Hypermedia
    Model
Aliases, Web server, 57
All element types partition, 77
Amaya authoring tool (W3C), link
    support through, 210
Amsterdam Hypermedia Model, 17
ancestor axis
  and point, 145
  in XPath, *107*, 109–110
ancestor-or-self axis
  and point, 145
  in XPath, *107*, 110
Anchors, 7, 10, 49, 50, 51. *See also* Links
  and <a> element, 9
  definition of, 39
  lack of overlapping, 13–14
  and nontextual links, 34

  overlapping, 45–46
  and SMIL, 36
Animation, 22, 43
Application Programming Interface
    (API), 81
Application-specific hyperlink
    definitions, 169
arc elements, 179, 183
arcrole attribute, 54, 61, 195
  and link semantics, 216
  and link typing, 64, 65
  in XLink, 183
arcrole value, 194
Arcs, 49, 52, 53, 54
  inline extended link with, *175*
  out-of-line extended link with, *176*
  and presentation semantics, 202
  roles, 54
  titles and roles for, 63
  and traversal attributes, 188
  in XLink, 178, 183
arc type, 175
arc value, in type attribute, 181
Association
  and arcs, 52, 53
  levels of viewing, 37–38
  selection by, 22
  and typed links, 64
Association semantics, XLink support
    of, 81
Associative links, 18, 30
"As We May Think" (Bush), 22
Asymmetric digital subscriber line, 5
attribute axis
  of point, 145
  in XPath, 110

Note: Italicized page locators refer to
figures and/or tables.

attribute information item, 83
Attribute-list declarations, 73
Attribute location, and covering
    range, 147
Attribute names, in XLink, 170
Attribute node, in XPath, 99, 100
Attributes
    and Hyperwave document
        management, 33
    and SMIL, 36
    in XLink, 170
Audio, 22, 34
    clips, 38
    and RTP, 70
Audio data, pattern matching for, 41
author attribute, 117
Authoring
    complex, 208–209
    tools, 196
Authoring approaches, 213–220
    accessibility and usability, 219–220
    controlling linking and ensuring link
        integrity, 215
    identifying things to link, 213–215
    link semantics, 216–219
Authoring aspects
    complex authoring, 208
    lack of presentation semantics,
        201–203
    legal issues, 207–208
    loss of context, 206–207
    tool support, 206
    unclear processing model, 203–206
Axes in XPath, 106–115
    ancestor, *107*, 109–110
    ancestor-or-self, *107*, 110
    attribute, 110
    child, 106, *107*, 111
    descendant, *107*, 111–112
    descendant-or-self, *108*, 112
    direction of, 106–107
    following, *108*, 112
    following-sibling, *108*, 112–113
    namespace, 113
    overview of, *106*
    parent, *108*, 113–114
    preceding, *109*, 114
    preceding-sibling, *109*, 114

principal node type of, 107
    self, *109*, 114–115

B
Bare names, 150–151, 153
base element, 79
Base URIs, rules for calculating, 79
begin attribute, 37
Behavior attributes, 184–187
    actuate, 184–185
    show, 185–187
    XLink, 180, 184–187
Berners-Lee, Tim, xxvii, 7, 8, 69
Bidirectional associations between
        information, 25
Big Bang approach, 234
Big Bang transition, 224, 225
body element, 73
book element, 193
Bookmarks, 213
Boolean functions, XPath, 125–126
boolean object type, 96
Boolean type, 146
Boolean values, and boolean
        functions, 125
Broken links, 13, 57, 141
Browsers
    and content misuse, 238
    and content negotiation, 232
    copyright issues and design of, 208
    support within, for XLink and
        XPointer, 210–211
    XML supported by, 142
Bush, Vannevar, xv, xxvi, 22, 23

C
Cable modem, 5
Cached resources, and XLink, 194–195
Cache identifiers, 182
Canonical XML, 87
Cascading Style Sheets (CSS), xxv, xxix,
        48, 69, 90
    and XSL-FO, 92
CC/PP. *See* Composite
        Capability/Preference Profiles
CDATA sections, 84, 102
CDF. *See* Channel Definition Format
ceiling function, 127

CERN, xxvii
CGI programs, and dynamic links, 40
Channel Definition Format
    (Microsoft), 93
chap elements, 133
chapter elements, 117
@ character, and attribute axis, 110
Character escaping, XPointer, 162–163
character information item, 84
Character points, 145, *146*, 148
Checksums, 182
  algorithms, 167
  and XLink extension, 195
child axis
  of point, 145
  in XPath, *107*, 111
child elements, and prefixes, 77
child information items, 82
Child nodes, 99, 102, 145
children locator, 63
Child sequences, 151–153
Client diversity, and authoring
    content, 231
Client-side transformations, of XML
    resources, 203
Cluster collection, 32–33
Code libraries, XML, 211
Coleridge, Samuel Taylor, 23
Collapsed range, 146
Collection head, 32
Collection hierarchy, 31, 32
Colon (:)
  within qualified name, 75
  and XML Namespaces, 78
comment information item, 85
Comment nodes
  and child axis, 111
  and XPath, 101
Complex authoring, 208–209
Complex links, and processing model, 204
Composite Capability/Preference Profiles
    (W3C), 232
Computed link filters, 30
concat function, 128
Conceptual associations, representation
    of, 37
Container nodes, 144, 145, *146*
contains function, 128

Content
  embedding, 47–48
  link semantics and embedding of,
    47–48
  locating appropriate links, 213–215
  transclusion of, with XLink, 206–207
  in transitioning to new model, 223
Content management
  and linkbases, 195–198
  and link checking, 215
Content migration, and transitioning to
    new model, 233–235
Content model, link data model
    integrated with, 196
Content negotiation
  flexibility of, 233
  and internal hybrid, external
    hybrid, 230
  and transitioning to new model,
    231–233
Content structuring and management,
    restrictive, 18
Context
  controlling, 48
  loss of, 206–207
  in XPath, 97
Context node, XPath, 97
Context position, in XPath, 97
Context size, in XPath, 97
Contextualization, 11
Convergence, xxv
Conversion level, and XLinks, 196
Cookies, xxviii
coords attribute, 37
Copyright issues, 220, 238–239
  and conventional HTML pages, 44
  with transclusion, 198, 205*n*, 207–208
  and XLink's success, 198
Cost-benefits analysis, with new model of
    handling hypermedia, 221
count function, 131
Covering range, 147
Crosshatch character (#), and fragment
    identifier, 71, 139
Cross-linking, rich, 42
Cross-referencing, universal, 64
Cross-site references, 30
CSS. *See* Cascading Style Sheets

D

Data capture, and building new sites, 235, 236

Data creation, integration layer, migration strategy and, 234

Datagrams, 5, 6

Data model, versatility and power with, 239

date attribute, 117

DCS. *See* Document Control System

Deep linking, 198, 238

Default namespaces, 76, 77

defs.xml file, 45

descendant axis
  of point, 145
  in XPath, *107*, 111–112

descendant-or-self axis
  and point, 145
  in XPath, *108*, 112

Descendants, XPath, 99, 100

Design
  browser, 208
  data model, 236
  of links, 214
  usage-centered, 215

Destination anchors
  and link semantics, 17
  and simple Web links, 26

Destination links, xxvii

Development tools, for XLink and XPointer support, 213

Device Independence Activity, 239

DHTML. *See* Dynamic HTML

Dial-up connections, 4, 5

Dictionaries, universal cross-references in, 64

Digital fingerprints, fragment, 215

Digital Millennium Copyright Act, 239

Directional associations between information, 25

Directional links, 39

Direction of axis, 106–107

Discussion forums, 42

Displays, and content negotiation, 231, 232

dl element, 154

DMCA. *See* Digital Millennium Copyright Act

DNS. *See* Domain Name System

Document collections, 31

Document Control System, 28

document document type, 73

document function, 124

document information item, 82

Document management, Hyperwave, 31–33

Document Object Model, xxv, xxix, 48, 70, 81

Document order
  determining in XPointer, 147
  of XPath nodes, 98

Document Style Semantics and Specification Language, 90, 91

document type declaration information item, 85

Document Type Definition, xxix*n*, 73–74
  document for sample, 74
  and external entities, 80
  for XLink content, 191

Document types, reuse of, 75

DOM. *See* Document Object Model

Domain Name System, 3, 6, 56

DSSSL. *See* Document Style Semantics and Specification Language

DTD. *See* Document Type Definition

dt element, 154

Dublin Core, 65
  meta-data keywords, 92–93

Dynamic HTML, xxx, 48

Dynamic links, xxvi, 40
  Web, 26, *27*

E

EAI. *See* Enterprise Application Integration

ECMA. *See* European Computer Manufacturers Association

ECMAScript, 70*n*

e-commerce, xxv

Editor-type applications, 88*n*

Electronic mail (e-mail), 3, 4

element information item, 83

Element node, in XPath, 99–100

element node type, 107

Element type attribute, XLink, 180–181

Element type declarations, 73
Embedded anchors, 11, 41
Embedded links, 46
embed value, for show attribute, 186
end attribute, 37
Endpoint, 145, 149
end-point function, in XPointer, 157
Engelbart, Doug, xxvi, 23
Enterprise Application Integration, 229
ENTITY attribute type, 83
Entity-Relationship Model, 235
Escaping mechanisms, XPointer, 162
ETags, 215
European Computer Manufacturers
     Association, 70*n*
Examples
    selecting nodes from XML documents,
      120–121
    XPath, 133–136
expanded-name, 98
    for attribute nodes, 100
    for namespace node, 101
    for processing instruction node, 101
Expressions, in XPath, 96, 121–123
extended element, 178, 179
Extended links
    DTD declarations for, 192
    and href attribute, 181
    remote resources in, 178
    XLink, 172, 174–177
extended type element, 174, 175,
     177, 181
extended value, in type attribute, 181
Extensible Hypertext Markup Language,
    xxix, 70, 88–89, 94
Extensible Markup Language, xxv–xxvi,
    xvii, xxviii–xxx, 20, 49, 70, 94
    and B2B scenarios, 238
    and building new sites, 235
    as catalyst for information
      management paradigm, 222
    core standards, 71–74
    design goals for, 72
    escaping rules, 162
    external entities, 80
    and hypermedia implementation, 237
    and linking, 50, 52
    namespaces, 75–78

XLink built on top of, 188, 189
Extensible Stylesheet Language, xxviii,
    69, 89–92, 94
    formatting semantics defined in, 74
    XSL Formatting Objects, 92
    XSL Transformations, 90–91
External linkbases, 44
External links, 46, 215
External transition, to new model, 224

F

False function, 125
figure descendants, 117
Filtering, 143, 165, 226
Filter Manager, 28
Filters, and XPath, 134
#FIXED attributes, 191
Floating-point arithmetic, 128
floor function, 127
Folders, bookmark, 213–214
following axis
    of point, 145
    in XPath, *108*, 112
following-sibling axis
    of point, 145
    in XPath, *108*, 112–113
Formatting semantics, 74, 90
Forward axis, 106, 111, 112, 113
Fragment digital fingerprints, 215
Fragment identification
    development tools for support of, 213
    XML, 167
Fragment identifiers, 9, 71, 139, 141, 210
    persistence of, 57, 59
    and processing model, 204, 205
Fragment reference, 59
"Framing," 198, 238
from attribute, in XLink, 188
Full XPointers, 150, 153–156
Function library, XPath, 97
Functions
    boolean, 125–126
    node set, 131–133
    number, 125, 126–128
    overview of XPointer, *157*
    string, 128–131
    XPath, 96, 123, *124*, 125
    XPointer, 156–161

G

Gecko browser engine (Netscape), XML
    support through, 210
General hyperlink specification
    mechanism, 169
General model-XPath, 96–103
    attribute node, 100
    comment node, 101
    element node, 99–100
    namespace node, 100–101
    processing instruction node, 101
    root node, 99
    text node, 101–102
Generation level, and XLinks, 196
Generic anchors, 41
Generic links, xxvii, 27–30, 44–45, 46,
    63–64, 66
    definition of, 40
    patterns for creation of, 41
    with simplification of Webcosm
        server, *28*
Generic locators, 64
Global attribute partition, 77–78, 170
Global attributes, 77, 78
Glossaries
    example, 197
    universal cross-references in, 64
Gnome XML Library (*libxml*), XML
    support with, 212
Google, 13
Graphics, 22
GSM mobile communications
    standard, 237
Guided tours, 20

H

Hand-coding, XLink, XPointer and,
    212–213
heading element, 73
Here function, in XPointer, 158
Hierarchies of linkbases, 61
Highlighting links, 64
href attribute, 9, 37, 181, 182
h3 element, 153, 154
HTML. *See* Hypertext Markup Language
HTML-capable clients with scripting
    capabilities, and content
    negotiation, 232–233

HTML clients with no scripting support,
    and content negotiation, 233
HTML Tidy, 88*n*
HTTP. *See* HyperText Transfer Protocol
HTTP cookies, and dynamic links, 40
http scheme, 56, 57
Hybrid systems
    migration strategy in, 234
    and transition to new model, 224, 225
Hypercard, xxviii, 23
Hyper-G, 23, 31
Hyperlinks
    semantics, 74
    used with XML documents, 169
Hypermedia, xvii, xviii, xxx, 237
    dearth of high-quality, 208–209
    definition of, 23–25
    description of, 21–22
    history of, 22–23
    new model of handling, 221–222
    systems, 20, 49
    and XPointer, 142–143
Hypermedia concepts, 25–42
    dynamic Web link, 26–27
    generic link, 27–30
    nontextual link, 34–37
    set-based association, 33–34
    simple Web link, 25–26
    spatial hypertext associations, 33
    structural links, 30–33
Hypertext, xv, xxvi, 21
    history behind, 23
    and nonlinearity, 24
    spatial, *34*
    systems, xxvii
Hypertext Markup Language, xxvii, 8,
    49, 71
    base element in, 79
    as common content format, 69–70
    and copyright lawsuits, 238
    difficulties with links supported by, 13
    and illegal links, 198
    links, 50, 214
    multiple-source links implemented
        in, *16*
    and overlapping anchors, 13–14
    and success of Web, 20
    transition from, to XHTML, 89

HyperText Transfer Protocol, xxvii, 6, 69, 70, 71
  content negotiation supported by, 231–232
  ETags provided by, 215
  protocol, 7, 8
Hyperties, 23
Hyperwave, xxviii, 17, 23, 31, 38
  server, 20
  structural links in, 30–33
  structural links with simplification of, *31*
Hyperwave Web page, structural links in, *32*

I
id attribute, 36
Identifiers, 50, 51
  persistence of, 56, 57, 66
IDREF attribute type, 83
IDs
  and embedded anchors, 41
  and fragment identifiers, 141, 142
  and persistence, 166
"Illegal links," 198
Image data, pattern matching for, 41
Image maps, and link anchor definition, 35–36
Images, 11, 34, 38
<IMG> links, 184
Immediately preceding node, 147
#IMPLIED, 100
Inbound links, 173
include statement, 80
Inclusion, 42, 208
  definition of, 41
  XML, 80–81
Incremental development, with hybrid systems, 224, 225
Incremental transitions with dual systems, 224, 225
InDelv client, and XML support, 211
Indexes, 22, 144, 145
  linking, 13
  of node point, 145
Information architects, 222

Information associations
  conception of, 37
  representing, 25
Information items, XML
  Infoset, *82–86*
Information linking, xxvi–xxvii
Information management, richer user experience and, 48
Information modeling, 235
"Information trails," 22
Infrastructure, and transitioning to new model, 223
Inline extended links, *174*
  with arcs, *175*
Inline links, 174
  out-of-line links converted into, 211
Inlining of content, xxx
Input devices, and content negotiation, 231, 232
Integration, and internal hybrid/external hybrid, 230
Integration layer, and migration of content, 233–234
Intellectual property rights, and XLink's transclusion features, 238
Interactive groupwork, 42
Intermedia, 23
Internal transition, 224
Internationalization
  and title elements, 180
  and XLink, 193
Internet. *See also* World Wide Web
  connecting to, 4–5
  datagram, 5
  environment, 3–6
  host names, 56
  hosts, 6
  way it works, 5–6
Internet Explorer, 210
Internet Protocol, 5, 6
Internet protocol suite, 3
Internet service provider, 4
Interoperability issues, resolving, 222
IP. *See* Internet Protocol
IP addresses, 6, 56
isbn prefix, 77
ISOC. *See* Internet Society
ISP. *See* Internet service provider

J
JavaScript, 18, 19, 70
JScript, 70

K
key function, 134
KMS, 23
Knowledge Interchange Format (KIF), 93
Knowledge representation, and
    RDF, 93

L
label attribute, in XLink, 188
lang function, 125
LANs. *See* Local area networks
last-call ID, 154
last function, 132
Leased lines, 5
Legacy content, 223
Legal issues, with transclusion, 198, 205*n*,
    207–208, 238
Link-adding proxies, 44
Link authoring, development tools for
    support of, 213
Link anchors, 44–45
Linkbase filter, 28
Linkbases, 60–62, 66, 198, 201, 205
    access to, 197–198
    and arcrole attribute, 183
    and control of links, 215
    development tools for management
        of, 213
    richer, 209
    and XLink, 195, *196*
Link data model, behind processing
    model, 205
linker function, 19
Linking, xxix, xxvi–xxvii
    controlling, 215
    formalizing concepts of, 37–42
    identifying items for, 213–215
    indexes, 13
Link lens, 220
Links, 7, 50, 52, 53
    adding to read-only material, 44
    associative, 18, 30
    broken, 13, 57, 141
    complex, 204

definition of, 39
difficulty in backtracking through, 13
directional, 39
dynamic, xxvi, 40
effective design of, 214
embedded, 46
embedded unidirectional, 11
embedding into XML documents,
    170–171
extended, 172, 174–177, 178, 181, 192
external, 46, 215
generic, 27–30, 40
highlighting, 64
information presentation, 37
inline, 174, 211
inline extended, *174*
integrity of, 215
multidirectional, xxix–xxx, 173
multiple-destination, xxx
multiple-source, xxvi–xxvii, *16*, 41
multiple-source, single-destination, 27
nontextual, 34–37
number of, 219
origin of, 220
outbound, 173
out-of-line, 173, 174, 195, 201, 211
out-of-line extended, 173, *176*, 212
out-of-link, 212
overlapping, 220
placement of, 219–220
references *vs.*, 49–54
semantic, 10
simple, 172, 173–174, 181, 212
simple Web, 25, *26*
single-source, single-destination, 15–16,
    31, *26*, 204
and SMIL, 36
specific, 30
static, 40
structural, 10, 17, 18, 30–33
third-party, 44, 45, 59–61, 198, 204
traversing in XLink, 184, 185
typed, 64–66
unidirectional, 11
untyped, 12, 16–18
and URI references, 139
Web, *26*, *27*
XLink support of, 171–172

Link semantics, 74
  controlling context, 48
  definition of, 39
  embedding content, 47–48
  and untyped links, 17
links.xml file, 216–217
Link traversal, and processing model,
    203–204
Link typing, 64–66
link.xml file, 45
Local area networks, 5
Localization, and title elements, 180
Local link, 30
local-name function, 132
Local part, 75
Local resources, in XLink, 178, 181
Location, and covering range, 147
Location paths
  and XML documents examples,
      120–121
  and XPath abbreviations, 118–119
Location paths in XPath, 96, 103–121
  abbreviations, 118–120
  axes, 106–115
  examples, 120–121
  location steps, 105–106
  node tests, 115–116
  predicates, 116–118
Locations, XPointer, 143
Location sets, 50
  XPointer, 143, 144
Location step predicates, location paths
    in, 117
Location steps, in XPath, 105–106
Location types, XPointer, 143
Locator attribute, in XLink, 180, 181–182
Locator elements, 52, 178, 179
Locators, generic, 64
locator type, 174, 175
locator value, in type attribute, 181
Lycos, 13

M
Magic lens, 220
mailto URLs, 57
Mapping
  and content negotiation, 233
  and transition to new model, 222

XML documents to relational
    structures, 228
Market success, unpredictability
    of, 238
Master linkbases, 61–62
Mathematical Markup Language
    (MathML), 77, 89
MCF. *See* Meta Content Framework
MD5, 167
Memex, xv, 22
Menus, 30, 32
Message passing, in Microcosm link
    service architecture, *29*
Meta Content Framework
    (Netscape), 93
Meta-data, 11, 65, 66, 219
  and building new sites, 235, 236
  RDF definition of, 92
meta element, 92
Meta tags, 11
Microcosm, 23
  linkbases in, 30
  link service, 28
Microcosm link service architecture,
    message passing in, *29*
Micropayment systems, 23
Microsoft, 7
  and CDF, 93
Microsoft Internet Explorer (version 6),
    XML support through, 210
Microsoft XML implementation, to
    support XML-related
    functionality, 210
Migration issues, and support of old data
    model to new, 228–229
Migration of content, and transitioning to
    new model, 233–235
MIME. *See* Multipurpose Internet Mail
    Extensions
MIME types, XML documents associated
    with, 139
Mobile phones, 231
Modem, 4
Modularization, advantages with, 89
MSXML. *See* Microsoft XML
    implementation
Multidirectional links, xxix–xxx, 173
Multi-ended links, 62–63, 66, 198

Multimedia
  and link semantics, 17
  pattern matching for, 41
Multiple-destination links, xxx
Multiple selections, making, 149–150
Multiple-source anchors, supporting, 19
Multiple-source links, xxvi–xxvii, 41
  benefits with, 16
  implementing in HTML, *16*
  lack of, 15
Multiple-source, single-destination
    links, 27
Multi-property-set XSL-FO formatting
    object, 48
Multipurpose Internet Mail
    Extensions, 139*n*
Multi-switch XSL-FO formatting
    object, 48

N

"Name clashes," 75
name function, 132
namespace axis
  of point, 145
  in XPath, 113
Namespace conformance, 78
Namespace declarations, 76
  and namespace axis, 110, 113
  in XML documents, 86
  in XPath, 97
namespace information item, 86
Namespace location, and covering
    range, 147
Namespace nodes, in XPath, 99,
    100–101
Namespace partitions, 77
Namespace prefixes, 75, 76, 83
Namespaces
  XML, 75–78
  and XPointers, 163–164
namespace-uri function, 132–133
Name test, node test used as, 116
NaN (Not a Number) value, 126, 129
Negative infinity, 126, 129
Negative sign-magnitude numbers, 126
Negative zero, 126, 127, 129
Nelson, Ted, xv, xvii, xxi, xxvi, 23, 42, 45
Nested anchors, HTML support of, 13

Nested collections, 34
Netscape, 7
  Meta Content Framework, 93
Netscape Navigator (version 6), XML
    support through, 210
new value, for show attribute, 185
Nielsen, Jakob, 219
NLS. *See* oN-Line System
Node points, 145, *146*, 148
Node relationships, XPath, 99
Nodes, 51, 149
  definition of, 38
  examples of selecting from XML
    document, 120–121
  selecting text spanning number of, 149
Node selection, and location paths, 117
Node set functions, in XPath, 131–133
node-set object type, 96
Node-set of document, and location
    paths, 104
Node sets, 117, 146
Node sizes, determining, 38
Node test
  in location step, 106
  in XPath, 115–116
node test*
  and attribute axis, 110
  and child axis, 111
  and descendant axis, 111
  and namespace axis, 113
Node tree, in XPath, *103*
NodeType, extension of XPath's
    definition of, 144
none value
  for actuate attribute, 185
  for show attribute, 187
  for type attribute, 181
Nontextual link, 34–37
Non-zero index, 145
normalize-space function, 129, 135
NOTATION attribute type, 83
notation information item, 84, 85
NoteCards, 23
not function, 126
number function, 127
Number functions, in XPath, 126–128
Number object type, 96
Number type, 146

O

Object-Oriented Hypermedia Design
    Model (OOHDM), 215
Object types, in XPath, 96
OmniMark, XML file processing with, 212
onclick event, 19
oN-Line System (NLS), 23
OnLoad value, for actuate attribute, 184
onRequest value, for actuate
    attribute, 185
Ontology, 93
Open eBook (OEB) format, 93
Opera browser, 10n, 210
Operands, in XPath expressions,
    121, 122
Operators, in XPath, 121, *122*, 123
origin function, in XPointer, 158
other value
    for actuate attribute, 185
    for show attribute, 187
Outbound links, 173
Out-of-line extended links, *176*
    with arcs, *176*
    support for, 212
Out-of-line links, 173, 175, 201
    converting into inline links, 211
    converting into simple links, 212
    and XLink, 195, 198
Overlapping anchors, 11, 45–46
Overlapping links, 220

P

Palm-top computers, 231
Paragraph nodes, 149
parent axis
    of point, 145
    in XPath, *108*, 113–114
Parentheses, for grouping XPath
    expressions, 122, 123
Parent nodes
    and parent axis, 113
    XPath, 99, 102
parents locator, 63
Parsers, in XML, 211
part elements, 133
Participating resources, 172
Path notation, 96
Pattern matching, 41, 212

PDAs. *See* Personal digital assistants
PDF. *See* Portable Document Format
People element, 87, 102
Per-element-type partition, 78
Perl, 131
Permanent connection, 5
Permissions, and attributes, 33
Persistence, 162, 215
    of identifiers, 57, 66
    of references, 57–59
    resource identifier, 59
    of XPaths, 134
    of XPointers, 166–167
Persistent URLs, 56n
Personal digital assistants, 70n
PICS, xxv
PNG, xxv
Pointers, 41, 49, 50
Point location, and covering range, 147
Points, marking with document, 148
Point-to-Point Protocol (PPP), 4
Portable Document Format, and XSL-FO
    processors, 92
position function, 133
Positive infinity, 126, 129
Positive sign-magnitude numbers, 126
Positive zero, 126, 127, 129
preceding axis
    of point, 145
    in XPath, *109*, 114
preceding-sibling axis
    of point, 145
    in XPath, *109*, 114
Predicate2, 121
    in location step, 106
    in XPath, 116–118
Prefixes
    namespace, 75, 76
    and XPointer scheme parts, 164
Presentation level, and XLinks, 196–197
Presentation nodes, size of, 38
Presentation semantics, 211
    lack of in XLink and XPointer,
        201–203
Primitive link types, 30
Principal node type of axis, 107
Processing instruction information
    item, 84

Processing instruction nodes, 102
  in child axis, 111
  in XPath, 101
Processing model, unclear issues with in
    XLink and XPointer, 203–206
product element, 218
products.xml file, 216
products.xsl file, 217
Profiles, 72
Properties, in XML Infoset information
    items, 82
Proximity position, of node in node
    set, 117
Publishing by reference, 42
PURLs. *See* Persistent URLs

Q
QName definition, from XML
    Namespaces recommendation,
    116
Qualified names, 75
Quality control, 222
query, 55

R
Range, 49, 145–148, 149
range function, in XPointer, 158
range-inside function, in XPointer,
    158–159
Range location, and covering range, 147
range-to function, in XPointer, 159
RDF. *See* Resource Description
    Framework
Read access to data, integration layer,
    migration strategy and, 234
Read-only material
  inability to link from or into, 12–13
  links added to, 44
Real-time data transmission, 70
Real Time Protocol, 70
References
  links *vs.*, 49–54
  persistence of, 57–59
  publishing by, 42
Relational data model, and XML's data
    model, 227–228
Relative location paths, 104
Relative URIs, 79, 101

Remote resources
  and href attribute, 182
  in XLink, 178, 181
replace value, for show attribute, 186
resource attribute value, 174
Resource Description Framework, xxv,
    xxix, 8, 65, 92, 93, 94, 219
resource element type, 178
Resource errors, for XPointer, 155*n*
Resource fragments, 57
Resource identification, 54–56, 66
  with URIs, 55
  URLs as, 70–71
  with URLs and URNs, 55–56
Resource identifier persistence, 59
Resources, 49, 50, 51, 52, 53, 57
  and inclusions, 80
  in link, 172
  origin of, 220
  and persistence, 166
  separation of linking from, 201
  short life span of, 141
  and topic maps, 197
  in XLink, 178
resource type, 174, 175
resource value, in type attribute, 181
Reverse axis, 106, 114
Reverse document order, XPath
    nodes, 99
Richer approach, example strategies for
    achieving, 226–230
Richer linking functionality, scripting
    languages used for, 18–19
Richly linked applications, approaches
    to, 213–220
Robustness
  and fragment identifiers, 204
  of XPaths, 134
  and XPointers, 165, 166
role attribute
  and link semantics, 216, 217, 219
  and link typing, 64, 65
  and traversal rules, 175
  in XLink, 182–183
Root location, and covering range, 147
Root node, in XPath, 99
round function, 128
RTP. *See* Real Time Protocol

S

Satellite connections, 5
Scalable Vector Graphics, xxv, 89
Schema definitions, for XLink elements
    and attributes, 192
Scheme parts, evaluating in XPointer, 156
Schemes, XPointer, 154–155
Scripting, 212
Scripting languages, 15, 48, 69, 70
    richer linking functionality with, 18–19
Search engines, 13
section elements, 73
self axis
    and point, 145
    in XPath, *109*, 114–115
Semantic associations, 25
Semantic attributes
    arcrole, 183
    role, 182–183
    title, 183–184
    XLink, 180, 182–184
Semantic links, 10
Semantic net, 197
Semantics
    formatting, 74
    link, 17, 39–40, 74, 216–219
Semantic Web, 8
    emerging vision of, xxv
Semistructured data, XML representa-
    tion of, 228
Sequence collection, 33
Servers, 5, 20
Server session variables, xxviii
Server-side transformations, of XML
    resources, 203
Set-based association, xxvi, 33–34
SGML. *See* Standard Generalized
    Markup Language
SGML tools, and XML support, 212
Short Message Service, 237, 238
show attribute, 36, 185–187
show = "embed" attribute, 47
show = "other" attribute value, 48
simple element type, 177, 183, 191, 192
Simple links
    and href attribute, 181
    out-of-link links converted into, 212
    and XLink, 172, 173–174

Simple Mail Transfer Protocol, 6
simple value, in type attribute, 181
Simple Web link, 25, *26*
Single-destination anchors, 39, 52
Single-source anchors, 39, 52
Single-source, single-destination links,
    xxvii, 26, 204
    problems related to, 15–16
    structural, 31
Site maps, 20
Slash characters, and location steps, 106
SMIL. *See* Synchronized Multimedia
    Interchange Language
SMS. *See* Short Message Service
SMTP. *See* Simple Mail Transfer Protocol
Software reuse, with XPath, 95
Sophistication, and specialization, 231
Source anchors, 9
    and Linkbase filter, 28
    and link semantics, 17
    and onclick event, 19
    overlapping, 14
    and simple Web links, 26
span element, 77
Spatial hypertext, *34*
Spatial hypertext associations, 33
Specific link, 30
Standard Generalized Markup Language,
    xxviii, 72, 91, 228
Startpoint, 149
    of range, 145, 146
start-point function, 156, 160
starts-with function, 129
Static link, definition of, 40
Storage level, and XLinks, 196
Storyspace, xxviii
string function, 129
String functions, in XPath, 128–131
string-length function, 130
string-range function, 156, 160
String type, 146
String-value, 98
    of comment node, 101
    of element node, 100
    of namespace node, 101
    of root node, 99
    of text node, 101
string value object type, 96

Structural associations, 25
Structural links, 10, 17, 18, 30–33
  in example Hyperwave Web page, *32*
  with simplification of Hyperwave, *31*
Structural relationships, 30
Structured text, pattern matching for, 41
Style sheet languages, 69
Style sheets, 10, 11, 48
  little XSLT programs as, 91
  and nodes, 38
Subfolders, bookmark, 213
Subresources, 50, 63, 143, 162
  errors, 155
  and processing model, 204
substring-after function, 130
substring-before function, 130
substring function, 130
SVG. *See* Scalable Vector Graphics
Synchronized Multimedia Interchange
    Language, xxv, 18, 36
Syntax
  for child sequence, 152
  for fragment identifiers, 141
  full XPointer, 153
  of location paths, 104–105
  for XPath expressions, 121
Syntax errors, for XPointer, 155*n*

T
table descendants, 117
table element, 89
TCP. *See* Transmission Control Protocol
Technology stability, and transitioning to
    new model, 224
TEX/LaTeX, 92
Text
  anchors, 9
  files, 38
  selecting for spanning number of
      nodes, 149
  selecting within one node, 149
Text nodes, 149
  and child axis, 111
  in XPath, 101–102
Third-party links, 44, 45, 59–61, 198, 204
title attribute, 193
  and link semantics, 216
  and link typing, 64, 65

  in XLink, 183–184
title elements, 193
  multiple, appearing as children, 180
  XLink, 178
title element type, 178
title value, in type attribute, 181
to attribute, in XLink, 188
Tool support, with XLink and
    XPointer, 206
Topic maps, 197
Transclusion, xvii, xxvi, 12*n*, 23, 43,
    44–45
  definition of, 41
  and embed value, 186
  legal issues with, 198, 205*n*,
      207–208, 238
  and linking control, 215
  and origin of resources, 220
  and processing model, 205
  supporting access to source, 47
  supporting composition, 46–47
  and XLink's success, 198
Transcopyright, xvii, 23, 208
Transitioning to new model, 221–236
  alternative approaches, 222–226
  building new sites, 235–236
  content negotiation, 231–233
  example strategies, 226–230
  external transition, 224
  internal: Big Bang—external: Big
      Bang, 225
  internal: Big Bang—external: no
      change, 225
  internal: dual system—external: no
      change, 225
  internal: hybrid—external: hybrid,
      226, 230
  internal: hybrid—external: no change,
      225, 226–229
  internal transition, 224
  issues in, 222–224
  migration of content, 233–235
translate function, 130
Translets (Sun Microsystems), 91
Transmission Control Protocol, 4, 6
Traversal, 52, 53, 54
  and arc elements, 178
  and multi-ended links, 62

and out-of-line extended links, 176
and typed links, 64
with XLink, 174
Traversal attributes
from, 188
to, 188
label, 188
XLink, 180, 188
Traversal semantics, XLink support
of, 81
true function, 126
type attribute, 180–181, 191
TypeB element type, 171
Typed associations, 25
Typed links, 64–66
Types, nodes tested for, 116

U
unexpanded entity reference information
item, 84
Unidirectional associations between
information, 25
Unidirectional links, 173
embedded, 11
Unified Modeling Language (UML), 235
Uniform Resource Identifiers, xix, 8, 51,
55, 56, 79, 162, 189
Uniform Resource Locators, xvii, 7, 55,
56, 57, 69, 70–71
Uniform Resource Names, 55, 56, 57
Unique identifiers, for element nodes, 100
Universal cross-referencing, 64
Universal resource identifier, 7, 50, 71
unparsed entity information item, 85
Untyped associations, 25
Untyped links, 12, 16–18
URI Infoset property, base, 79
URI references, 139
namespace prefix mapped onto, 75
semantics specified with, 182
XInclude support of, 80
URIs. *See* Universal Resource
Identifiers
url-path, 55
URLs. *See* Uniform Resource Locators
URNs. *See* Uniform Resource Names
Usability
and content sophistication, 231

engineering, 219
Usability issues, in XML-based systems,
219–220
Usage-centered design, 215
Usage scenarios: hypermedia support for
information utilization, 42–48
adding links to read-only
material, 44
generic links, 44–45
link semantics-controlling context, 48
link semantics-embedding content,
47–48
overlapping anchors, 45–46
scenario description, 42–43
transclusion-supporting access to
source, 47
transclusion-supporting composition,
46–47
User-defined schemas, RDF, 93

V
Values, in type attribute, 181
Variable bindings, XPath, 97
Video, 22, 34, 41, 70
VIKI, 34, *35*
Virtual Reality Modeling Language
(VRML), 33

W
WAP. *See* Wireless Application Protocol
Warwick Framework, 93*n*
W3C. *See* World Wide Web Consortium
Web Accessibility Initiative (WAI),
xxv, 219
Web browsers, 6
bookmarks in, 213–214
Web content
accessibility and usability of, 219–220
and transitioning to new model,
221–236
Webcosm, xxviii, 20, 27, 30, 38, 64
Webcosm server, generic link using
simplification of, *28*
Web links
dynamic, 26–27, *27*
simple, 25–26, *26*
Web Markup Language (WebML),
xxv, 215

Web metadata, RDF for definition of, 92
Web pages, 6
  assisting technologies for, 69–70
  Hyperwave, *32*
  transition issues with, 221
Web scenarios, 222
Web server aliases, 57
Web servers, enhancing, 20
Web sites, 10
  building new, 235–236
  link-poor, 209, 213
Whitespace, 88, 102
Wireless Application Protocol, xxv,
    70, 238
World Wide Web, xxvii–xxviii, 3–4,
    7–8
  basic linking components, *9*
  broader view of linking in, 10–11
  current solutions to linking problems,
    18–20
  growth of, xxv
  information linking in, 8–20
  and link destination unpredictability,
    14–15
  linking model, 8–10
  as open hypermedia system, 239
  overwhelming success of, 69
  resource, 50
  shortcomings of linking model, 11–18
World Wide Web Consortium, xxv,
    xxviii, 7, 72, 141
  Composite Capability/Preference
    Profiles, 232
  and device independence, 239
  and RDF generation from
    XLink, 93
  snapshot of technical reports page,
    140, 165
  WAI group in, 219
  and XLink processing model, 203
  and XML Infoset, 88
  XML introduced by, 71
  XML Linking Working Group
    within, xxix

X

Xanadu, xvii, xxvi, 23, 208
XForms, xxix

XHTML. *See* Extensible Hypertext
    Markup Language
XInclude, 81–88, 94, 212
XLink, xv, xvii, xviii, xxix, xxx, 12, 13,
    15, 20, 21, 44, 49, 66, 69, 94, 221
  attributes, 180–188
  built on top of XML, 188
  as catalyst for information
    management paradigm shift, 222
  conformance described by, 189–190
  cross-referencing with, 227
  embedding links into XML documents
    in, 170–171
  emerging support for, 209–213
  extending, 194–195
  future of, 198, 237–239
  and global attributes, 78
  hand-coded support, 212–213
  interpretation of, 188–190
  and linkbases, 195, *196*
  link flexibility in, 39
  link types and element types,
    171–180
  multi-ended links supported by, 62–63
  and namespace conformance, 78
  parsers and code libraries, 211–212
  processing, 188–189
  and publishing by reference, 42
  RDF generated from, 93
  relation between link and element
    types, *172*
  richness of link semantics in, 40
  show="other" attribute supported
    by, 48
  support in existing browsers, 210–211
  and third-party links, 59–61
  transclusion features with, 80–81,
    206–207
  traversing links in, 184, 185
  typed links supported by, 64–66
  usage, 190–198
  XML as foundation of, 189
  XML Base required by, 80
  and XML Infoset, 86
XLink attributes
  behavior, 180, 184–187
  element type, 180–181
  locator, 180, 181–182

semantic, 180, 182–184
traversal, 180, 188
XLink-capable clients, and content
        negotiation, 232
XLink element types, 177–180
    arcs, 178
    attribute use patterns for, *179*
    locators, 178
    relationships, *177*
    resource, 178
    title elements as children of, 179
    titles, 178–180
xlinkit.com, 212
XLink locators, XPointers used in
        definition of, 51–52, 54
XLink namespace URI, official, 170
XLink standard, comments on definitions
        in, 53–54
xlink:type attribute, 171
XLink usage, 190–198
    extending XLink, 194–195
    using XLink for linkbases, 195–198
    XLink element and attribute
        declaration, 190–194
XML. *See* Extensible Markup
        Language
XML Base, 79–80, 94
    support for, 212
    XLink applications implementing, 189
xml:base attribute, 79
XML documents
    embedding links into, 170–171
    examples of selecting nodes from,
        120–121
    hyperlinks used with, 169
    Infoset information items with, 86
    and MIME types, 139
    and nodes, 38
    node types illustrated in, 102–103
    XLink attributes for embedding link
        formation in, 180
XML DTDs, 81
XML editor, 73
XML fragment identifiers, XPointer
        goal of defining mechanism for,
        143–144
XML Inclusions. *See* XInclude
xmlinfo link, 19

XML Information Set (Infoset), xxix,
        81–88, 94, 143
    Information items, *82–86*
xml:lang attribute, 100, 180
XML Linking Language. *See* XLink
XML Namespaces, 69, 94
    effect of naming rules on, 78
    recommendation, conforming to, 86
    XLink's use of, 189
    and XML names, 170
xmlns, 154 155
xmlns attribute, 101
xmlns:html attribute, 75
xmlns prefix, 75
xmlns scheme, 163, 164
xmlns:xlink attribute, 171
XML Path Language. *See* XPath
XML Pointer Language. *See* XPointer
XML Query (XQuery), xxix, 95,
        136–137
XML resources, transformation of by
        XSLT style sheet, 203
XML Schema, xxix, 136
    information models specified in, 235
    for XLink content, 191
    XPath used by, 95
xml:space attribute, 100
xml:xlink:href attribute, 171
XPath, xv, xxix, xxx, 20, 21, 49, 51, 66,
        69, 91, 95–137, 165
    abbreviations, *118*–120
    axes in, *106,107*–115
    document order of nodes, *98*
    example node tree, *103*
    examples, 133–136
    expressions, 121–123
    functions, 123–133
    future developments with, 136–137
    general model, 96–103
    location paths, 103–121
    and namespace conformance, 78
    node set functions in, 131–133
    node sets and XPointer location
        set, 144
    node tree example, *103*
    number functions in, 126–128
    operators, 121, *122*, 123
    overview of XPath functions, *124*

XPath (*continued*)
  and pattern definitions, 41
  performance suggestions about,
      133–134
  string functions in, 128–131
  and XML Infoset, 86, 87
  and XPointer, 165
  XPointer built on top of, 156, 168
  and XSLT, 165
XPath 1.0, 136, 137, 167
XPath 2.0, 136, 137, 167
XPath data model, XPointer's extension
     of, 147, 156
XPath object types, in XPointer, 146
XPath specification, location path
     syntactically described in, 104
XPath Visualiser, 212
XPointer, xv, xvii, xviii, xxix, xxx, 20,
     21, 49, 66, 69, 91, 139–168, 221
  built on top of XPath, 156, 168
  capabilities of, 50–52
  as catalyst for information
     management paradigm shift, 222
  character escaping (examples 1
     and 2), *163*
  emerging support for, 209–213
  end-point function in, 157–158
  error types defined by, 155*n*
  escaping rules, 162
  evaluating scheme parts in, 156
  extensions of to XPath data
     model, 147
  fragment identifiers, 39
  functions, 156–161
  future developments with, 167–168,
     237–239
  general model, 143–150
  generating for point within
     document, 148
  and generic links, 44–45, 63–64
  hand-coded support, 212–213
  here function in, 158
  and namespace conformance, 78
  origin function in, 158
  overview of functions in, *157*
  parsers and code libraries, 211–212
  and pattern definitions, 41
  and publishing by reference, 42

range function in, 158
range-inside function in, 158–159
range-to function in, 159–160
requirements for using, 139, 141–142
schemes, 154–155
standardization problems with,
     167–168
startpoint function in, 160
string-range function in, 160
support in existing browsers, 210–211
XLink complementary with, 198
and XML Infoset, 86
XPath object types in, 146
XPath used by, 95
XPointer data model
  point, 144–145
  range, 144, 145–148
XPointer data model examples,
     148–150
  making multiple selections, 149–150
  marking point within document, 148
  selecting text that spans a number of
     nodes, 149
  selecting text within one node, 149
XPointer forms, 150–153
  bare names, 150–151
  child sequences, 151–153
xpointer keyword, 154
XPointers
  client support of, 142
  composing, 165–166
  as fragment identifiers for XML
     resources, 71
  and namespaces, 163–164
  persistence of, 166–167
xpointer scheme, 163
XPointer specification, container nodes,
     node points, and character
     points, *146*
XPointer usage, 161–167
  composing XPointers, 165–166
  persistence, 166–167
  XPointer character escaping, 162–163
  XPointers and namespaces, 163–164
XQuery, 136
XSL. *See* Extensible Stylesheet Language
XSL Formatting Objects (XSL-FO), xxix,
     90, 94

xsl:key element, 134
XSL style sheets
  and nodes, 38
  XML documents formatted by, 187
XSL Transformations (XSLT), xxviii, 51,
      90–91, 94, 136, 197
  evolution of, 136
  support for, 212
  and XPath, 95, 165
XSL Transformations style
      sheets, 210
  and hand-coded support, 212

and link semantics, 217–218
  transformation of XML resources
      by, 203
XSLT Virtual Machine (Oracle), 91
XTooX, XLink linkbases supported
      with, 211
X2X, XML support with, 212

Z
Zero, dividing zero by, 126
Zero index, 145
ZOG, 23

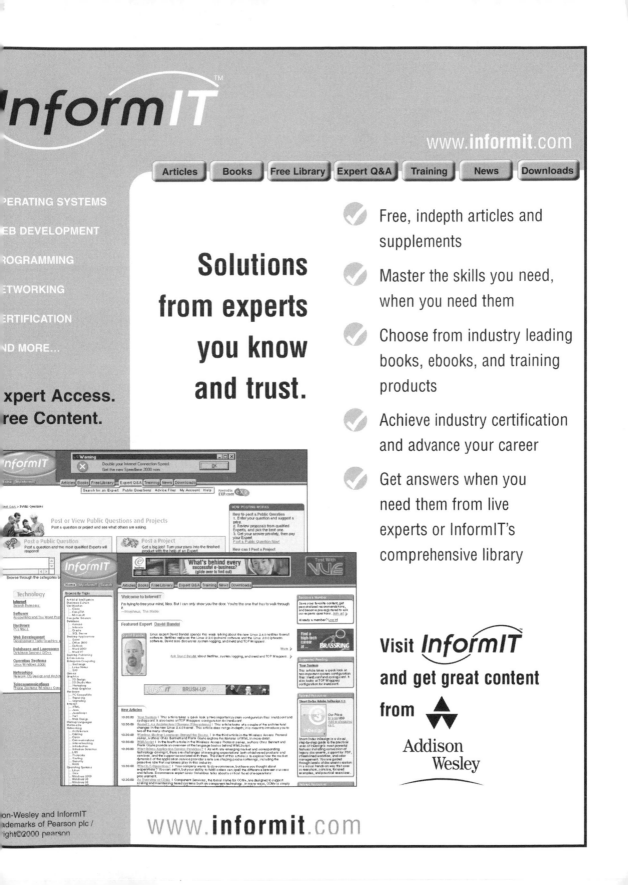